# The House of LIES

## RENEE McBRYDE

hachette
AUSTRALIA

Pseudonyms have been used in this book and other details altered where necessary to protect the identity and privacy of people mentioned. While every effort has been made to recall past events accurately, the memories contained within this book are the author's own and may differ from those of others.

 hachette
AUSTRALIA

Published in Australia and New Zealand in 2017
by Hachette Australia
(an imprint of Hachette Australia Pty Limited)
Level 17, 207 Kent Street, Sydney NSW 2000
www.hachette.com.au

10 9 8 7 6 5 4 3 2 1

National Library of Australia
Cataloguing-in-Publication data

McBryde, Renee, author.
The house of lies / Renee McBryde.

978 0 7336 3721 6 (paperback)

McBryde, Renee.
Children of criminals–Australia–Biography.
Abused women–Australia–Biography.

364.1092

Cover design by Christabella Designs
Cover photograph courtesy of Trevillion Images
Text design by Bookhouse, Sydney
Typeset in 12.2/17.4 pt Adobe Garamond Pro by Bookhouse, Sydney
Printed and bound in Great Britain by Clays Ltd, St Ives plc

*For John. My light, my laughter, my love. Always.*

*There is no agony like bearing an untold story inside you.*

Zora Neale Hurston

# Prologue

Strip clubs, prostitutes, drugs, corruption; or maybe just one last drink? No matter what your vice is you'll find it in Sydney's Kings Cross. It's 1981 and the lure of the Cross is at its peak: raw, edgy and laced with danger. The laws are loose and the morals are looser; the streets a playground for the misfits and transients who have nowhere else to go, nowhere to rest their heads between the darkness of the night and the breaking of a new day.

Knowing the Cross makes it easier for me to imagine *them* there. To see them walking hand in hand around El Alamein Fountain or to glimpse them through the window of the video arcade where they met only months ago. Gemma and Michael, Gem and Mick; two troubled hearts seeking salvation among the wreckage of broken lives in the Cross. These two swear they're going to be different. They are going to leave the Cross behind and really make a life together.

Gem is so young and pretty it hurts to look at her, especially like this standing outside Central Station. Her athletic swimmer's body had always made heads turn, but now she looks too starved to swim even a single lap, let alone in under twenty-five seconds. Her thick chestnut mane is pulled back loosely from her face, her smile exposing perfect white teeth. From a distance you might think she's collecting money for her school charity, a walkathon perhaps, but if you get close enough and strain against the whipping wind, you'll hear she's begging, pleading with the passers-by for some loose change. She hasn't eaten properly in days. Gem tries to make eye contact with those desperate to avoid her. The scabby infected sores beneath her unwashed jeans begin to ache.

Hours later she carefully counts her meagre collection, enough for just a couple of cheeseburgers. She decides to call it a day, setting off towards William Street, back to the Cross, back to him.

Her hunger pains fleetingly satisfied, Gem lets herself in to Michael's place and sits staring at the four grubby walls, waiting for him. The door handle turns and Michael walks in, and they lock eyes, each breaking into a smile. Everything is tolerable now. Intoxicated by his authority and control, she wonders how they ever drew breath without each other. In his arms, in his bed, she is consumed by him.

Whispering in her ear, he says, 'Tomorrow let's just go and get away from all this shit. The drugs, the squats, all the sick child fuckers with their filthy money! We don't need it! We are done. As of tomorrow, babe, we are going to live the good life!'

She nods into his shoulder, believing his words because at nineteen, he knows these things, and because growing in her belly is their reason to start afresh: a tiny new life that will soon rely solely upon them to nurture her and guide her in life. A new beginning.

In this moment they are bound to each other. Him and her. Their baby. Everything else falls away. They fall asleep entwined, full of hope and the promise of a new day, a new life.

Neither stirs as the wailing sirens and screeching tyres pull up outside their window; both have lived rough for too long to be disturbed by the sounds of the Cross. It's not until wood cracks as the door detaches from its hinges that their eyes fly open to see the door momentarily airborne before it settles inches from their tatty mattress. Six armed police officers storm the room, jaws clenched.

'Michael Caldwell, you are under arrest.'

Gem draws the discoloured sheet around her as they drag him from the bed. Clawing at him, at them, she is confused, desperate, her fifteen-year-old eyes wide in disbelief. 'Mick, what's happening? What's going on?' He is silent, doesn't look at her, so she turns to the officers. 'Please don't take him from me, he hasn't done anything wrong!'

Then she is alone, sitting silently in Michael's room, not knowing what to do or where to go next.

# 1

The weekend started like any other. Nan appeared at the door of my classroom well ahead of bell time as she always did on Friday afternoons. Twenty-two pairs of eyes flew to the doorway as she filled it with her round frame. She wore her good black slacks and a red knitted jumper, and it was no accident that Nan's freshly permed hair and carefully painted nails were the exact same shade of vermillion red as her jumper. She sailed into the classroom like a vibrant splash of paint on a tired canvas, beaming at Manly West's most infamous kindergarten teacher. 'Good afternoon, Mrs Beltcher. Would you mind if I steal Renee away a little early today? We have quite a way to travel this afternoon.' With a wink and a grin, Nan collected me by the arm and we made our getaway, only just managing to hold on to our giggles until we were out of the room with my bag. If only Mum knew!

And then the journey home: bus to Manly, ferry to Circular Quay, train to Redfern and finally the slow walk up to the big sky-scraping units, stopping every few minutes so that Nanna could catch her breath. In the lift we would count the floors 3, 4, 5 . . . 12, 13 . . . 14! *Ding!* Every leg of the well-trodden journey taking me further away from my weekday life with Mum.

As soon as we were in the door, Nan stripped down to her bra and knickers, peeling off the steaming layers that, in spite of the heat, she insisted on wearing, because, 'Rennie, darling, everybody knows winter clothes make you thinner!' I wondered if this was the latest pearl of wisdom from Nan's Weight Watchers meetings.

The zip of my uniform was barely undone before Nan was sashaying down the hall in one of her Ken Done–inspired house dresses, elbows flapping in an attempt to release the heat of the day.

'Why didn't you just wear that to pick me up, Nanna?'

She looked at me as if I'd suggested she leave the house nude. 'Doesn't that mother of yours teach you anything? It's important that we always try to look our best! I can't just wear a house dress out in public, I could run into anybody – or worse, be hit by a bus! I don't want to die in a house dress!'

She sauntered off to make one of her endless cups of tea, and I made a beeline to my room to make sure all was just as I left it. My heart leapt – sitting on my bed was the biggest package I'd ever seen. It was covered in inky red stamps from the post office, and my name was written prominently on the front in thick black texta. It was from my daddy.

Nan appeared behind me with the scissors. Setting down her mug of tea, she sliced the masking tape carefully along the creases before stepping away so I could fold back the flaps. The room became scented with wood chips and something strong and heady like Nan's nail varnish. Pulling at the sea of plastic bubbles, I uncovered the most magnificent jewellery box.

'Wow, Nanna. Look! Isn't it beautiful?'

The wood was the same colour as the cherry juice that stained my fingers at Christmas time; so polished that my own smile reflected clearly back at me.

'It's called rosewood, possum,' Nan said.

When I opened the lid there were no dancing ballerinas or music, just a gleaming glass mirror and a glamorous bed of emerald green velvet, soft but scrunchy beneath my fingers.

It was the most beautiful thing I had ever seen but presents like this from my dad were not unusual. Everything my dad had ever sent me was handmade, specially carved with me in mind.

Whenever he sent me things he always told me on the phone that, 'Any dad can just go and throw something in a trolley but my little girl deserves the most beautiful things. Everything I send you is made with love, by me. Special and one of a kind, just like you, sweetheart.'

The presents were my dad's way of saying sorry for never being home like other daddies. I found it hard to understand why I couldn't see my dad after work or on weekends like all the other kids, so I always made sure to tell everyone that my dad was the big boss of Cottee's Cordial and he was so important that his work simply couldn't be without him. All my friends were suitably impressed, especially because I punctuated my stories with a well-versed rendition of the Cottee's jingle – which every child knew and loved – as if it was about my very own dad.

Clearing a space on my dressing table for my new prized possession, I fussed over where exactly the centre was, trying to make it look just perfect. I felt so grown up, so loved.

That next morning I woke up hungry, the smell of eggs and toast wafting from the kitchen as I sing-songed the news that the lady of the house was now awake. 'Nanna! Grandpa! I'm awake! And you better come quick 'cause there's a big lump in your bed!'

Giggling, I scrambled under the sheets and doona, quickly pulling up the lilac-embossed bedspread so that the bed looked made. *Slap, slap, slap*, I could hear their slippers getting closer along the linoleum floors.

'My goodness, Betty, look at that big lump in your bed,' Grandpa said in his thick Irish accent.

'Perhaps we should lie on top of it and squash it out?' said Nan. Jumping on top of the bed, they rolled back and forth. I gasped for air as I heaved under their weight, laughing and choking and laughing.

'Listen. The lump is making a noise!'

After a few more moments giggling, the covers were thrown back.

'It's me!' I squealed.

A kaleidoscope of shock, disbelief and relief patterned their faces. 'Oh thank goodness, it's you! Now come on, you big lump, it's breakfast time!' Every morning waking up at Nan and Grandpa's was the same.

The day was supposed to be a scorcher, thirty-five degrees by lunchtime, so before it got too hot Grandpa and I set off for Prince Alfred pool, laden down with all the things Nan deemed necessary for the day.

'What have you packed in here, Betty? The bloody kitchen sink?'

'You leave the packing to me, Michael Kevin bloody Neville . . . smart mouthing me! The hide! You just concentrate on getting Rennie to the pool in one piece, and mark my words, you big Irish

sod, if you let anything happen to her, even one little scratch . . .'
She wagged her finger at him, the threat hanging in the air.

'Yes, yes, woman! I know!'

The threat of Nan's words were obviously still echoing in
Grandpa's cauliflower ears as we walked down Elizabeth Street,
because he was on guard: 'Come back here, missy! How many
times do I have to tell you? You must never walk next to the gutter!
Always walk next to the houses. A car could leap from the road at
any moment and crush you – and what would we do then? What
would we do if we didn't have you anymore?'

I grabbed his hand and started to swing our arms back and
forth, trying to pull him into a skip. His Irish eyes smiled; he never
could manage to stay mad at me for long.

'You'll be the bloody death of me, you will, my girl.' Then
suddenly he pulled my arm, skipping ahead as he chortled out the
words to one of his beloved Irish ditties, waiting for me to join in
with his ponderings about how just far it was to Tipperary, which
always made us smile.

———

Pushing through the turnstiles to the Prince Alfred pool, my
nose filled with the smell of chlorine and my heart swelled with
happiness. It was here that Grandpa first taught me to swim, and
it was practically our second home in the summer; when we were
there, just me and him, the hours seemed to melt away like the
endless ice-creams I always sweet-talked out of him. Hours and
hours of somersaults, splashing and big strong arms throwing me
high into the air, as I shouted, and always got, 'More, more, more,
Grandpa!'

Eventually, I would spy a friend to play with and Grandpa was allowed to retire to the bench to complete his beloved crosswords. With one eye always watching my latest trick, Grandpa would sit patiently until I emerged, red-eyed and stomach rumbling, announcing, 'Okay, we can go home now.'

That Saturday, back at Nan's after bolognaise and a bath, I dressed for bed in my favourite nightie – an oversized Boy George T-shirt that only just covered my scrappy knees. Like a spoilt cat I sprawled out on the lounge, all tanned legs and sun-bleached hair, fingertips curling over one cool leather arm of the lounge and toes stretched to the other. Saturday night meant two things: watching *Young Talent Time* and my weekly phone call from the Cottee's farm. I started to think about all the things I needed to tell Dad.

'Nan, do you think I'll get to speak to Big Bird tonight?'

Sometimes Dad put me on the phone to some of his Cottee's farmers. They always told me what a great man my dad was to work with and how lucky I was to have a dad like him. Big Bird was always my favourite. He had a smooth, deep voice just like Dad, and he always asked me fun questions like, 'What's the name of Dorothy's dog in *The Wizard of Oz*?' Once a long time ago I had asked Dad if Big Bird was the same Big Bird from *Sesame Street*. Dad had erupted in laughter, a great big belly laugh that kept on going and going until it infected the phone line because, before I knew it, I was laughing too, although I wasn't sure why – it seemed a reasonable question to me. Before Nan could answer me about Big Bird, the phone rang. I sprang out of the lounge even though I wasn't allowed to answer the phone; we all knew it was for me.

'Yes, we'll accept the call, thank you,' Nan said into the receiver and then moments later, 'Hello, Michael. How are you, love?'

At her hip, I pulled the spiral telephone cord until it was rigid. 'My turn now, Nanna . . . Hi, Daddy!'

'Sweetheart! I miss you! How are you?'

We fell into our weekly exchange. Dad always began with the same questions:

'Are you being a good girl?'

'How's Mum? Nan? And what about Grandpa?'

'What did you learn at school this week?'

And then it was my turn, always replying with my own scripted questions too:

'When can I come to visit the farm, Daddy?'

'When are you coming home?'

That week I couldn't wait to tell Dad about my new trick on the monkey bars at school.

'Guess what I can do, Dad? I can swing around the monkey bars with no hands, just holding on with the backs of my knees! Only me and one other girl in the entire junior school can do it. Maya Bray did it first but she can only do it seventeen times and I can do it twenty-two times now!'

'Are Nan and Grandpa still with you, sweetheart?' he interrupted. 'I have something important to tell you, but it's just our secret for the moment okay?'

I wasn't sure that he had understood the importance of my monkey bar trick. Did he hear me say the trick was with no hands? Did he hear me say *twenty-two* times? Perhaps if I told him how the backs of my legs were scarred and bloodied, raw from the friction of the metal bar rubbing against my skin, he would better understand the difficulty of the trick.

'So, the way the trick works is –'

'Sweetheart, stop! This is important, you're not a baby anymore and you need to know the truth. I don't want you to say anything to Nanna or Grandpa until I've finished speaking, okay?'

*Young Talent Time* was on. I wanted to hear the important news, but Dannii Minogue had just appeared on screen wearing a shimmery strapless dress with her crimped hair styled into a side pony. She was poised to sing. I felt torn.

'Okay, Dad.'

'Darling, it really is time for you to know that I don't really live on the Cottee's farm, or work for Cottee's Cordial.'

Now I was listening.

'I want you to come and visit me, I want to be able to see you, so you need to know the truth for that to be able to happen, okay?'

What was he talking about? Was I finally going to the Cottee's farm?

'I don't live on the Cottee's farm. I live in a place called jail.'

'Jail?' I whispered.

'Jail is a place people have to live if they do naughty things.'

I was confused. 'I do naughty things all the time and I don't live in jail!'

'Only grown-ups go to jail, sweetheart, grown-ups who do very naughty things.'

'What sort of naughty things?'

At home Mum was always asking me, 'Renee, are you deaf?' and it popped into my head at that moment that maybe I was deaf, because even though I was trying to listen, my brain felt tangled, and I could only hear bits of what Dad was saying.

'We killed two men . . . it wasn't supposed to happen . . . we had a knife . . . you'll understand better when you're older.'

*Silence.*

'Say something, sweetheart.'

'Are you sure you don't just work for Cottee's Cordial?'

'No, sweetie, I'm in jail.'

I burst into tears.

The phone was taken away. Angry words were shouted into it, but I couldn't hear them.

On the TV, Johnny Young was surrounded by the whole *YTT* gang, singing 'All My Loving'. It was the end of the show and Johnny's smooth, velvety voice wrapped itself around me, as if trying to comfort me, but all I could think about was that my daddy didn't work for Cottee's Cordial.

# 2

In the immediate aftermath of the phone call, a state of emergency was called. My nan wasn't sure what to do, or how much to say. There was much arguing and indecision, with Nan and Grandpa unable to agree on how this bombshell should be handled until Grandpa said, 'There's no bloody way around it, Betty, call Gemma and face the music. She's the girl's mother and she has a right to know. She should be here for this.'

Mum hadn't known about the weekly phone calls with Dad and once I knew she was coming I became terrified about how much trouble I would be in for not telling her. I started to worry about how I would be punished, knowing that if Nan and Mum got into a big fight, I would most likely be banned from seeing Nan and Grandpa. It had happened before after they had rowed – Mum had refused to let me see Nan and Grandpa for three months. Nan and Grandpa often recounted how they had sat and waited for Mum and me all day Christmas Day, with a table full of food, and a tree with presents underneath, and we never showed up. They didn't know that I had cried myself to sleep every single night until eventually Mum had given in. There was no doubt that threatening separation had become Mum's trump card, and if there was one thing that would make Mum fly off the handle, it was talk of my father. I was scared.

Mum knew that I had spoken to my dad on the odd occasion because sometimes when I got home on a Sunday evening I would slip up. She always knew about the gifts because Nan would find a way to subtly mention something to Mum like, 'What? Oh, you haven't seen Ren's new jewellery box before? Mick made it for her. Touch the velvet, go on, it's so soft!'

I would be sent into my room at the mere mention of my father's name: 'Go and play with your Barbies, Ren. I need to have a talk with Nanna.'

I could imagine Mum on the other side of the paper-thin walls, hands on hips, foot stomping as her voice travelled through to most of the units in the building. 'Mum, I've told you and told you and told you! I don't want Renee to have *anything* to do with him. No letters, no phone calls and definitely no gifts! If she wants to know him when she's older then that's up to her, but I don't want him in my life, I'm done with all that shit.'

Nan would reply, 'We're not all fairweather friends, Gemma. Just because you abandoned him, doesn't mean the rest of us have to. The girl's got a right to know her father, doesn't she? Besides, it's just a phone call and a gift every now and then.'

'Mum, I don't give a fuck if it's every now and then. It should be *never*. She's my daughter, not yours, so it's my decision. If you want to speak to Mick then you go ahead and do whatever you want but Renee is not to talk to him anymore. Why do you keep trying to tie him to me? Are you trying to punish me?'

Sometimes they fought long and hard and other times I could hear Nan give in. 'Fine, fine, fine, Gemma, whatever you think is best. Are you staying for dinner?'

Whichever way the fight went, Nan's house rules stayed the same, largely underpinned by the ethos 'What your mother doesn't know won't hurt her,' and 'What happens at Nanna's stays at Nanna's!'

My phone calls with Dad were really just the tip of the iceberg in a lifetime of lies and betrayal between Nan and Mum. Even at the age of six I was acutely aware of the necessity to tread very carefully when they were both in the room; it could be very easy to upset either of them, with the other around. When Nan picked up the phone that night to summon my mother, I knew life was about to change.

Mum didn't own a car, so her boyfriend, David, must have dropped her off for her to have arrived at such breakneck speed. Long after the doorbell had rung, Nan and Mum stood whispering to each other in the hallway. Just before they rounded the corner I heard Nan say in a voice she never would have used with me, 'Pull it together, Gemma, I'll handle it.' Her hand was on Mum's back, propelling her forward.

Looking at Mum it was clear that Nan's living room was not the destination she had in mind when getting ready for the evening. Dressed to hit the town, Mum's eyes were rimmed with thick black eyeliner and had a rawness that betrayed her lipstick smile. She looked beautiful but sad, just like the crying clown masks Nan collected and put on the wall near the kitchen. Mum knelt in front of me, as she always did, and held out her arms. 'Come and give Mummy a cuddle,' she said. She was shaking.

Wrapping my arms around her neck I whispered into her ear, 'Hi Mumma!'

At the sound of my voice, her lips contorted, lipstick disappearing into her mouth. She kept looking to the ceiling, trying in vain to stop her tears from spilling over and drowning us all. It was a trick she had taught me when some of the kids in our street were picking on me and I had run home bawling. *Just keep looking up to the sky. Don't let them see how much they've upset you; don't ever let anyone see you cry.*

Her voice cracked into a million pieces. 'My baby girl, my baby girl, I'm so sorry, I'm so sorry, I love you so much.' I felt her hot tears start to pour down her cheek onto mine, matting our hair together.

And I felt so, so sorry for not telling her about all the phone calls and for making her feel so sad.

———

Nan made herself a fresh tea and set it down at the head of the table, then went to the linen closet to retrieve the big bottle of Johnnie Walker she kept hidden behind the tea towels. She poured two generous glasses of scotch, added a splash of Coke, and then slid them over to Mum and Grandpa. Strangely, neither of them uttered a word of complaint about her customary heavy-handedness. There was not one sarcastic smile or any dramatic gagging as per their usual carry-on because on this occasion they were both grateful for a little extra of Nan's Dutch courage, which everyone clearly deemed necessary for facing a wide-eyed six-year-old, and the past.

And then they began. Nan and Mum. Counsel and co-counsel. Grilling me for every word, intonation and thought that had been exchanged between me and my father. Looking back now it was one of the rare times I saw them act as a team. Perhaps they weren't as different as they thought?

13

'What *exactly* did your father say to you?'

'Tell us word for word.'

'Are you sure he said *he* killed someone? Or did he say *his friend* killed someone?'

'How did he say the men died?'

'Did he say anything about Mummy?'

'So, let's get this straight, he started by saying, "Where's Nan and Grandpa?" Is that right?'

'Try to remember exactly . . . Let's go over it again.'

I now realise they were trying to find out how much I knew, how little they could get away with telling me and how many of their lies could be salvaged, but at the time I felt worried that if I said the wrong thing, or reported back incorrectly, I would get into even more trouble. It seemed paramount that I not make a mistake, that I report every word perfectly.

'Okay, petal. Well, we had thought we would talk to you about all this when you were a little older, but your dad obviously had a few other ideas in his head, so tonight we're going to tell you about some very important grown-up stuff, okay? Everything we talk about tonight is a secret, one that you can never tell anyone else about. It's just for family. Do you understand?' asked Nan.

I nodded. My very first round-table discussion about my father's colourful past.

Nan feverishly set about conjuring a new portrait of my father, her beloved would-be son-in-law. She was a generous artist, my nan, manipulating her palette and canvas with expertise; heavy brush strokes in some places and barely visible sketching in others. Truth and lies bleeding into each other and, like any child, I was easily distracted by all the pretty colours.

'It's true that your dad *is* in jail, sweetie, but it's a very complicated situation. When your mum and dad were younger, before you were born, they knew some very bad men. These men did some very awful things to people and one day your dad and his friend Andrew tried to stop them from doing bad things.'

'What did the bad men do?'

'They used to hurt young children.'

My eyes had grown wide as I looked to my mother for confirmation, but Mum was someplace else, back out on the periphery of my life, where she often sat when Nan was around. So while Nan concentrated on filling my head with a more abstract version of the truth, Mum focused on refilling her glass. Nan was always the boss, even when she was commandeering the conversation while wearing a Sylvester and Tweety Pie nightie.

'What did they do to the young children?'

'You're too young to know all the details. But your dad and Andrew tried to stop them, they were very courageous, but then the bad men tried to hurt your dad and they all got into a fight.'

'So . . . Nanna, was it just like in Grandpa's Chuck Norris movies, the goodies fighting the baddies? And my daddy won, right?'

'Gosh, you're a smart girl! That's exactly what it was like.'

'So the baddies died, right? And my daddy killed them?'

'Yes, they died. Your dad and Andrew had to kill the bad men, just like in the movies.'

'So why did they have to go to jail if they got the baddies? Chuck Norris never goes to jail . . . Does Daddy have a gun? Is he a policeman?'

Perhaps it wouldn't be so bad if my dad didn't work at Cottee's Cordial, especially if he was a policeman, or, even cooler than that, a trailblazer karate expert like Chuck Norris. I could just picture the faces of the kids at school, awestruck, as they huddled around me on the handball courts, hanging off my every word.

'No,' Nan said, 'your dad isn't a policeman and he doesn't have a gun. The police wouldn't do anything about the bad men, so your dad did. He got the baddies but what he did was still against the law, so he had to go to jail, and he has to live there until the policemen say he can come out.'

'Oh.' It made sense. My dad was even braver than a policeman because he had to fight the baddies with no gun. Like Chuck Norris.

My mind ran away, fantasising about going to school on Monday. My two best friends, Elleni and Alicia, and I would race to the top of the fort, our favourite place to sit and talk about everything we had done over the weekend. I would wait till last to tell them my news. Elleni had the nicest, most normal dad I had ever met, and Alicia's dad wasn't around much because her parents were broken up like mine. Alicia's dad worked nights and weekends in a nightclub that my mum sometimes went to. They already thought my dad was cool for working at Cottee's so they would be super-impressed when I told them he was actually like Chuck Norris. Elleni's hands would fly to her mouth, Alicia's eyes would grow big, both of them wonderstruck as I regaled them with brave tales about my dad fearlessly fighting evil.

'Do you think it would be okay if I just tell Elleni and Alicia about Dad?' I pondered aloud.

Sprays of tea and scotch flew as both Mum and Nan spluttered, 'No!'

'You can't tell anyone! No one at school, none of the grown-ups you know, not your teachers, not even any of Mummy's friends, okay? No one! It's our secret. A family-only secret. Lots of families have big secrets.'

'Why do we have to keep it a secret from *everyone* if Dad's a goody? Elleni and Alicia wouldn't tell anyone anyway!'

Nan opened her mouth but Mum jumped up, spilling some of her drink on Nan's nightie as she came around the table.

'Mum! Stop filling her head with rubbish! Haven't you caused enough trouble? None of this would even be happening if it wasn't for your obsession with Mick! He's not your bloody son, okay? Your loyalties should be to me and Renee! Not to a fucking murderer you barely even know!' The scotch was making Mum brave.

Mum knelt down in front of me again and cupped my face hard in her hands, her fingers pressed into my cheeks. 'Look at me and listen! This is not a game. This is serious. Do you like having friends? Do you like having sleepovers with Elleni and Alicia?'

Of course I did. I nodded as much as her grasp would allow.

'Well, let me make this very clear. Elleni and Alicia will never be allowed to play with you again if anyone finds out you have a murderer's blood pumping through your veins, okay? No one will. You will sit in the playground all by yourself! Your father is not Chuck Norris. He killed somebody. Stabbed them to death. Do you understand?'

It seemed important that I did understand so I nodded, but I was confused, because I still thought he was the goody and someone always has to die in fights between good and bad.

'Listen, Rennie,' Nan said. 'Your mother's right. If you ever tell anyone anything about this, not only will no one want to play with you or be your friend, but you could be taken away from us. Do you understand? Do you want to be taken away from us and have to live with strangers? You might never see me or Grandpa again!'

Now I was worried. 'What about Mummy?'

'Not Mummy either. Is that what you want?'

'No. That would make me very sad.'

'That's right, you would be so sad! So button those lips and not a word to anyone, okay? Ever. If you want to ask any questions or talk about your dad, you come to Nanna, Grandpa or your mother. No one else. It's our secret, okay?'

'Okay.'

And just like that the innocence of my childhood bubble had burst. I was catapulted into a dark and complex world, where my father was serving life in jail for double murder and I somehow had to learn how to carry the weight of who I was and where I came from without ever breathing a word of it to anyone. It was on this night, at the tender age of six, that I was initiated into my lifelong role as a Secret Keeper.

Mum would have killed me if she had known how far we roamed. In the evenings we would play in the park at the end of the street until the first stars began to twinkle in the blackening sky and then our names would be called one by one, screeched from the high heavens until we could ignore it no longer without painful repercussions of the wooden-spoon variety. It was time for dinner.

Fairway Close was the type of street that all our mothers aspired to get away from, but for me it was the most cherished home of my childhood. It was the first real home Mum and I had ever had and I would have been happy living there in our shared bedroom – beds less than a metre apart – in the bubble of childhood forever.

Before we moved to Fairway Close, Mum and I had moved around a lot – in and out of refuges, different Housing Commission units or renting a spare room from one of Mum's friends. We also had long and short stints living with Nan and Grandpa until, inevitably, Mum and Nan would have another falling out. The fights were usually over Nan pulling rank on Mum for disciplining me, like the time just after my fourth birthday party when we were all living in Nan's big house at Airds in Campbelltown before they moved to Redfern. Mum had been out all day with David and when I saw them pull up, I ran downstairs to greet her. Mum was sitting in the car for ages, not getting out. She kept turning to me and holding up a finger, mouthing, 'One more minute.' After what must have been at least a hundred one more minutes, I bent down and picked up a handful of grey garden rocks and threw them at David's pristine white van. I bent down and picked up another handful and another before Mum's and David's doors flew open, looking for the culprit. I hated him and his sandy-blond hair. I'm not sure why I hated him, but he took my mum away from me all the time. Nan hated him too, which was good enough for me. Mum and David were yelling, their words jumbling into each other's, him yelling at her, her yelling at me, faces bursting with rage. I knew I was in serious trouble, so while Mum was apologising and David was looking at the damage, I made a run for it.

I ran in the front door, screen door slamming behind me, and straight past the living room and kitchen, then up the two flights of stairs on all fours. My heart was pounding, and I kept thinking that if I could just put some distance between me and them, then Nan and Grandpa would have time to come and save me. I heard the screen door slam again so I knew Mum was inside and then she started screaming.

'Renee! *Renee!* Get here now! When I get hold of you I am going to pull your pants down and smack your bum so hard you won't sit down for a week!'

At the top of the stairs I turned left into Grandpa's room and slid down behind his bed, my back jammed up against the cold wall. I congratulated myself – she would find it hard to smack my bum over the bed and next to the wall. Grandpa wasn't allowed to sleep in Nan's bed because he snored and I knew Mum would probably look in Nan's room for me first. I could hear her thundering up the stairs. Nan's room. My room. Bathroom. And then she loomed in Grandpa's doorway, her eyes wild and teeth gritted. She was practically panting.

'Get out from behind that bed now. NOW! I said.'

Grandpa was behind Mum in a second; he was quite spritely in those days and still had his gardening gloves on.

'Don't you dare hit her, Gemma. She's just a little girl.'

Mum turned to Grandpa but was backing closer and closer to the bed.

'Shut up! You're not my father! Don't tell me what to do! What would you know about parenting?'

'Apparently nothing, but this is my room and you are not welcome in it. Get out, Gemma. Now. You will not touch that child in this room.'

Mum wasn't scared of Grandpa. She turned back to me.

'Get out from behind that bed, you little brat.'

I didn't move, peeping over Grandpa's itchy green tartan blanket, watching.

And then Nan appeared, circling like a lioness. 'You lay one finger on her and not only will you be out of this house, you will feel the back of my hand like never before. My house, my rules. Now get downstairs.'

—

When we first moved into Fairway Close it was as if Mum and I were playing house with no real grown-ups around to tell us what to do, but it quickly became the most normal life we'd ever had. When I started primary school, Mum got a job working at a factory just a few minutes' walk away from school. She had to pack a certain amount of bathroom hooks into boxes per hour and the monotony of it drove her crazy. But the crazy usually started much earlier in the mornings, with the whole of Fairway Close forced to listen to Mum.

'Come on, Renee! Toast, hair, teeth. Get moving! Why are you so slow?'

No matter how hard I tried to focus on the tasks, my mind was always elsewhere, so after a while I started sneaking my uniform on at night under my pyjamas in the hope that there would be less yelling in the mornings.

Once we were out the door we would begin the thirty-minute walk/run to school and work, with Mum metres ahead of me, craning her neck around to shout back at me: 'Stop dragging your feet, you'll ruin your shoes, I've told you I can't afford to buy you another pair of shoes! Hurry up! No, I am not going to carry you! Come on, I will lose my stupid job if I'm late!'

Mum has always been renowned for her fast-paced walking and her absolute intolerance for lateness, neither of which married well with a six-year-old's legs and attention span.

Finally we'd arrive at the empty playground where I would sit and wait for the other children to arrive. Keith, the school garbage man, was always there and he promised Mum he'd keep an eye on me because he could see me clinging to her, not wanting her to go. Mum would hold my face with her hands, the anger of the morning gone.

'I love you as big as the world, okay? Be a good girl!' She would lean in and smother me in red lipstick kisses and then she would prance out the gate, gone in a cloud of cheap perfume, leaving both Keith and me staring after her.

———

Life with Mum was exciting because I never knew what to expect. When the other kids were being called in for the night I was often heading straight back out. Mum never liked to stay home so we were always going somewhere: moonlit walks to visit her friends or off to our favourite Italian restaurant in Manly where kids ate free if they could solve a puzzle. Even on the coldest nights we were always walking somewhere. I never minded because there was never any yelling, just singing, and we were always arm in arm.

One night Mum announced we were going to visit her friends Sharon and Mark, who lived about a half-hour speed-walk away in the middle of Manly. I loved Sharon and Mark and I loved the view from their big skyscraper unit, but I didn't want to walk all that way, I wanted to fall asleep in my own bed instead of on someone else's lounge.

'Pleeeease can we stay home, Mum?'

'No.'

'Can we get the bus, then? My legs are tired.'

'No. Don't be lazy. Sing me one of your choir songs and we'll be there before you know it.'

We were about the same distance down Kenneth Road as I was through *Aladdin*'s 'A Whole New World' when I saw colourful lights ahead of us. As we got closer I could hear music playing and people laughing, and the flashing lights got brighter and brighter until they were unmistakable – rides!

'Look, Mum, look!' I pulled her arm, dragging her until we were in front of a huge red-and-yellow tent.

There were rides and fairy floss and people everywhere. A big flashing sign was screaming at us: *Circus! Circus! Circus!* I turned to my mother, eyes pleading. 'Please, pleeeease can we go to the circus?'

Mum laughed and I saw an opportunity.

'Pretty, pretty please with a cherry on top? It will be so fun!'

'Not tonight, Renee, but if you behave yourself, we'll see. Maybe next week.' She turned and started walking again. Then stopped. Rifling through her bag she said, 'Oh no! I think I left the keys in the door at home.'

Digging deeper and deeper into her bag she looked worried, and then I heard her say, 'Oh my goodness me . . . look what's in my bag!'

She turned to face me, hands behind her back. 'Guess what I found, Rennie.'

She flung her arm out and held up two tickets. My breath caught in my throat and my eyes started welling. Could it be possible?

'What is it, Mumma? What do you have?' I needed to hear her say it out loud.

Her beautiful face broke into a smile. 'Let's go to the circus, baby girl!'

I was so happy I started to cry. How did she know I would even ask to go? Mum linked her arm through mine and we ran back towards the music. It would be impossible to ever love her more than I did in that moment.

# 4

It had been over a month since I found out The Secret and I still hadn't seen or spoken to Nan. For as long as I could remember, Nan had called every night at eight o'clock to say goodnight, and if for some reason she couldn't get through, she would ring at 7 a.m. the next day. Grandpa didn't trust technology, so instead of talking on the phone he mailed me a letter every week. But after The Secret all of that stopped. It wasn't that Nan and Grandpa didn't try: the phone rang day and night, but I was no longer allowed to answer it. Letters came too, even more than usual, but they went straight in the bin. Consumed with worry that I might never see them again, I barely even thought about The Secret or anything to do with my dad. I begged and pleaded and cried myself to sleep at the injustice of it all, but Mum stood firm.

'Why aren't I enough for you?' she asked, which was ironic because I often wished I could ask her the same thing.

Mum was twenty-two, and her weekends belonged to David and her friends, and therefore the stalemate with Nan could never have lasted. None of Mum's friends had children because, like her, they were all in their early twenties. All in the prime of their lives, with no responsibilities, which meant that they often planned things at the last moment, leaving Mum pulling out her hair at what she should do with me, so she didn't miss out on the fun. Having me home meant that her social life suffered.

Whenever I was with Mum on the weekend, we rarely stayed at home. Sometimes we went to the pool or the movies, if Mum could afford it, but mostly we went to barbecues at her friends' houses. By early evening the barbecues would take on a distinct party atmosphere. Madonna or Prince blared so loud that the window panes shuddered in protest. Glass after glass of wine or scotch or beer was drained and refilled and the grown-ups would get louder and more fun by the hour. Most of the drinking was done outside, although everyone made regular trips inside when it was their turn to have what they called a cone. Sometimes I would sit inside pretending to read my books and secretly watch them as they put their mouths inside a big colourful vase-like contraption they called a bong. They would light the pipe and draw in their breath so that the water in the bottom of the vase bubbled furiously. Each and every one of them would shut their eyes and hold their breath in their lungs for as long as they could before finally exhaling and filling the room with a disgusting grey smoke that made both the smoker and me in the corner cough. The bong would be passed around and around and around; cones and scotch and dancing. Dancing, scotch and cones.

Inevitably someone would suggest that they all go out and 'have a boogie' in Manly. It would be a crime to keep these dance moves confined to the lounge room and an even greater crime for the group to go dancing without Mum. Mum was the prettiest and most outgoing of them all, the life of the party, but seeing as though we lived off beef-flavoured two-minute noodles and barely had enough money for the essentials, Mum would often say, 'Ooohhh, I'd love to go out, but I really can't afford it this week . . . and besides I've got Ren.'

Sometimes Mum was adamant about not going out and we would start walking home just as her friends were pouring themselves into a taxi to hit the town. Other times, like the Saturday six weeks into the post-Secret stalemate, I could see the desire in Mum's sparkling, glassy eyes; she was desperate to go with them. Tapping her leg in time to the music, Mum exclaimed, 'Oh, I *love* this song, it makes me want to dance!'

Seeing their window of opportunity, the girls pulled Mum to her feet. 'Yes! Let's go out for a dance! It's been ages!'

'Yeah! Come on, Gem! You know you want to.'

'It'll be fun!'

Prince was persuading her too, crooning in her ears about his 'Little Red Corvette' and making her body sway in time with the beat.

'Come on!' Jodie cajoled, and Mum's eyes snapped back open to the moment. 'I'll even shout you! You can't say no to a free night out!' Jodie always had lots of money because she was the one who sold everyone the pot; sometimes it was small sticks of tightly wound foil and other times big stuffed sandwich bags of stale-looking mowed grass.

'How about you just leave Ren next door with Judy? Or we could call Sharon's brother Paul?'

'How about that, Ren?' They turned to me, faces bright and encouraging as if they were offering me something too good to refuse. 'How would you like to go and sleepover at Judy's next door? Wouldn't that be fun?'

I didn't want Mum to go with them. I wanted her to stay with me. I wanted to go home and crawl into bed together and talk like we always did if I stayed home on weekends.

'I don't want to stay at Judy's. I want to stay with my mum.'

Mum didn't say anything, so Jodie continued.

'What if I gave you twenty dollars, would you stay at Judy's?'

I had stayed at Judy's before and it was okay, but the last time I had her ex-husband threw a brick through the front window, right next to where Judy's eldest sons and I were camping out in the lounge room. The police had to be called. Blue lights filled the room, making the shards of broken glass glint like diamonds on the threadbare carpet, as they asked us question after question about what had happened. I definitely didn't want to stay there again.

'No. I don't want to stay at Judy's! I don't ever want to sleep over there again!'

'Well, your mum needs a night out, Rennie. A little break from being a mummy for a while, so where do you want to stay? With Paul?'

Sharon came over to where I was sitting and put her arm around me. 'How about I call Paul and he comes and picks you up?'

'No, I don't want to stay with Paul either.'

'You have to choose, Paul's or Judy's?'

'None.' And then I had a lightbulb moment, a thought of how we could both get what we wanted. 'Mum can go out but only if I can go and stay at my nanna's house.'

They all looked at each other. I could see Mum was torn – she really wanted to go. They discussed the options among themselves. How would they get me to Redfern? There had been far too much alcohol and marijuana consumed for anyone to drive and neither Nan nor Grandpa had a licence.

'What if we put you in a taxi to your nan's place? Could your mum come out with us then? Are you sure you won't be too scared in a taxi by yourself?'

'I won't be scared, I'm pretty grown up.'

Less than an hour later I was strapped into the back of a taxi and Jodie handed me a fifty-dollar note.

'Thirty is for the taxi driver and twenty is for you to buy yourself some of those *Baby-Sitters Club* books, okay?'

They all kissed me goodbye and waved from the kerb until the taxi turned and I couldn't see them anymore. Twenty minutes later, I was delivered to the base of Redfern's Housing Commission towers. Grandpa was downstairs waiting when the taxi pulled up, his anxious face illuminated by the building's security light. He ran to the taxi and opened the back door, bundling me out.

'What took so long? Are you all right? I thought the taxi driver must have run away with you. Come on, it's dangerous out here, let's get inside before we get mugged!'

Inside the security doors, Grandpa knelt down and looked me over, turning me to one side and then the other, searching for any hairs that might be out of place. Satisfied, he folded me into his arms.

'Thank God you're okay! You've grown so much in six weeks! We've missed you, you know!'

'I know. I missed you too, Grandpa.'

In his arms I didn't have to be a grown-up, I was instantly a child again: small, safe and loved.

# 5

Before I was born, Mum and Nan had sixteen years of complic-ated life together, each of them consistently falling short of the other's expectations. Nan never loved Mum enough and Mum never behaved in a way that was worthy of Nan's love. Nan, a single mother, worked shifts as a nurse and when Mum was only five she put Mum in a boarding school – two hours away on a train – and rarely came to see her. Nan thought she was doing her best by trying to give Mum a good education. But Mum felt abandoned.

When the boarding school became too expensive for Nan, Mum was moved to a Catholic home at Ashfield run by 'The Nuns'. All the other children at the home were orphans, with no parents to speak of. On weekends Mum sometimes went home to Nan's, but she was just as frequently farmed out to foster carers and, later, her sympathetic swimming coach, who was trying to nurture her raw talent. No matter how nice people were to Mum, she always wondered what she had done to make her mother not want her at home. What could she have possibly done to be dumped in a place whose core mission was beating the spirit out of every child who crossed their threshold, in that special way that only deviant Catholics seem to know? Why didn't her own mother want her?

The resentment and mistrust between them had, over the years, manifested into near hatred. Nan had too many boyfriends; Mum became a truant and a runaway. Nan used to belt Mum with an electrical cord, trying to 'whip some sense into her'; Mum fell pregnant at fifteen . . . to a murderer. By the time I was on my way they were like beaten-down boxers, exhausted from going round after round with each other; sullen and bruised by the bitter disappointment they continually inspired in each other. They couldn't see that no matter how hard they fought there would never be a winner. But maybe for the sake of a baby there could be a ceasefire?

Because of my father's high-profile court cases, Mum and her pregnancy became known to the Department of Family and Children's Services. They told Mum if she couldn't provide proof of a stable home for me they would take me into care after birth.

My mother cried for most of her pregnancy. I know this because she told me – Mum and Nan both liked to tell me. Mum shut herself away from the world for days and weeks at a time, doubled over and heaving with grief, while inside her my little limbs grew to the symphony of her tears. Eyelids, nose and lips all taking shape while waves of grief continued to engulf her. She cried for my father, for herself, for the life they would never have. And she cried because she was so very alone. Everyone told her she should have an abortion. Or give me up for adoption. Anything but raise me herself.

'Wait for the father's court case and if he's innocent you can try for another baby in happier times, when you're both older.'

'What sort of life can you offer the child, Gemma? You're just a child yourself!'

Every refuge, counsellor and nun tried to convince her to put 'it' all behind her. Start afresh. But she wouldn't or couldn't hear of it. Couldn't possibly fathom losing him and me both. One organisation offered Mum food and accommodation for as long as she needed it, if she agreed to give me up for adoption to one of the loving families they had on their waiting list. But she couldn't.

'I had to have you, Ren. I would have done anything to keep you. I was so alone, so miserable, but I knew if I had you, you would change my life. You would love me. Real, unconditional love for the first time in my life and I could be happy, because *you* would make me happy.'

Eventually, with the Department of Family and Children's Services watching and waiting, Mum had nowhere else to turn but to Nan and they momentarily allowed the idea of my impending birth to right all the wrongs between them, the way only a baby and the promise of new life can.

For as far back as I can remember, that was my role, the pre-ordained olive branch between them. Mum and Nan. Nan and Mum. The two ever-battling lionesses. I was the reason for peace after yet another bloody battle between them. No matter how many hateful words flew from their tongues, or how ragged their gaping heart wounds became, the bitter stand-offs would always come to an end eventually. They had to, because Mum needed Nan to look after me and Nan needed Mum to ler her be a part of my life. I was their road back to each other, the bridge that allowed them to reconnect without losing face or ever uttering, 'I'm sorry.' Never forgiving, never forgetting and certainly never explaining, Mum and Nan would suddenly just set down their weapons and abandon the fight, both acting as if nothing had ever happened at all. Grandpa, who had met and become engaged to Nan when Mum was ten, said they had always fought this way. He said they were both crazy and it was best not to get involved, because if you did, they might join forces and turn against you instead. He said he never liked to get involved but I know he used to sneak Mum money, clothes and food when she was living on the streets, making her cross her heart and promise not to tell Nan. I took his advice to mean that it was best to be on each of their sides without letting the other one know, that way you could keep both of them happy. It was something I ended up doing a lot.

The day after the stalemate over my father broke, Mum came to pick me up from Nan's instead of Grandpa taking me home on the ferry. It was the only deviation from the old routine and if it wasn't for the orange twenty-dollar note screaming to be taken out of the confines of my Rainbow Brite purse and straight down to Dymocks, I could have been convinced the last few months had been a bad dream.

# 6

The phone calls with Dad started up again about a month after I was allowed back to Nan's. It was as if nothing had changed, the weekday–weekend routine just went back to how it had always been. Except now I had The Secret to keep, too.

My dad wanted me to come and visit him and post-Secret, every phone call we had centred around this wish: 'When are you coming, sweetheart? I can't wait to see you, don't you want to come and visit your old man? Maybe you could meet Big Bird too?'

'I don't know when I can come. I don't think Mummy would want me to.'

I didn't want to upset Mum or Nan but when it was Nanna's turn to speak, I heard her say, 'Don't worry, Michael, I'll speak to Gemma, I'm sure I can get her to come around to the idea.'

Visiting hours at Long Bay Correctional Centre were Saturdays and Sundays from 8.30 a.m.–11.15 a.m. or 11.45 a.m.–2.15 p.m.

Despite having been up since six o'clock preparing, Nan and I didn't arrive at the gates until the 11.45 a.m. session. There'd been a lot to do before we'd finally got out the door. Nan had to unwrap all the rags she'd put in my hair the night before and pull and twist each ringlet, so they would drop perfectly in time to see my father. Nan usually only put rags in my hair for special occasions like my birthday, because they took so long to do and it hurt her back to sit for that long.

Nan had laid out our clothes carefully the night before. She chose her good slacks and a teal knitted jumper, because green really only ever looked good on redheads, she said. For me, Nan had chosen one of my best outfits: a pink dress with fur trim around the bottom and a matching pink hooded cape with fur around the hood. My mother hated the outfit. Every time I wore it she said, 'God, Mum, why do you have to dress her so woggy all the time? She looks like a Russian bride!' But when I was in it I felt like Red Riding Hood, only prettier, because I was in pink. I could not have imagined a more perfect outfit to wear to meet my father for the first time, certain he would be overwhelmed by how beautiful I looked. Nan thought so too. New white ballet shoes, white socks with a lace frill around the ankle and white gloves completed my look. Nan said I looked just like Shirley Temple.

While Nan and I got ready for the big day, Grandpa was sent down to Kentucky Fried Chicken to wait for its doors to open. My dad had requested Nan bring a bucket of fried chicken, chips and potato and gravy because prisoners were allowed to eat food from 'the outside' during family visits and Kentucky was his favourite.

With the chicken secured, Nan focused again on my hair. She sprayed it with stronghold hairspray three times before Grandpa finally convinced her that we would never get there if she poisoned me to death with another face full of godawful spray.

'Shoosh up, you big Irish sod, what do you know about hair? I have to spray the curls so they stay – can't you see they're dropping?'

Eyes rolling, Grandpa shut the door and the three of us set off laden with an esky of food and coats to brave the fierce winds that Grandpa was certain would be waiting for us all the way out at Malabar. At Bondi, Grandpa put Nan and me on the right bus. 'I'll be waiting right here on the bench for you at three o'clock,' he said. Grandpa didn't want to visit my father and no matter how much Nan bullied him, he refused to give in. Grandpa walked alongside the bus waving until we were going so fast I couldn't see him anymore.

The bus out to Malabar was mostly empty and it seemed to take forever. I kept moving around on the seats, pretending I was a grown-up catching the bus by myself, and before long I was entranced in a game of make-believe, pretending I was Mary Poppins, and singing at the top of my lungs about spoons full of sugar and medicine going down. Really getting into my game, I pointed my finger, in my Mary Poppins-ish white gloves just like I had seen Mary do in the movie a thousand times, before swiping it along the window sill of the number 400 bus. I was suprised to see that my glove did not stay white; in fact, my finger was instantly covered in black soot.

Nan spied what I was doing and perhaps for the first time in my life, she shouted at me. 'What on earth are you doing? Come here! Look how filthy you are! Your father is going to think you're a street rat!'

Pulling out one of the tissues that she kept stashed in her bra, she wet it with a bit of spit, and then started rubbing furiously at my glove, trying to get it clean. The wetness and the vigour of the rubbing just made the thick black dirt spread further and soon the contrasting black and white bled together, turning most of my right glove a smudgy grey colour. Nan sighed. 'What's the use?' She yanked both gloves off my hands and stuffed them in her bag. I sat very still next to her.

Eventually the driver shouted to Nan as she had requested, 'It's your stop, missus,' and suddenly we were gathering everything and jumping down the back steps of the bus in front of a big, fortress-like building. The walls were built so high that I had to stretch my neck right back like a Pez dispenser to see the top. Along the ridge of bricks was rolled barbed wire that tumbled around the edges and seemed to reach all the way up to the sky. I was a pretty good climber but I was certain there wasn't a person alive who could get over those walls.

Seeing my furrowed brow, Nan grabbed my gloveless hand and said, 'Don't worry, poppet, everything's okay. There's nothing to be worried about, okay? You didn't need the gloves anyway.'

Ahead of us there were lots of people lining up to go inside. I could even see a few little girls like me, standing with their mothers or grandparents. I gripped Nan's hand tighter. When we were almost at the entrance, I saw some serious-looking men taking people's bags and looking inside them. Other people were being patted down with a black wand-type thing. Suddenly Nan let go of my hand. She dipped her head and covered her face with her fingers. 'Oh God, oh God, what am I going to tell your father?'

I didn't know what was wrong. It looked like Nan was going to cry. What could she possibly be so worried about telling my father?

She took her hands away from her face and looked at me. 'We left the esky on the bus . . . We left your father's Kentucky Fried Chicken on the bus!'

Inside the walls there were more walls, and then another wire fence to go through. We were mustered like cattle from checkpoint to checkpoint, before finally being released into a huge yard where we were faced with a small army of washed-out green overalls and bulging biceps.

Everywhere I looked, inked arms thrust themselves towards loved ones. Each tattoo was supposed to mark out the men's individuality, but somehow they all looked the same to me. One of these men was my daddy.

And then there he was, arms outstretched like all the others but bounding purposefully towards me. I had thought I would *know* him, recognise his face, but I didn't. In his prison clothes he looked the same as all the other men in the yard.

'Come here and give your dad a big kiss and hug, it's so good to see you.'

I burrowed behind Nan's well-padded frame and attempted to tuck my head under her armpit. I wasn't ready for hugging yet. Suddenly the idea of having a real live dad that I could visit seemed less exciting and more terrifying. This wasn't what the other kids' weekends with their dads were like. Nan moved her arm around to touch the small of my back, dragging me forward, so that I was again standing next to her.

'Go and give your dad a big hug and kiss, Rennie, we've come all this way and now you're hiding.'

With another less discreet shove from Nan, I lurched into my father's kneeling embrace. He held me to him for a long time, my arms pinned at my sides, face buried in his chest. Breathing in, I smelled my father for the first time. Imperial Leather soap and shaving cream, a bit like Grandpa but without the familiarity or Old Spice. Still pressing me to him, he began stroking the back of my head, saying over and over again, 'Oh, my little girl, my little girl – you're so big! Not a little baby now, are ya?'

'You're holding me too tight, I can't breathe!'

Letting me go, Dad touched the fur around my hood, laughing as he said, 'This fur tickles.' He leaned in to kiss my cheeks and I gave a small smile because he had pink fluff on his smooth jaw from holding me against him.

'Take that hood off so I can see your pretty face. Want to see my tattoos? I have your name right here on my arm. Look! Come on, come over here and sit on my lap. Your mum used to bring you here to see me when you were just a baby, you know?'

No, I didn't know that. I thought Mum hadn't seen Dad at all since before I was born.

Dad wouldn't, or perhaps couldn't, stop touching me – my arms, my back, my face. It made me wriggle and squirm to be free.

'I want to get down.'

'Don't get down. Stay on my lap. I've waited so long to see you.' He tightened his arms around me. I was trapped. Trapped in his heavy arms, inside the prison yard, behind the biggest walls in the world. I wanted to get down and run away, to go home.

Seeing I was about to make a fuss, Nan beckoned me over.

'Come here, Ren. I need to speak to your dad about some grown-up things anyway.' Digging deep into her black leather handbag, Nan started depositing fistfuls of coins into my open hands. 'Where can we buy some snacks, Michael?'

Dad pointed to a vending machine across the yard. 'Straight over there, sweetheart, near those guards, and make sure you get lots of salt and vinegar chips, I just can't get enough of those, I love 'em.'

Walking across the yard, I was worried that my white ballet shoes would sink into the muddy ground and be ruined. Around me there were kids playing and laughing, families eating in the sunshine and couples huddled together on benches, kissing, touching and crying. Each different group was marked out by their very own tattooed giant. I didn't want to get salt and vinegar chips, I wanted to get chicken Twisties, but I bought all the salt and vinegar chips that were left in the vending machine because I knew that Nan would want me to do as my father had asked and I wanted to make her happy after dirtying my glove and making her leave the chicken on the bus.

Walking back with my hands gripping an excessive amount of magenta foil bags, I noticed the guards in the yard weren't the only ones watching us all. Above me more guards paced back and forth in the towers, eyes intently focused over the yard and into other places I couldn't see. Watching and waiting and pacing. They had guns.

'It was so good to finally see you, my girl. Promise me you'll come again soon, sweetheart? I love you.'

'Can we go now, Nanna?' I said trying to talk without moving my mouth, like a puppeteer.

'Where have your manners gone? Say goodbye to your dad.'

'Goodbye.'

'Ren! Tell your dad you love him and go and say goodbye properly! Don't be so rude.'

Brow furrowed, jaw set, my silence echoed around the almost empty yard. I didn't want to tell him I loved him and hadn't we already hugged enough? By then Nan and I were the last visitors in the yard. The gate was open and the guards were waiting patiently for us to say our final goodbyes. It seemed like everyone was watching and waiting for me to say a 'proper' goodbye. But I couldn't make myself do it. In that moment I really didn't want him to feel loved by me.

And so I ran.

As I reached the guards I heard them ask, 'Is everything okay, little girl?' They let me through the wire fence where I stood next to them looking back into the yard. 'It's okay, little girl, just stand here with us and wait for your gran.'

On the safe side of the fence my heart started to beat rhythmically again. I pushed my face up against the wire, fingers and eyes peeking through, as I watched my nan apologising and saying her goodbyes. I could almost hear her saying in her best prim voice, 'I'm so sorry, Michael. She is normally such a well-behaved little girl. I don't know what's gotten into her today.'

# 7

After the first visit to meet my father, The Secret started to bubble inside me, brought to life by the physical reality of his existence behind *those* walls. The Secret was no longer about a fictitious Chuck Norris character, or a gravelly voice I heard down the phone line each week. I had a real physical father and a place where I could picture him. A place where I had stood beside him.

I now knew with absolute certainty just how different my dad was to the dads who came to pick my friends up from school. In many ways, meeting my father for the first time affected me far more than the murderous revelations. The Secret was no longer just a concept bobbing around in my head – the story was real and I was a central character.

At home, the visit elevated me to a new 'security clearance' within The Secret club and for something we weren't supposed to ever talk about, we ended up talking about it an awful lot. Nan was very nonchalant about The Secret, always trying to downplay the details with humour.

One night, I sat twisting forkfuls of spaghetti bolognaise round and round like cotton onto a spool. Thinking. Waiting for my dad's call.

'Nan, when Dad isn't in jail anymore will he come and eat bolognaise with us instead of calling?'

'Of course,' Nan said. 'He'll probably come over for dinner all the time. I'll cook him my famous roast – I bet he hasn't eaten anything decent in years! But we'll have to hide all the knives, just in case.' She winked at me to let me know she was joking and went on, 'Well, I guess we could leave the butter knives but we should probably hide the big carving knives, just to be safe. Hmm, but if I cook a roast, how will we carve it then? That's a pickle!' She was talking to herself more than me. 'Maybe you're right, Ren, I'll probably just have to stick to bolognaise.' She sighed heavily for dramatic effect.

Nan's 'hide the knives' joke became one of her favourites over the years but despite the humour, I'm not sure if any of us were convinced that the knives wouldn't miraculously disappear for real if my dad ever did present himself for dinner.

Even though Mum never wanted to talk about my dad or The Secret, it was my relationship with her that actually changed the most after the visit with my dad. The revelation that I too knew his voice, his face, his touch, seemed to prove to Mum that we were really in this secret life together, bonded by blood and baggage. Mum began to confide in me, offloading little pieces of her pain, safe in the knowledge that I would always climb into her lap and wipe away her tears. Mum knew that I would love her no matter what, because that's the only way a young child knows how to love their mother.

Late at night, when Elton John crooned from the record player and I should have been sleeping, Mum told me stories about her childhood, about her life with Nan and what it was like to be cast off to 'The Nuns'. If we stayed up late enough, Mum would tell me about her life on the streets and the people she encountered: prostitutes, drug addicts, social outcasts from all walks of life. Mum had come to think of many of these people as her best friends – her street family. Mum's stories were full of danger, darkness and desperation, and always tears.

Mum's life on the street sounded hard but she also talked about a sense of camaraderie and loyalty among the community, everyone bonded by the constant search for a warm place to sleep and money for their next meal. Mum said her friends often went missing for days or weeks at a time when they were off trying to 'crack it' or 'get on', and she would wonder if she would ever see them again. One night her friend 'Punk Chris' disappeared and she really did never see him again. After months of silence, Mum heard his name on the evening news and looked up to discover that his body had been found decapitated. I didn't know what decapitated was, but the way Mum whispered it, I knew he must have been dead.

'I'm sorry about your friend, Mumma.'

'They just cut his head off, Ren. Right off his body. And the police couldn't find it, you know. It wasn't even next to his body.'

I sat on the floor next to her with my legs crossed, nodding.

'That's terrible, Mumma!' And it was, but that sort of stuff had become pretty commonplace in my world by then.

---

The Secret was beginning to occupy more and more of my real life. The number of things I had to keep secret from people kept on growing. Most of the kids at school barely knew what sex was, but I knew all about Kings Cross and people having sex for money. While lots of the other kids talked about visiting relatives in America and the UK in the next school holidays, Nan and I were talking about how we would get to Orange now that my dad had been transferred to another facility.

Children are not the best secret keepers and the pressure to keep quiet, to never talk about who I was, or where I came from, slowly began to fester inside me. Sometimes I felt like I would implode if I didn't tell someone. Every phone call, visit and grown-up confession took me further and further from the playground into this complex adult world, but the more we talked about The Secret at home, the more normal my abnormal life became. I began to wonder if maybe it really wasn't that big a deal. Maybe everyone had secrets? Maybe I could tell just one of my friends?

Before long The Secret became like money burning a hole in the pocket of my childhood. I wanted to take it out and look at it, turn it over in my hands and examine the details closely, but at the same time I was worried about what would happen if I did. Would my best friends, who I played with every single day and whose houses I stayed at, really not be my friends anymore if I told them the truth? Surely not.

One hot summer's day, I decided to test the boundaries. It was the end of lunch; Maya Bray and I were standing at the bubblers, out of breath from another intensive session on the monkey bars. We were the last ones in the playground because we had been working on our routine. I could feel the trickles of sweat running down my back, my yellow-and-white checked uniform clinging to me.

The second bell rang – we were going to be late. Maya reached for my hand so we could run together and my heart felt so light. She hadn't been at the school long but I already really liked her. I was just thinking how great it would be if Elleni, Alicia, me and Maya became a group, when abruptly Maya stopped running, yanking me backward to a standstill. She looked at me intently, her head cocked to the side and her damp hair sticking out at odd angles. Our sweaty palms were still clutched together as she said, 'Do you want to be best friends?'

My heart leapt. She liked me. She really liked me.

I smiled so hard, I could feel my lips cracking from too much sun and the salt of my sweat.

'Yeah! Of course I do!'

And then I heard it. A whisper. *She wouldn't like you so much if she knew the truth about you. No one would . . .*

My heart felt defensive, but not decisive.

*No! That's not true. Best friends stick together! Right?*

*Find out for yourself then . . . go on!*

'Hey Maya. I want to tell you something . . . a secret.'

'What is it? We're gonna be so busted if we don't go!'

'You might not wanna be my best friend if I tell you.'

'Yes, I will.'

'No, really. You might not. It's serious.'

She slid her hand out of mine and looked at me. 'What is it?'

'It's about my dad. He did something really awful . . . He's in jail.'

Her cornflower-blue eyes grew wide and she started jigging on the spot like she needed to go to the toilet. 'Please don't tell me,' she said 'We've got to go.'

'But I went there . . . to the jail . . . I saw him.'

'Renee Davidson and Maya Bray, get up these steps immediately! The bell went ten minutes ago!' Mrs McNaughton was out the front of the classroom, brow furrowed, using her best shouty voice.

Maya started running towards the classroom and my heart sank. I shouldn't have said anything. The voice was right.

I started to run too and when I caught up to Maya I looked at her and said, 'Hey, Maya, I was just kidding about what I said, ha ha ha, like you know, April Fools!' But it wasn't April and I don't think she believed me for a second. We went into the classroom and sat down in our chairs. We didn't end up being best friends after all.

# 8

After Maya, I tried my best to just get on with being a regular kid, but it was hard, because I knew I wasn't and the memory of Maya's face after I shared The Secret with her made sure I didn't forget it. Mum had been right all along and I just knew I couldn't let the truth slip out again, but I didn't know how to keep it separate, how to be the right version of me so that everyone still liked me. I became increasingly self-conscious about what image I needed to present, but it wasn't just The Secret, there were other things that kept popping up and began separating me from the herd too.

We were of an age where we had started to notice everything about each other, determining what was cool, what was normal and what wasn't. If anyone strayed from the norm, they were picked on. It's just the way school works, part of being a kid, and it was always clear when it was my turn to be picked on. Sometimes the girls in my gang would ignore me from the moment I stepped onto the play-ground, clearly marking the day as one of *those* days. At recess they would run away from me and I would follow, asking, 'What have I done wrong? Can someone just tell me what I've done?' At lunchtime the silence would usually be broken by whoever had been elected by the group to speak for them, usually Chantel, or Justine, with Alicia hanging back as the boss of the group, and Elleni and Amelia on the fringe, hoping to avoid being roped in to the confrontation.

'Hey, we've decided to talk to you again . . . how about you talk to us about why your mum's so thin and pretty and you're so fat and plain?'

'Yeah, or you could tell us why your mum is so much younger than all the other mums?'

'My mum says it's because you must have been an accident – she said your mum is too young to have a child our age, and that's why you don't have a dad or any brothers or sisters.'

I never knew where to begin with this stuff. I hadn't really noticed that all these things were different about me until they all made it so glaringly apparent, and it hurt because these girls were supposed to be my best friends. 'Why are you guys saying this stuff to me, I wasn't an accident, my mum always tells me how much she wanted me –'

'Well, how come you're the only one of us who doesn't have their own bedroom? None of us share with our mums and dads, so why do you? It's because you're too poor, isn't it? Your mum can't afford you.'

By the next day it was often someone else's turn to be left out and I was allowed back in the group. Relieved to be liked again, I always forgave them instantly, but I could never forget the words they'd said, instead I embedded them in my head like a checklist of things I needed to fix about myself. If I wanted people to like me, if I wanted to fit in, then I had to be more like the other girls. I had to be normal, I just had to figure out what normal was first.

—

Ruby Tuesday was a gift my grandfather gave to me the day I was born. It started out as a joke, a nickname he stole from those 'long-haired louts, the Stones', because I was born on a Tuesday and my birthstone is a ruby. As I got a little older, Ruby became the persona Grandpa and I blamed bad behaviour on, the makings of an alter ego, who did things Renee would never dream of.

'Who drew on the wall here, Rennie?' Grandpa would say.

'Not me, Grandpa.'

'Are you sure?'

'Grandpa, you know I would never do that!'

'Hmm, let's scrub it off before your nanna sees . . . I guess it must have been that bloody troublemaker Ruby Tuesday again, huh?'

'I'm not a dobber and I'm not one hundred per cent sure, but I guess it *could* have been Ruby.'

'Well,' he would say, eyes twinkling, 'next time you see Ruby, you tell her that if she draws on the walls again, we'll have no choice but to take her off to the naughty little girls home, okay?'

Sometimes Ruby was entrusted with tasks that I wasn't quite sure about. At the park, if I was being picked on by some of the older Housing Commission kids, Grandpa would pull me aside. 'Come on, Ruby Tuesday, you've got to keep a stiff upper lip! Show me your lip.'

When I offered my stiffest upper lip to Grandpa for approval he would say, 'All right, now show me your bunch of fives!'

Clenching my hand into a ball, I would punch the air like Grandpa had showed me.

'That's my girl, now if they upset you again, you just introduce them to Ruby's bunch of fives, okay? I'll be just sitting over here if you need me.'

Grandpa had been thrown out of the Irish Guards when he was younger for having his own powerful bunch of fives land squarely on his boss's chin, and Nan was constantly telling him not to teach me to punch anyone. Grandpa would never have directly gone against Nan's wishes, so instead of teaching Renee, he taught Ruby to punch instead.

Towards the end of primary school I started to think of Ruby as a character that I liked to play. I watched other children carefully, particularly the ones I perceived to be popular and perfect, and I worked on emulating them, slowly adding their phrases and behaviours to my Ruby mindset. Ruby was like a mask I put on when I felt out of my depth; she didn't have secrets to hide, she was whatever I wanted her to be. Or whoever the other kids thought she should be. Mostly being Ruby involved not saying things that would make me unpopular or stand out too much for the wrong reasons. She consciously, desperately, tried to fit in and be like all the other kids, but to firm up her existence, I also gave her a more normal backstory. Ruby wasn't the child of a factory worker or a murderer. Ruby's parents were high-school sweethearts, much like Mary Anne and Logan from *The Baby-Sitters Club* books I loved so much, but before Ruby was born her dad died in a terrible car accident, leaving her mother pregnant and all alone.

One week at school I was Renee whose dad worked at Cottee's and the next I was Renee whose dad was in jail. Renee who had The Secret to keep. That was the week I began wearing my Ruby game face. For a few days I even tried to make my friends start calling me Ruby, but when they refused I realised it was probably best if I left her in my head.

# 9

Shortly after I turned ten, Mum and David decided to get a place together. They had been together since I was four, and even though I always told Nan and Grandpa that I didn't care about David, I desperately wanted him to like me. When we moved in together, I started spending a few more weekends at home, sometimes joining Mum and David on their big adventures. One weekend we all went skiing and David, who was a skiing enthusiast, was very impressed at how natural I was despite having never skied before. I glowed with pride at his praise.

David had never made any secret of the fact that he didn't want to have children, but I wondered if after years of him and Mum being together, I was finally starting to win him over. I noticed that when I was good at something, David liked me better – in fact, everyone liked me better.

Mum and David fought a lot. I guess they had always fought, but I was never usually around to see it. They fought in ways that I had never seen people fight before: big screaming matches that would end in threats and upturned furniture. I could hear them from where I sat in the back of the van, or from inside my room, where I spent a lot of my time, especially since Nan and Grandpa had bought me a television, Sega Mega Drive and endless new *Baby-Sitters Club* books so that I could lock myself away from the drama until the next weekend escape.

One weekend when I was kept home with Mum and David, I was lying tummy down on my bed, engrossed in a special summer edition of Kristy, Stacey, Claudia and Mary Anne's enviable Connecticut babysitting lives, when I heard Mum and David start. We had had a barbecue at our place and after everyone had gone home, they had kept drinking.

The fight got louder and louder. I could hear them moving from room to room. Uncharacteristically, David just would not give in. He knew Mum would never back down, but still he didn't leave. The fight raged on and on into the evening, each trying to conquer the other, but eventually words weren't enough and I heard something smash.

'Don't you even think about touching me or I'll call the police.'

'You're a fucking psychopath, Gemma. What the fuck is wrong with you? Two can play that game –'

'What the fuck are you doing? Put that down! Don't you fucking dare,' I heard Mum scream.

I came out of my room to see David with the glass coffee table poised over his head, eyes wild, threatening to throw it at Mum. Neither of them noticed me so I screamed, 'Stop! Stop! Please stop fighting!' They paused, panting, full of adrenaline.

Not taking her eyes off David, or the table, Mum shouted at me, 'Renee, get back in your room.'

I stood transfixed in the doorway.

'GET BACK IN YOUR ROOM NOW! I'll be there in a minute.'

I slipped back inside my room and waited. *Why was she shouting at me? I wasn't the one going to throw a table at her, I was just trying to help!*

After a while I could hear softer voices and crying but it was quieter, further away. They must have moved to their bedroom. I sat down in my bean bag and turned on my Sega Mega Drive, waiting for Mum to come in. I played level after level, world after world, focused and determined that tonight I would save Wonder Boy's princess. Eight worlds, four levels in each, minutes melting into hours. I was unstoppable. Consumed by a sense of duty, I couldn't sleep until I saved her. And I did. Sometime in the wee hours of the morning when the rest of the house was dark and calm, I finished the game, and love hearts filled the screen as Wonder Boy and his beloved were reunited. Exhausted, I pulled myself from the bean bag and put myself to bed, realising that Mum probably wasn't going to come in to say goodnight after all.

———

Of a morning, Mum drank coffee and David drank tea, because his parents were English. If I brought steaming mugs to their closed bedroom door, I was usually forgiven for the intrusion, unless it was ridiculously early. The morning after the coffee table incident I wasn't sure what I should do. I knocked on the bedroom door and said, 'Mum, I'm awake. Should I bring you a coffee?'

Mum groaned, which I took as a yes, and then David shouted back, 'Make me a tea too, please, Ren.'

I was enraged that he was in there with her, even though of course I knew he would be. I stomped off to the kitchen, wondering how adults could go from throwing furniture at each other to lolling about in bed together.

As I filled the kettle and waited for it to boil, I began getting all the bits and pieces from the cupboards, spooning coffee into Mum's special mug and getting a teabag in David's. As I thought about Mum and David in the bedroom, I stood scowling at the kettle, willing it to hurry up, and that's when I noticed it: next to the kettle stood a long cylinder of powdered Ajax™. It should have been under the sink with all the other cleaning bottles, but it wasn't and an idea popped into my head.

Could I?

I finished making Mum's coffee, thinking it through, and then I turned to David's tea. I took the bag out and added milk, a teaspoon of sugar and then I grabbed the Ajax™ cylinder, sprinkling in a heap of the white powder before manically whipping it into a teacup whirlpool, making sure that all the powder had dissolved into the liquid. Once satisfied, I walked purposefully back to their bedroom, careful not to spill the mugs. *It's done*, I thought, *we won't have to worry about him anymore.*

I put Mum's coffee down on the bedside table and then carefully took the tea around the foot of the bed to David's side. He sat up and smiled at me as he took the steaming mug. Neither of them mentioned the fight or the night before, so neither did I.

As David drained his cup I wondered if at ten years old I was going to end up in jail for murder, just like my father.

My eyes kept darting towards David, watching, but nothing happened. The poison must be killing David's insides slowly. Any moment now his body would start to shut down and he'd collapse right before my eyes. I began to worry. *What have I done? What have I done?* But nothing happened, everyone got dressed and we went to the beach, so David could check out the surf.

For days I monitored David closely when he wasn't looking, checking him over for any signs of sickness. I was less worried about David dying than I was about how on earth I would manage to explain everything to my mother should we come home to find David's body lying at the bottom of the stairs. But despite the worry, I didn't crack. I never told a soul about what I had done, having become devoutly committed to this business of secret keeping since my failed truth experiment with Maya Bray.

A week later, after watching and waiting, I finally allowed myself to breathe again. God, or someone out there, had granted me redemption, given me a pass. David was obviously going to live and it seemed I wasn't destined for a life behind bars just yet.

# 10

The Department of Housing offered Nan a transfer in October 1993 and she moved to a tiny one-bedroom unit in Cremorne, finally on our side of the Harbour Bridge. I was thrilled until I discovered she was moving without Grandpa. 'There's nothing to be upset about, petal, it's just there's no room for him there, okay? I mean just look at the big Irish sod! He won't fit in the tiny shoebox the department have given me! But the main thing is I'll be close to you. Grandpa and I have agreed to do this because it's what's best for you.'

I didn't know what it all meant, so I asked Mum.

'Nan hasn't loved Grandpa like *that* for a very long time, she's incapable of it! They're not living together anymore because she doesn't need his rent money. It's what she does – she just uses and manipulates people until she sucks them dry, leaving a trail of destruction in her wake.'

'Nan isn't like that at all! She loves everybody! Just look how much she loves me!'

'Yes, well you're the exception to the rule, aren't you? But it's because you're her last living hope. She doesn't have anybody else!'

Grandpa moved to a men's boarding house in Surry Hills so he could still be close to work. He said I wasn't allowed to see where he lived because the boarding house had a very strict 'No girls and no nuisances' policy and seeing as I was both, he definitely couldn't risk sneaking me in. Grandpa was still at Nan's every Saturday and Sunday, arriving bright and early and leaving late in the afternoon, sometimes even after dinner. Aside from not sleeping under the same roof anymore, nothing else between Nan and Grandpa really changed. Nan still cooked for Grandpa, and Grandpa still gave Nan all the money from his pay packet. My days were still spent with Grandpa at the pool or park hopping, but the nights now belonged solely to Nan. Not even my father called anymore but I didn't really notice that with all the change, although I am sure it would have been a condition of Mum's, seeing as though Nan was now going to have unlimited access to me.

Nan moved to Cremorne on a Tuesday morning, and that very afternoon I arrived on the bus straight from school. And every afternoon after that. Nan insisted on waiting at the bus stop to meet my bus and once we got to know the area we would stop at Bill's corner shop for a chat and Nan would buy me far too many bags of chips, lollies and ice-cream, convinced there was a direct correlation between how much she loved me and how much food I ate. My friend Elleni said her *yiayia* was the same. 'It's a Greek thing,' she said, but my nan wasn't Greek, she was Tasmanian.

Sometimes I was so full of Nan's love that she would give me fistfuls of Ford Pills and rows of chocolate laxatives to clear me out, and if that didn't work, she would use an enema and make me sit on Grandpa's lap until the kitchen timer went off, at which point I would be marched back to the toilet. Once I was all cleaned out, Nan then worried herself sick that I would be too weak and empty to face a day at the park with Grandpa, and so the feeding process would start again.

My diet was a constant source of contention between Mum and Nan, the two of them arguing back and forth on a weekly, sometimes daily, basis.

'She's a growing girl, Gemma. I don't want her to be as scrawny as you are, look at you!'

'She doesn't need any of that junk, Mum! It's not you that bloody has to listen to her cry every morning before school because the kids at school said she's too fat!'

'She's not fat, she's pleasantly plump.'

The fights were a moot point, though, because Nan was too set in her ways to know another way of loving and Mum couldn't monitor what food Nan put in front of me, because she was never there. Some of Mum's friends had started to comment on my weight too, as did David on a regular basis, and I think it made Mum embarrassed, because she started watching what I ate like a hawk, always screeching, 'If you're hungry eat an apple, you're not having any junk! You eat enough rubbish at your nan's.' I often wondered just how many apples Mum thought it was possible for one child to eat.

———

Mum stood behind the mesh of Nan's security door as Nan tried to find the right key to let her in. We weren't expecting her.

'It's over,' she said.

'What's over?' said Nan.

'I just can't face another day, another hour, or another screaming match with that bastard.'

'What are you talking about?'

'Me and David of course! What do you think I'm talking about?' Behind Mum I could see Noddy, the most ancient and unreliable Holden Gemini you could ever hope to escape purchasing, still running on the street. Mum gestured to Noddy, whose seats were piled high with black garbage bags. 'I've just got mine and Ren's clothes with me, I'll have to go back and get the rest of our stuff later, when we find a place. Would it be okay if we stay here for a few days? Just until I sort something more permanent out?'

I was shocked. I had left for school the day before and everything was fine, and now after eight years together they were just over?

'Well, it will be a little cramped but of course you can, Gem. It's about time you left that good-for-nothing, I've never liked him. Now go and turn that car off before someone complains about all the fumes!'

———

For a few magical weeks it was like a giant sleepover. The three of us got ready for the day together, we ate breakfast and dinner together, and best of all, at night the three of us all slept in the same bed. Lying side by side, the three of us talked about silly nothings. One night we talked for hours about our favourite children's names. I was adamant that I was going to call my future children Johnny Young and Maria, like the stars of *Young Talent Time*, or perhaps maybe something glamorous, like Melissa. Mum said if she ever had a son she would love to name him Daniel.

'Well,' Nan piped up, 'if I had my time again, I would have a daughter called Patsy. It's such a beautiful name. So eloquent and charming, don't you think?'

'Um, no! Retch! That's probably the worst name I have ever heard!'

'No way, Nanna! Mum's right, that's a hideous name.'

'Who in the world would call their child Patsy?'

'Yuck!'

Mum and I started giggling uncontrollably, unable to catch our breath. Whenever one of us stopped the other would say, 'Patsy!' and we would both start up again. It was contagious.

'If you are going to be so rude to me, and insult such a beautiful name, then I'm going to sleep.'

'Really? You're joking, right?'

Nan rolled over, huffing, 'So rude! The both of you!'

Mum and I laughed harder at Nan's annoyance, unable to believe she loved the name that much.

It was times like this when I would indulge my constant fantasy and pretend that Mum and I were sisters, and Nan was mum to both of us. That would have been better. That night I fell asleep between a huffy nanna and a smirking mum, a wide smile spread across my face, content.

~

In January 1994, Mum and I moved to a noisy two-bedroom unit on the main road of Balgowlah. The unit could at best be described as scrappy, with peeling linoleum and frail windows that shook when the buses flew by every few minutes. We had to start again, so for a while the place was pretty empty, except for the huge bunches of flowers and balloons that were delivered to Mum daily for weeks on end from David. Mum didn't read the notes, but I did and all of them begged her to come back to him: 'I love you, Gem, come home and I promise everything will be different'; 'I'm sorry, forgive me.'

I was impressed, and thought for sure we would be moving back, I certainly would have. It was like something out of a movie, all the romantic deliveries. But then what did I know about relationships? I hadn't even kissed a boy.

'None of this means anything, Renee, don't you see?' Mum said. 'It's all too late for flowers and balloons, people don't change! Take it from me: once you leave you *never* go back.'

Mum, Nan and I settled into a weekday routine, bookended by Saturdays and Sundays with Grandpa. Things between Mum and Nan slowly started to change and I wondered if it was because Nan had finally listened to Mum and stopped the contact between me and my dad. We never talked about it, the sporadic school holiday visits and the phone calls just never happened anymore. I guess it was the same way fights were never talked about, sorry was never said and Grandpa didn't live with Nan. What could there possibly be to talk about? Whatever it was that changed between them, I got a vague sense that maybe Mum and Nan might be starting to like each other again and that made me very happy.

# 11

It would have just been another ordinary Year 6 school day in September if Mum hadn't appeared ahead of the bell to pick me up. I didn't see her at first, because my seat didn't face the door, but John Fitzgerald did, and he alerted me and likely half the school to her presence. 'Renee,' he shouted, 'your mum's here! Hi, Mrs Davidson, you look awfully pretty today, would you like to have a seat in my chair?'

I whipped my head around to see Mum at the door smiling at me. John was right – she did look pretty and I felt a surge of pride. What was even more exciting than her pretty face, though, was that she had come to pick me up from school – she never did that anymore, not since she'd escaped the factory and started climbing the car insurance career ladder at AAMI.

'I finished a little early today and I thought I would surprise you!' Mum explained on the way to the car. When we got home, she asked me to come and sit with her on the lounge. She needed to talk to me. I frowned, rummaging through my mind to see if there was anything I had done to be in trouble.

'You're not in trouble,' Mum said, obviously seeing the look on my face. 'I just want to talk to you.'

I sat facing her on the lounge beneath the window that was parallel to the main road. It was hard to hear her because all the school buses were roaring past.

With the afternoon sun streaming through the glass pane, she looked like an angel tinged in gold, her eyes were moist and glistening.

'Come here and give me a cuddle. I love you so much.'

'I love you too, Mum. What's wrong?'

'I have to tell you something. I didn't really finish work early today, I didn't go to work. I was with Nanna.'

'Why? What happened?'

'She had to go to the doctor's, not Doctor Small, a proper specialist, and she asked me to drive her.'

'Why? What's wrong?'

'I don't want you to worry, okay? The doctors are going to try and make Nanna better. I promise she will get better.' Mum's voice was shaking and the way she was talking scared me.

'What's wrong with her?'

'The doctors said Nanna is very, very sick. She needs lots of medicine to make her better.'

'Why? I want to speak to Nanna. I'm going to call her.'

'You can't call her right now, she's not at home. We'll call her later.'

'What do you mean she's not at home? Nan's always at home!'

'She's not at home because she has cancer, Ren. The doctors think it will be better if she stays in hospital for a little while, gets some rest, before she starts treatment. We can go and see her tomorrow.'

When Mum said those words I literally did not know what they were going to mean. I didn't know anything about cancer, but I did know about hospitals and I knew they were bad. You had to be really, really sick to be in hospital. I didn't want Nan to be sick. I started to cry. Seeing me cry made Mum cry, which made me more scared, because I knew then it had to be serious. Mum would never cry over Nan if it wasn't really bad. Outside, the buses kept roaring past, trying to compete with our sobs.

———

Walking into Nan's room at Royal North Shore Hospital, all I could think about was how white everything was: walls, floors, sheets; every surface gleamed like a toothpaste ad. The place smelled white too, or at least the way I imagined white would if colours had a smell. Even the doctors and nurses wore white and, as if to fit in, so did the patients. Everywhere I looked there were slow shuffling bodies wearing stiff hospital gowns, with open backs that exposed flashes of beige underwear or bare bottoms.

I think it was the stark white backdrop of the hospital that made the colour of Nan's skin so shocking. She was yellow. Every single part of her. Her skin, nails, tongue and most memorably the whites of her eyes had all turned a dull mustard colour like some sort of ghoul in a scary movie. I wondered what had happened. She hadn't looked like this two days ago. Mum agreed, she said it happened right after Nan was diagnosed. 'The doctor turned to your nan and said, "Betty, I'm so sorry to have to tell you this, but you have cancer," and seriously, Ren, she turned yellow instantly. I'm not even joking, it was like the shock of his words made her change colour.'

———

The hospital had to run more tests to see how aggressive the cancer was and if it had spread to any other areas of Nan's body. Once all the results were back, the doctors could talk to us more about a treatment plan.

For months Nan had been feeling under the weather, blaming it on winter and getting old. Everyone, including Nan, had thought she had the flu. But when she still couldn't shake it, Nan's doctor finally referred her to a specialist, who diagnosed Nan and recommended she be admitted to hospital right away.

The cancer was more advanced than initially thought. 'Your mother is in the advanced stages of liver cancer and it has spread to her kidneys, lungs and pancreas. We need to start an aggressive course of chemo and then see how she responds. Once she completes this round and we do some follow-up tests, she can go home until the next round.'

If she could come home then I was sure everything was going to be all right. We filled visiting hours with talking about school, a guy at Mum's work that she really liked and Nan's hope to be well enough to come to my choir concert the following Friday. Nan and Grandpa had bought tickets months ago and Nan was darned if she was going to miss it.

Once the chemo started, Nan's face became even more sallow and drawn. There was less talking when we visited and more running back and forth to the bathroom to empty Nan's silver vomit bowl. The chemo was making her even sicker, the silver bowl overflowing with the blood that Nan kept heaving up. Red blood, white walls and yellow eyes. The colours of cancer.

If all continued as planned, then Nan could come home on Wednesday, 17 August. On the Sunday before Nan was due home, Mum and I went over to her flat and cleaned the whole unit. We put everything she loved to eat in the cupboards and fridge and changed all the sheets, so that when she came home she could just sit and get better. On Monday I went to school and called Nan's hospital from the payphone near school.

'Hi Nan, how are you feeling?'

'Well, I'm much better now that I'm talking to you, my little one! How are you?'

'I'm good! Last day of chemo today and then you'll be home on Wednesday, are you worried?'

'I'm not worried and neither should you be, I'm tough! Besides, I've got an important concert to go to on Friday!'

I laughed but there was something about her voice that made me not believe her and the memory of her yellow eyes popped into my head.

'I could come to the hospital, you know, and spend the day with you?' I had never gone anywhere by myself on the buses other than Nan's before, but I was pretty sure I could do it.

'Absolutely not! You have to go to school; today's the last rehearsal, isn't it? Aren't you all going into the Town Hall to practise?'

'Yes, but I don't have to go. I'd rather be with you anyway.'

'No way José, you go and practise for that concert, I want you to be all ready for Friday night, okay? I don't want you to spend the whole concert vomiting in the green room because you're too nervous like last year. Go and practise and have fun! I'll talk to you tonight.'

'Okay, Nan. Loves ya!'

'Love ya more, you knows I do.'

I thought about walking back to the main road and getting the bus to the hospital, but I also knew I should practise for the concert so I went to school. By the time we got back from the Town

Hall rehearsal in the city, it was the second half of lunch. I bought an iceblock with the last of the money Nan had given me at the hospital and I joined the end of the handball line, hoping to get a turn before the bell rang. A couple of the girls from my class were playing and when they saw me waiting they said, 'Hey, Renee, did you see your mum?'

'My mum? No. Why?'

'She came to see you after recess and spoke to Mrs McNaughton. She said she forgot you were at choir and that she would come back.'

My heart sank. Something was wrong.

I found Mrs McNaughton in the playground, but she wouldn't say why my mum had come, just that she would be back. 'Don't worry,' she said, 'I'm sure everything is okay.' But we both knew that it wasn't. I could see it in her eyes.

The car pulled up near the gates and Mum and Grandpa got out and started walking towards me in the playground. Mum *and* Grandpa. My heart was pounding. Everything seemed to be in slow motion – it was like they were walking on the moon. Around me I knew my classmates were running, laughing and shrieking, but I couldn't hear them, all of their joy drowned out by the *thump, thump, thump* of my heart and head. When we reached each other, I already knew. Mum had rivers of mascara streaking down her face and Grandpa's head hung so low that his chin almost touched his chest.

I waited for someone to say it out loud, but instead Mum put her arm around me and said, 'Come on, let's go get your bag.'

I looked towards the classroom but before my feet had lifted from the asphalt, Grandpa said, 'She's dead, Ren. Your nan's dead.' His voice broke and he looked away.

# 12

The car trip was like riding in a fog, I was there but I wasn't really. Still clutching the wooden stick from my red Icy Pole, I sat in the back seat trying to comprehend a world without my Nanna. When I had bought this iceblock, Nan was still in my life, preparing to come home, and everything was going to be okay. I wanted to go back in time, stop Mum and Grandpa coming into the school, go back to this morning and decide to skip the choir practice and go to the hospital to be with Nan. Maybe things would have been different then.

I'd been crying for so long that up front Mum and Grandpa had stopped trying to console me and were already making arrangements. As my heaving sobs gradually scaled themselves back to wet whimpers, I caught snippets of their words.

'I can't believe you just blurted it out to her like that in the playground! What's wrong with you?'

'Well, I can't believe we're taking her to see her grandmother's dead body. She's too young, Gemma. She should remember Betty the way she was at home.'

'She *will* remember her that way but she's just a child, off with the fairies most of the time, she doesn't know what death is and she needs to understand that Mum is really gone.'

'You're going to scar her for life, twelve-year-olds don't need to see dead bodies.'

'Let's just get to the hospital first and decide then. There is so much to do! We have to sort out the funeral and then we should go back to Mum's place to sort out all of her stuff.'

My head was pounding in time to the flashing words in my brain. *Nan's dead! Nan's dead. Dead, dead, dead, gone, gone, gone. She's left me. But she wouldn't, would she? No, she couldn't. I just spoke to her this morning! People don't get diagnosed with cancer and then die just a few weeks later, especially without saying goodbye!*

⁓

She was laying on a gleaming silver bench not unlike the ribbed sides of the sink where you pile up the dirty dishes. The outline of her round body, covered in a starched white sheet, was so still. Only her arms, shoulders and head were outside the sheet. Nan would have been annoyed about them laying her underneath the fluorescent lights, *no one looks good in poor lighting* she would have complained, and she would have been right. Nan's trademark fiery curls had faded to sombre rust, as if aware that fiesta red was inappropriate for such a sad occasion, and were pushed back off her forehead in an unfamiliar style. Her face was chalky and white, like someone had come in and patted her down lightly with talcum powder just before we arrived, or maybe it was just that all of life's colours had drained out of her with her last breath, leaving only the washed-out canvas.

71

Grandpa refused to come into the room. He stood in the doorway, his face turned to the corridor.

At twelve, I had never met death before. I thought Nan and Grandpa were invincible, that the trips to the park, Chinese dinners and movie nights would go on forever. I still didn't really believe that I would ever grow taller than Grandpa's belt or get to use a calculator for maths when I went to high school, so how could I fathom death? My world was very limited and so much of it was lying cold on the table before me.

'You can touch her if you want to,' a lady in a white coat said.

So I did. I edged my way over to the sink until the people behind me had faded and it was just Nan and me. I stroked her cold doughy cheek. 'I love you,' I whispered. I picked up Nan's limp hand in mine and clasped it tight, *Wake up Nanna, please don't leave me.* Up on my tippy toes I leaned over her swollen frame and pressed my face to hers, nose against nose, our last ever eskimo kiss, and I felt engulfed by sadness. I whispered to her, 'I love you, please don't leave me.' I felt myself heaving against her. *Please, Nanna, please!* If she was ever going to wake up I knew it would be me she would do it for. *Please wake up, please.*

Standing in that stark, cold room, I made all sorts of silent deals with Nanna: *If you wake up I will be so good. If you wake up I'll leave Mum's and come and live with you like we've always talked about.* But she stayed silent.

Then I thought, *I'm obviously making deals with the wrong person! It's God I have to convince, not Nan; He's the one who's taken her from me, she wouldn't leave me.* So silently I begged God, *Please don't take her, take anyone else, anyone . . . How about my mother, God? Take her instead?*

And then a miracle. Nan's nose started to bleed. A trickle of brilliant red blood on powder white skin. You don't bleed if you're dead.

'Mum! She's alive, she's alive!' My arms still wrapped tight around Nan, I swivelled my head to Mum, who was crying quietly in the corner behind me. 'She's bleeding Mum, look!' *I did it*, I thought, *I brought her back*, and for a second the loneliness of a life without Nan disappeared.

The white coat swooped in, her arm around me, gently pulling me back from the sink, away from my nan. 'Come away, sweetie. Go to your mother.'

'No, let me go! She's alive, look!'

'I'm so sorry, I'm so sorry, she's not alive. Sometimes this happens, a capillary bursts and there's blood . . . she's not alive, sweetheart. She's not alive,' she repeated more firmly, pulling me back and depositing me with my mother as she moved swiftly to wipe the blood away.

Turning back to us, the white coat avoided my eyes, instead focusing on my mother. 'I'm sorry, Mrs Davidson, sometimes this happens when the body is out for a while, it gets too warm, we may need to finish up here, if that's okay?'

Trying to pull out of my mother's arms, I reached desperately for my nan. 'Nanna! Nanna! Don't worry, I won't leave you.' I pleaded, 'She's not dead, she's just sick, look at her, she's bleeding.'

My grandpa stepped out of the doorway and into the hallway, his eyes spilling over, unable to hear the desperation in my voice anymore. 'Get her out of there, Gemma, please. Let's go.'

As we walked out of the automatic doors of the hospital and into the brilliant August sunshine, I caught Grandpa's hand and tried to stop myself crying. *There is no reason to cry if she isn't really dead*, I told myself.

# 13

Even though I tried to tell myself Nan wasn't dead, Mum insisted that we plan the funeral and clean out her flat anyway. It must have been a painful process for Mum to have go through all of Nan's belongings with me sitting there as the gatekeeper, unwilling to part with anything. 'What about this?' Mum said, holding up a heaped armful of Nan's tent dresses. 'Surely all of these rags can go?'

'No!' I cried. 'They're Nan's favourites!'

In the end, exasperated, Mum gave me one box and said, 'Keep whatever you want so long as it fits in this box, but absolutely nothing more!' I negotiated a separate box for all of my collector Barbies that Nan still had displayed on the dresser for me and set about trying to choose the things of Nan's that would remind me most of her. Mum and Grandpa set aside a few things to keep too, and then there were the piles of paperwork that we had to keep to sort through when we got home; bits of paper were apparently very important to grown-ups when someone dies. Everything else went into the charity bins, and then that was it – Nan no longer had an address.

In the days leading up to Nan's funeral, there were many people to call. Mum and I went through her address book and took turns calling all the names in it, not really knowing who was important and who wasn't. There were old nursing cronies, a sister in Glebe and then three others in her native Tasmania. She had brothers too but they had already died.

'Hi, I'm Renee, Betty Cooley's granddaughter? I am calling with some very sad news. My nanna just passed away.'

After a few calls, I wanted Mum to do the phone calls herself, because I felt like every time I said the words, Nan became more dead. For most of the phone calls my grief was met with polite condolences and indifference, and in some cases our calls were met with relief, that it wasn't *that* Betty from Prince of Wales hospital or Betty, Gerry's wife, from down the road. At least with polite indifference there was still some concern and respect that someone's life had been lost. This wasn't so much the case when we finally got on to Nan's sisters.

You don't speak ill of the dead. I think it's an unwritten rule, everywhere except for Tasmania. Perhaps in 1994 the rule hadn't yet spread from the mainland or, if it had, it hadn't made it as far as rural Tasmania, where Nan's sisters lived. All of the secrets Nan had carefully packed with her to take to her grave found a new life in the mouths of her sisters. Dulcie, Sheila and Rosie all fell over themselves to set us Sydney folk straight about the real Betty Cooley, each of them desperate to be the one to give voice to Nan's life before us.

'Gemma, didn't your mother ever tell you she was married here in Tasmania? Not just married but married with *four* children – she just up and left one day, gallivanting off to Melbourne, I think it was, left those poor kids with no mother!'

Nan had four children? She lived in Melbourne? Mum was beside herself – she had always wanted brothers and sisters. But we didn't know what to make of all this. How could we not have known? We called June, the only Sydney sister and the only one Nan still saw occasionally.

'She tried to leave Bayden, her husband, several times, with the kids, but he always caught her leaving and brought her back. They married very young, you see, everyone wanted to marry her back then. Your mother was the life of every party, but Bayden was persistent, desperate to tame her wild ways. He was very controlling . . . I shouldn't be talking to you about this, none of the girls should. It should all be dead and buried with her.'

I don't know what happened with the Tasmanian gossip line but after we spoke to June everyone clammed up, no one wanted to talk to us about Nan's secret life, or about anything at all. They stopped taking our calls. Mum turned to the paperwork. Certain information had to be accurate to formalise Nan's death, including her date of birth, and Mum was having a hard time finding any documentation that matched up. There was paperwork with various names and many with different ages too. Mum enlisted the help of a solicitor who, after a hefty fee and a few days, gave it to Mum straight.

'Your mother was born in 1928, not 1944 as she led you to believe, which makes her sixty-six when she passed, not fifty. Births, Deaths and Marriages confirm that your mother was married in Tasmania and gave birth to four children there – two boys and two girls. There is a record of your mother's divorce, which she applied for after you were born in Sydney. Her application cited that she had left the marriage as her husband was violent and she was in fear for her life and she had had no contact with her estranged husband or children since she left Tasmania. Your mother gave birth to another child in Melbourne, a boy, and then years later to you in Sydney. After you there was one more child, a girl who died several months after being born. I can send you all the paperwork if you like, I'm sure it's a lot to take in.'

Nan left behind four sisters, six children and goodness knows how many grandchildren in addition to me, but the day we buried her at Frenchs Forest Cemetery, there was only Mum, Grandpa and me standing in the rain to say goodbye. The nurse who was with Nan when she died had told us that Nan's final words were, 'I can't take the pain anymore,' and as the three of us stood there listening to the minister talk about my nan being free of life's burdens now that she had been released back into the arms of God, I wondered if Nan had been talking about the pain of the cancer or the pain of keeping all those secrets buried inside.

As her coffin was lowered into the ground, Wet Wet Wet's 'Love Is All Around' played on a portable CD player. *She really is dead*, I thought, and maybe for her it was a relief, but I couldn't even begin to imagine a life without her. I wanted to run and jump on the coffin and be dead and buried with her.

———

I didn't care about Nan's secrets, nothing could change how I felt about her, but for Mum and Grandpa the revelations caused a lot of pain. They'd spent so long knowing her and it was suddenly all lies and I don't think either of them ever forgave her. Along with the thousands of dollars of debt, Nan had now left Mum with a gaping hole in her identity. She still didn't know who her father was – Nan had remained tight-lipped about that for her whole life – and now with her passing, and all these secrets coming out, Mum was left not really knowing who her mother was either.

Mum tried to contact her newfound siblings through the solicitor, hoping that something good might come out of all of this. He wrote to them, seeking their permission to pass on their contact details to Mum, but all those still living refused, including the spokesperson for the family, Nan's daughter, Patsy.

I wanted to cry when Mum told me that one of Nan's daughters was called Patsy, my mind instantly taking me back to that night in Nan's bed when Mum and I had teased her mercilessly about liking such a wretchedly awful name. While I had drifted off to sleep that night with a smile on my face, Nan had been lying there thinking about her baby girl.

# 14

Six weeks after Nan died my mother became embroiled in a passionate affair with Peter, the love of her life. It had been months in the making, with Mum becoming more enchanted every time this blue-eyed, dark-haired dreamboat popped in to say hello to his sister, Mum's co-worker. Peter was often the topic of conversation between me, Nan and Mum, especially in Nan's final days as we sat whiling away the hours between chemo sessions. It was in the oncology ward that we decided that there had to be a limit to the number of times that even the most dedicated of brothers went to visit his sister, especially when they worked at a boring car insurance office.

Once Mum and Peter finally got it together, their love was like wildfire, engulfing all our lives and leaving nothing untouched. Our newly formed mother–daughter duo instantly became a trio, but it was different to anything I had experienced with David. With David, I had had my own life with Nan and Grandpa going on and David had his own life separate from Mum and me too.

But with Nan gone and me not being allowed to stay at Grandpa's boarding house, Mum and Peter's love cocoon left me feeling alone and angry. I felt like I had been pushed aside in my own house and it instantly became a source of raging, screaming arguments between Mum and me.

'Why can't you be happy for me, Ren? Why do you have to ruin it for me?'

'Why does he have to be here all the time? I don't even like him because you act like I don't even exist when he's around, everything is about Peter, Peter, Peter and I hate it!'

'Oh, the shoe is on the other foot now, is it? You feel left out! Well, I was the third wheel to you and your nan for years. All your private jokes and secret words. It's time for me to be happy!'

'I hate you! Nan was so right about you, all you care about is yourself. You don't love me, you only love yourself!'

'All I care about is myself? Do you know how much of my life I have sacrificed for you? Of course your bloody nan would say that to you, wouldn't she? She's dead and buried and still pulling all the strings on her little puppet. Well, guess what, kiddo? Now you can't go running off to hide behind your nan. You're stuck with me and I deserve to be happy too. Now get into your room.'

She was right, no longer could I pack my bags and threaten Mum that I was moving to Nan's and never coming back. When things got really bad, I still disappeared to the park for what seemed like hours on end, hoping that Mum would be worried sick and so grateful when I came home, dirty but safe. But whenever I came back, Mum never seemed bothered by how long I'd been gone, or even that I'd been gone at all.

'Do you have something to say to me?' Mum would say, not even lifting her head from her book.

*Silence.*

'I'm waiting.'

'I'm sorry.'

'Anything else?'

'I don't really hate you.'

The timing for Mum and Peter's romance was ideal for her, the euphoric feeling of new love distracted her from the loss of a mother she felt obliged to mourn. But for me, the timing was excruciating. In a matter of weeks I had lost my nan and my mother too. At night it was the worst – I could no longer jump into Mum's bed to cry or talk about Nan, because my spot had been taken. And the bedroom door was always shut. Again.

———

Lost in books, food and, perhaps most dangerously, my own thoughts, I spent far too much time alone for a twelve-year-old girl. Instead of going to Nan's after school, I was back to coming home to an empty house. I started thinking a lot about my dad, partly because I felt so alone now that Mum had Peter and Nan was gone, and I guess I also thought about my dad because without Nan, I knew he was probably gone from my life for good. Grandpa was my lifeline out of my lonely afternoons, my only saviour from my own thoughts. Every afternoon I called him at work and had him paged to a nearby desk and we would talk until his boss inevitably came to tap him on the shoulder: 'Neville, time to get back to work, these floors aren't going to clean themselves, are they?' When his boss was out of earshot, Grandpa would whisper, 'I have to go, lovey, bossy bugger he is! He thinks he bloody runs the joint! Next time I'll give him a piece of my mind –'

'He does run the joint, Grandpa, but you should tell him anyway. Just tell him in Irish, go on, shout, *póg mo thóin*, I dare you!'

'You cheeky little bugger,' Grandpa would chuckle and I could just picture his eyes sparkling, 'I will say no such thing and where on earth did you learn to speak that type of filth?'

'I learnt it from you, Grandpa!'

We would both hang up smiling, but when I put the phone down, I was alone again.

———

In the mornings Mum was gone by eight, and on weeknights and weekends the tiny unit seemed crowded now that Peter was spending every night at our place. There was nothing wrong with Peter on paper, I guess – he was funny, warm and genuinely seemed to care about whether I liked him or not – but it was hard to think of him as anything but staunch competition for Mum's attention, which was even more vital to me now that Nan wasn't around.

Peter and I had little more than awkward, forced interactions to start with, and my behaviour was closely monitored by Mum. I hated every second of it, however bribery is an excellent tool to crack the facade of most twelve-year-olds and Peter cottoned on to this idea early, often bringing me little gifts to try to win me over. Mostly he brought me new *Baby-Sitters Club* books, but sometimes he also tucked five-dollar notes into the covers for me so I could buy more books myself. Accepting Peter's presents made me feel a bit guilty about regularly offering his life up in exchange for my nan's as part of my nightly brokerage deals with God, but until God accepted my offerings, I didn't see the harm in expanding my already impressive book collection.

As soon as I could leave the two of them without seeming rude, I retreated to my room, book in hand, but before I allowed myself to read, I made my daily diary entry. Lying belly down on my bedroom floor with my lips millimetres away from the speakers of my pink ghetto blaster, I pressed PLAY/REC and started my secret diary tape to Nan. Every night I spoke to the tape recorder as if Nan was on the other end of the phone, telling her all about Grandpa, my woes with Mum, the latest development in The Peter Invasion and, of course, school. I didn't want her to miss out on anything just because she was dead. The hardest part of doing the tapes was always saying goodbye, because I treated every goodbye like it was the last time she would listen and no matter how many entries I made, I still never worked out how to properly say that final goodbye.

# 15

About five months after Nan died I started high school. I had always liked school, but I was nervous about finding my place among the hordes of girls who, like me, would be trying to navigate the vast Mackellar campus at the same time as the confusing web of adolescence.

Not long after I started, Mum announced that we were moving in with Peter. By this stage I was comfort eating my way through my grief and it was clear that the weight I was carrying was becoming a little more than puppy fat. Eating and reading were all that made me happy, all that were able to distract me from the gaping hole Nan's death had created and the sickening happiness of Mum and Peter sitting opposite me on the lounge each night.

When we unpacked everything at our perfect white cottage in Curl Curl, I found the box of my collector Barbies from Nan's place. This house had room for all my stuff, so I sat down and pulled out all of my old friends: Christmas Barbie 1989, Malibu Ken, the pink convertible they all liked to drive around in, and Skipper.

I had always enjoyed playing by myself, spending hours in complex fairytale worlds at Nan's and Grandpa's feet. But on this afternoon the dolls stayed silent. Somewhere between Nan's last breath and moving to Curl Curl they had turned their backs on me, and I wondered if maybe it was because they didn't want to play with a little girl whose mind was so cluttered with grown-up things.

It wasn't just my Barbies who had abandoned me: *The Baby-Sitters Club* did too. Almost one hundred perfect spines stayed lined up on my bookshelf, closed. Instead I buried my head in Mum's tattered old Virginia Andrews novels, enthralled by the deep, dark family secrets and complicated webs of lies. Finally, I found a world I could relate to. Maybe every family was keeping secrets like mine?

Perhaps predictably, the adjustment to being a live-in trio did not go smoothly. I didn't want to play happy families, and Mum, Peter and I began to fight constantly. I refused to do anything Peter told me to do, which resulted in me being grounded, which in turn led to more forced time together and more opportunities to fight.

The tension at home was becoming unbearable. I ran away several times, spending one night under the stars at the nearby netball courts, other nights at friends' houses and a long stint with a family I babysat for, but, being thirteen, it seemed inevitable that I would always wind up coming home. There was no peace at school either, with my primary-school friends Chantel and Justine taking to relentlessly bullying me day in and day out about anything and everything they could think of: I was too fat, I didn't have a boyfriend like they did, I hadn't gone to the movies with them on the weekend. It didn't matter what I did, it was wrong, until eventually it all came to a head and I was kicked out of the group. 'We just don't think you're cool enough to hang around with us anymore!'

'Yeah, you sort of bring down our image, I mean, it was probably always going to happen, wasn't it?' said Justine. 'I mean, even your own mum doesn't want to hang out with you anymore, does she? Weren't you just telling us she's totally dumped you for her new boyfriend?'

'We sort of feel the same, we've been putting up with you for too long now, but you're not in the group anymore, okay? You can't sit with us.'

It had been a mistake to share any of my feelings with them about the stuff at home, but I never thought they would use it against me like this. 'Guys, I'm sorry, I don't know what I've done wrong but I don't want to *not* be friends.'

'Well, you don't really have a choice, we just realised how much better the group is without you. Besides, you don't really fit in with us anymore . . . you don't really *fit in* anywhere do you, you're so fat now.' They started laughing.

'Yeah,' snorted Chantel, 'what happened to you anyway, your mum must be so ashamed, I mean look at her and then look at you . . .'

'Yeah,' Justine chimed in, 'I bet she wishes she never had you, especially 'cause she's probably going to have a new family with her boyfriend.'

'God, I bet her new kids are going to be beautiful,' said Chantel.

I hated them for knowing how to get to me. I tried to think of something witty to say back to them but while neither of them were beautiful, they were both thin and from pretty normal families, which is what seemed to matter most.

Every day I went to school and thought that the fight would be over and that we would be friends again, just like in primary school. But every day the teasing became worse, until they were hounding me for everything I did.

If I put food to my mouth they would shout across the playground, 'You shouldn't eat that, you stupid fat shit, you shouldn't be eating anything! You're already the size of a house.'

'You don't *need* that sandwich, do you?'

'Oh God, sir, don't ask her a question. She's so dumb, she doesn't know anything!'

I tried everything to make them like me again. I bought them things from the canteen when they asked me to, gave them some of the lunch money Grandpa gave me on payday, I even tried smiling at them when they were mean to me so they would think I didn't care, and then finally, out of desperation, I started to try to fix the things they were saying were wrong with me. I started skipping meals, going all day eating only an apple and then vomiting up everything Mum made me eat at home. I knew that if I got thin enough, they would eventually leave me alone.

I hated being at home and I hated being at school. I began begging Mum on a daily basis to let me change schools but she flat-out refused to even entertain the idea. 'No. Stop asking me, I'm not raising a coward. You have to face your demons, not run away from them and, besides, I'm sure it's not as bad as you think, you've always been an overly sensitive child.'

'Mum, it *is* that bad, it's *worse*, I swear. Why don't you even care?'

'They just want a reaction from you, they want you to get upset and I *know* you, I bet you give them exactly what they want every time! You just have to pretend it doesn't bother you.'

'I've tried that, they just won't leave me alone.'

When the words were no longer enough, Chantel and Justine started spitting on me from the balcony and pushing me on the stairs. I began to spend recess and the first half of lunch in the toilets and then dashed to the library when it opened in the second half of lunch. But when they couldn't find me in the playground it made things worse. One day, they found me in the E Block toilets. I was in the cubicle but they could see my shoes.

'We know you're in here.'

I didn't say anything.

'Come out, you gutless piece of shit, we've got something to tell you.'

'I'm not gutless, I'm going to the toilet!'

'Come out or we'll climb over.'

'Okay, I'm coming.'

I flushed the toilet to make my lie look authentic.

When I opened the stall, all of us stood looking at each other. Chantel was the tallest with cropped black hair. She was Maori with dark caramel skin that looked darker next to Justine's pasty white English skin that she got from her mother. Neither of them looked particularly threatening but it was their insides that were merciless.

'We're going to bash you after school,' Chantel boasted.

'Yeah, so you better watch your back, 'cause we are going to follow you home and get you when you least expect it.'

'But why? I haven't even done anything to you.'

'We just don't like you anymore.'

'Actually, we hate you.'

'That's just because you're both massive bitches!'

'Ooooh, she finally bites back!'

'And such a witty comeback! Let's see if you're still willing to call us bitches when we're beating the living shit out of you this afternoon.'

'Yeah, the boys are even coming to watch!' Justine crowed.

'So a whole group of you are going to come and beat me up, are you? Wow, that sounds like a fair fight, you're so tough!'

'You won't even be able to open that big mouth of yours when we're done with you, let alone talk so much shit!'

'Whatever,' I said as I moved past them out of the bathroom, 'I'm not even scared of you girls one bit, you're all talk.'

My whole body was shaking as I walked out of the bathroom. I wasn't really sure if they would beat me up – maybe they would, maybe they wouldn't – but hearing their cackles at my back, one thing was certain: I hadn't fooled anyone when I'd said I wasn't scared of them.

———

I went straight to A Block to use the school payphone to call Mum, the whole time trying not to cry because I was sure that one of the kids waiting in the long line behind me would report it back to Chantel or Justine. Finally it was my turn.

'Mum, it's me, I'm just calling to tell you that I'm leaving school early . . . I won't be wagging exactly, but I have to go home. If I stay they're going to kill me.'

'Who's going to kill you?'

'Chantel and Justine and I think some of the Balgowlah boys.'

'Renee, you are not leaving school because of two little thirteen-year-old bullies. You are at school to learn. We have talked about this – if you leave today then the problem will still be there tomorrow. You have to stay.'

'I'm not asking you, I'm telling you, I'm leaving. I don't even know why I bothered calling.'

'Don't you even think about stepping one foot outside that school. You can't run away from your problems, you have to face up to them. I am going to call the school the second we hang up and get them to check you are in class this afternoon. I mean it, Ren, don't run away, you will make it worse.'

'Please, Mum, they said they're going to follow me home and bash me! I have to leave!'

'I've told you what to do! Now I have to go, I'm at work.'

'Mum, please –'

'I'm going to call the school to check on you –'

'That won't be much good if I'm dead!'

———

Me, Chantel and Justine. The three of us sat in a row along the same work bench. Double science with Mr Murphy. Of course, when we had chosen our seats we had all been friends, but now it was insufferable. 'Today we're going to work in pairs. I need one of you from every second bench to join up with someone on the bench behind, come on, girls, hurry up, it's not rocket science.'

Of course Chantel and Justine paired up, so Elyssa from the bench in front came to be my partner. Elyssa was in the popular group but almost by default. She was blonde haired and blue eyed but didn't have an obnoxious or pretentious bone in her body. An elite gymnast, Elyssa could barely be bothered tying her hair back let alone trying to sneak make-up onto her face before school like the rest of her friends. Sitting alphabetically by surname for rollcall each morning meant Elyssa and I were placed next to each other, unlikely friends, but friends all the same.

The four of us worked on the bench side by side with our Bunsen burners, Chantel and Justine using every opportunity to remind me about what was happening after school.

'Look at her trying to act all cool, like she's not shitting herself –'

'I bet she bawls like a baby before we even touch her.'

The first bell rang, leaving one period to go. Maybe I could get to the bus before they held me back?

My stomach was in knots and I couldn't stop looking at the clock above Mr Murphy's head.

Elyssa whispered to me, 'What are they talking about, are they threatening to beat you up?'

'No, they're just being bitches, everything is fine.'

'It doesn't sound fine.'

Justine interrupted us with a time update. 'In half an hour you'll be face down on the ground, your bus will have left and no one will even notice you're missing until your mum gets home from work, although she'll probably be so relieved to get rid of you, she won't even come looking for you.'

'Hey, how about you bitches leave her alone, you've been trying to scare the crap out of her all lesson and I'm sick of hearing about it. You're both jerks!' Elyssa said.

There was a knock on the open lab door and everyone looked up at the excuse to stop working. The school messenger brought a piece of paper over to Mr Murphy and said, 'Excuse me, sir, Renee Davidson has to come to the office straightaway, they said she should bring her bag.'

I couldn't believe my ears, it was like I was in some sort of movie, saved by a guardian angel. I didn't care why I was being called to the office, I was just relieved to be getting out of that lab. Hopefully I was being expelled and I would never have to come back again. I could feel Chantel's and Justine's eyes on me as they watched me walk out.

Unbelievably, Mum was standing at the office in her grey-and-red AAMI uniform. I had no idea what made her change her mind and come to my rescue, but my eyes instantly filled with tears of gratitude and relief and I threw my arms around her. 'Oh my God, thank you, Mum, thank you for coming to get me.'

Peter was waiting for us when we pulled up in the driveway, a concerned look on his face. 'Is everything all right?'

'She's fine, I got her before the bell,' Mum said.

Inside, the three of us sat down and talked about what I should do. It seemed inevitable that there would be a fight so it was decided that I should at least know how to defend myself. Peter took me out to the garage and strung up his boxing bag. 'Show me how you punch,' he said. I held up my bunch of fives like Grandpa had shown me. 'That's good but you can't tuck your thumb in like that, it has to be on the outside, otherwise you could break it on impact. Watch me, okay?'

My eyes were round as I thought about breaking my thumb from punching someone. *I'm only thirteen*, I thought.

Peter continued, 'Now you have to stand with a split stance and always keep your hands up near your face. No, don't drop them otherwise they will have an opening and punch you right in the face!'

It was all very complicated and unnatural. 'But Peter, I don't even want to fight them. I'm too scared.'

'You may not have to fight them, it might not ever come to that, but at least you'll be prepared to defend yourself if it does.'

'Okay.'

Peter spent hours patiently training me in the garage. 'Jab, jab, hook, thumb out, Ren, good, keep your hands up, watch your stance!'

'Pete, I think if they actually hit me, I won't be able to remember any of this . . . it's too much!'

'Yes, you will, you'll be fine. The adrenaline will kick in and you'll be ducking and weaving like Mike Tyson.'

I loved him for all his efforts in preparing me for battle, but I knew in my heart I'd still probably be beaten to a pulp. When there was no more Peter could do with me, we went inside for dinner. As soon as we were at the table, I started.

'Mum, I really don't want to be in a fight. How come I just can't change schools? There are two schools in walking distance from here, I could probably take the test and go to Manly selective school, I think I would be smart enough to get in –'

'Ren, we've talked about this. You wanted to go to Mackellar with all your friends from primary school, that's the choice you made and now you have to stick with it. You should never run away from your problems. They won't hound you forever. They're just silly little girls.'

'Mum, please! I hate it, I hate going, please just let me change schools.' Tears and snot were leaking down my face.

Mum got up from her chair and bent down in front of me. 'Ren, I promise – one day you will thank me for this. I know it's hard but you will be okay. I'll tell you what, you only have two months left of school for the year. If you still want to change schools at the end of the year, we'll talk about it then. But I don't want you to ask me again beforehand, okay?'

I knew this was the only offer I was going to get. 'Okay.'

'Now about tomorrow, just because Peter has taught you how to defend yourself, it doesn't mean you can just start hitting people whenever you like. It is for defence purposes only. Under no circumstances are you to start a fight or throw the first punch. I don't want you to get suspended or expelled, okay?'

I looked over at Peter and we both laughed. Clearly Mum hadn't seen any of the 'training' going on in the garage, as she now seemed to think I was some sort of seasoned warrior.

Chantel and Justine were hunting for me the next day, furious that my disappearing act had upset their plans. We always started Wednesday mornings with dance class, jeté-ing up and down the dance hall with Mr Milne shouting, 'Legs straight, girls, and one, two, three, four, and next line, go! And one and two and three and four.'

'You think you're so smart getting yourself out of class yesterday, huh? I thought you said you weren't scared? You must have been scared to have organised to get out of class.'

'I'm not scared of you. I had nothing to do with getting out of class yesterday, I had an urgent family situation.'

'Yeah, well, nothing is going to save you today, straight after class, it's on! Everyone can watch now.'

After the bell rang, we all went outside the hall to put our shoes back on. I sat down, taking extra care to tie my laces in perfectly even double-knotted bows.

They waited for me to get up. 'Come on, you fat piece of shit, get up, we're going to fight and you can't run away now.'

I pulled myself up and looked Chantel and Justine in the eyes. There were lots of other girls standing around waiting to see what was going to happen.

'Look at you, scared shitless, no one's going to help you, you know, no one likes you.'

'Chantel, I don't even care what you're saying, if you're going to beat me up, just get on with it.'

Justine took a step back and it became clear Chantel was going to take the lead. Chantel edged up close to me and shoved me. 'Come on, fatso, are you afraid to fight back? Are you that pathetic you're not even going to defend yourself?'

'You're not even worth it, Chantel, if you want to hit me then hit me, you're the one always threatening to beat me up, so get on with it! I don't even want to fight. I still want to be friends.'

'Oh my God, you're so pathetic, as if I would be friends with you, you should just kill yourself and do us all a favour.'

'Fuck off, Chantel. Just hit me or leave me alone.'

'Come on, don't be such a pussy, Renee. Fight me!' Chantel shoved me again. 'Look at you, you're so pathetic.' Nose to nose, Chantel gave me three short, sharp shoves until I almost lost my balance over the school bags scattered on the ground. If I didn't do something soon, I was seriously going to have my arse kicked. It occurred to me that no matter what I did right now, we were never going to be friends again. For months I had been holding my tongue trying to win their friendship back, but for what? Why did I want it back? And if I didn't want it, why wasn't I hitting her?

As I looked into Chantel's taunting, smiling face, she begged me to fight her, dared me to hit her. She was so smug and safe in the knowledge that, after months of wearing me down, I would never have the guts. She and all the girls watching thought they had me pegged, thought they had defeated me. I wanted to be able to shock that cruel twisted smile right off her cocky face, but I was scared. Somewhere among all the indecision, I could hear a whisper of my old friend Ruby Tuesday's voice willing me to stop being such a massive pushover, because it was embarrassing: *Come on, Ren, Just do it!* she coerced. *Get your bunch of fives out and just punch her! Show her you're not some pathetic doormat she can trample all over, enough's enough!* But I could also hear Mum's voice at the forefront of my mind, shouting, *Don't you dare throw the first punch! You can defend yourself, but don't even think about throwing the first punch!*

It was like I had a little angel and devil sitting on each shoulder trying to convice me what to do.

*Bugger Mum*, I thought. *Let's do it, Ruby!*

As hard as I could, I shoved Chantel in the chest, watching as her eyes flew open in surprise. With an inch of breathing space between us, I tried to split my stance and clench my fists just like Peter and I had practised the night before. *Thumbs out, Renee, fists at chin height, okay that's about right, go!* Pulling my right arm back, I aimed for Chantel's nose, shutting my eyes just as I felt my hand connect with her face. *Shit I forgot to leave my thumb out!*

Very quickly, I felt Chantel's fist hit my nose in retaliation. *Bugger, I didn't keep my hands up like Peter told me either, I have to try and focus!* But then there wasn't any more time to think about technique, we just kept hitting each other, trying to land as many punches as we could. Peter had said I had to dance like a butterfly and sting like a bee: 'You have to be light on your feet and practise precision punches. It's not how many punches you throw – it's the accuracy and the impact.' Peter would have been mortified to see the brawling tornado that happened outside the dance room. There was no precision or grace, just listless arms and flying hair, until we were pulled apart by an outraged Mr Milne.

He took us straight to the principal's office. I should have been scared but I wasn't. I didn't care what sort of trouble I was going to be in, it would be worth it. The fight was over and I had come out okay – I wouldn't say that I had won, but I hadn't lost either, and I knew for sure that I wasn't going to let myself be anyone's punching bag ever again.

The fight made me realise that in my grief over Nan dying I had let my guard down. I had all but forgotten about protecting myself through Ruby until her indignant little voice popped into my head during the fight, demanding I stand up for myself. In forgetting about Ruby, I had stopped monitoring who I was, forgotten to keep my insecurities close to my chest and I had become vulnerable. I had allowed Chantel and Justine to use all my weaknesses against me and make me believe I was nothing. I had to get my act together, I was thirteen, not a baby anymore, and no one was going to swoop in and fix all my problems. I had to be less trusting. Less Renee and more Ruby. I needed to transform myself to be confident, funny, smart and thin! And not just some of the time, but all of the time. It wasn't enough for me to only mentally hide the truth about my dad behind Ruby, I had to wear her like an armour. And I had to be ahead of the game, instead of on the back foot like with Chantel and Justine. If I could just try to think of all the things about myself that were different from the other girls and try to fix them before they noticed, then no one could hurt me. In short, I had to be perfect. Just like the girls who put make-up on before school, I had to clear my head and put the Ruby mask on. I vowed to myself I wouldn't be vulnerable again. With Ruby as my armour, I would make sure that no matter how much people like Chantel and Justine tried to pull me down, I would never let them get to me. With secrets like mine, it seemed like turning myself into someone else was just what I had to do if I was to survive high school.

# 16

Mum had been right. After the fight, things at school did settle down a bit and I decided to stay on at Mackellar for Year 9. Mum, Peter and I moved to Narrabeen, right across the road from a cute surfer boy, Sam, and his gang of hot mates. Because I had been vomiting, taking handfuls of Ford Pills that I forced Grandpa to buy for me and doing two hundred and fifty Elle Macpherson 'pot belly crunches' every night before bed, I had high hopes of soon being attractive enough to get the attention of one of them.

Things at school were going well, and I'd seemed to gain a small amount of credibility for being in a fight, which helped me carve out a tough girl image for Ruby. I had finally settled into a good group of friends; I started playing netball, doing rock eisteddfods and I even joined the debating team, where my honed arguing skills were a force to be reckoned with. It turned out all the years of fighting with Mum – and now Peter – hadn't been in vain after all.

As my confidence grew, I became more disruptive in class, unable to keep any joke or witty observation to myself. I enjoyed playing the class clown and the harder people laughed, the more it fed into my Ruby persona. Funny people were popular, so I had to be more funny. Much to the fury of my teachers, it never affected my good grades; with a memory like mine I never had to work as hard as everyone else. Once I got a taste of doing well in things, I became obsessed with it. I didn't have to be the best all the time, I just had to be better than the majority – top five in the class was my cut-off. I loved beating all the girls whose parents paid for private tutoring and who spent their lives sucking up to the teachers. Just like being a smartarse, doing well at school was a way to get attention. I loved hearing Mum tell her friends how smart I was and I loved the look of surprise on teachers' faces when they returned highly graded papers to me, both of us equally unsure of how I managed to get the mark in the first place, let alone whether I really deserved it.

One of the things that separated me from the rest of the girls at school was how young and attractive my mother was compared to theirs. I now also had to explain Peter to anyone who slept over at our house, which was even more tedious. Apparently he was rather attractive to other teenage girls. It drove me crazy to have to lie on my belly encircled by friends I was supposed to be having fun with and instead answer questions about Peter or Mum. But it wasn't going to go away, so in maintaining my Ruby mask, I had to pretend it didn't bother me. I couldn't let people get wind of how awkward I felt about it all in case they used it against me, so I had to come up with some sort of emotionless and concrete way to respond when they asked. As a kid, Nan told me that when people ask you how you are, you should always say 'good', even if you're dying, because people don't really like to hear the truth, and so that's what Ruby did, she hid the truth. Ruby was happy and positive about everything, an emotionally impenetrable wall that refused to let anyone see any of Renee's vulnerabilities, flaws or tears. Ruby saved people from the uncomfortable truths of Renee's life.

'Peter's great, he makes my mum really happy, especially since my dad died before I was born. I don't think she thought she would ever find anyone to replace him.'

'It's great living together, it's like we're a real little family.'

'Mum and I are like sisters, that's how we grew up. My nan looked after us both, so when she died it was really hard. Luckily Mum met Peter almost straight after Nan died. He helped her grieve.'

Through Ruby, I magnified all the good in my life. Sometimes I had to extend the truth a little – or a lot – but it was worth it. People always like happy, uncomplicated, pretty girls better than fat, sad ones and the more I moulded myself into the Ruby mindset, the more I felt like I fitted in; that I was liked. Whenever a friend told me how pretty, smart or lucky I was, I felt like I had earned a gold star. If anyone commented on the weight I had lost, it made me feel proud and determined to lose more. But it was the negative comments that stuck with me – if someone even whispered the word 'fat' in my presence, it made me feel guilty that I wasn't doing more to be thinner, so accordingly I would eat less and work out harder. I realised I was in complete control of what people saw and knew about me. As long as I kept my guard up and my mouth shut, they could never know more than I was willing to share. Which, unless it was positive, was nothing. Other kids were always complaining about their parents being too strict or relentlessly hounding them about homework but I made sure I never complained about my home life to anyone. To be fair though, I didn't have much to complain about; if anything, I wished Mum would hound me more about homework and school, just to show she cared, but she never did. Sometimes Mum might ask, 'Have you done all your homework, Ren?' and I would reply, 'Yep,' but never once did she ever ask to check if I had or not.

The older I got, the more school work we got, which resulted in my friends being put under more pressure by their parents. Mum's indifference began to bother me.

'Don't you want to check my books to see if I've actually done the work or not?'

'No.'

'Why not? What if I'm lying and I haven't done any of my homework? Won't you be angry?'

'Not really, you would only be hurting yourself if you're lying. I'm not the one who wants to be a big fancy lawyer or whatever it is this week, so if you don't do your homework, then you'll fail and God knows how much it would pain you to fail.'

'What is that supposed to mean? Don't you want me to do well? Don't you want me to be a lawyer?'

'Ren, I don't care what you do, you could be a cleaner for all I care and I would be happy for you, if you're happy. School isn't for everyone; it's not the be-all and end-all you think it is.'

'So you're seriously saying you would be just as proud if your daughter was a cleaner, as you would be if I was a lawyer?'

'Yes, because I don't care what you do for a job. It's your life, you're the one who has to do it every day, not me.'

No matter what I said, Mum couldn't see how much I needed her to care. 'Why can't you be like other parents? Everyone else's parents actually care about school and what their kids do with their lives because they want them to succeed and be happy! You're my mum, you should *want* me to be a lawyer, because that's what I want. That's what parents do! I think it's insulting you would be happy for me to be a cleaner. Who wants their child to be a cleaner?'

'You're twisting my words. I'm just saying I don't care if you do your homework or not, it's up to you, you're the one who sets these ridiculously high standards for yourself, not me.'

'Well, someone has to care about my life, because you certainly don't! All you care about is Peter.'

It was in these moments that I felt so alone, like if I didn't push myself to achieve great things in life I would just end up being completely irrelevant. Like I was fast becoming to my mother.

# 17

Mum and I sat side by side on my bright blue doona cover, the one with the yellow-gold tulips on it. The sun was streaming in through my open window, a soft breeze blowing across our faces as we tucked our knees under our chins and our backs rested against the cool wall, talking and listening to the radio. Sometimes Mum did this, came in and closed the door, closed Peter out, so it was just me and her again. It made me happy to have her to myself, but also sad that it couldn't always be like this.

Sometimes we talked about Nan or Peter or Mum's jealous friends, who had all dumped her since she started going out with Peter. I liked helping Mum fix her problems; it made me feel useful to her, like she really did need me in her life.

One day Mum came in, her face brighter than the tulips on my doona cover, and I could tell she was bursting to tell me something but was trying to wait for the right moment. Finally, grabbing my hand, she said, 'I have something to tell you, Ren, and I really want you to be happy for me, okay? Say it, say you'll be happy for me.'

'Okay. I'll be happy for you. What is it?'

'Peter and I are having a baby! You're going to be a big sister! Isn't that exciting?'

In that moment I felt many emotions, but I can't say excitement was one of them. Mum might as well have told me she was dying. As far as I was concerned I had been put on notice, given nine months until I lost my mother to a baby born to a man she loved, not a man she hated, like with me and my father. It was overwhelming. In nine months' time she would be someone else's mother and at only fifteen I would be alone.

She was looking at me, waiting for me to say something. 'I'm so happy for you, Mum. That's so exciting.' I tried to smile at her, but my face wouldn't work and my eyes betrayed me by filling with tears.

'Don't be upset, be happy – you've always wanted a brother or sister.'

It was true I had begged for a sibling when I was younger, someone to share in my lonely world full of adults, but now that I was practically a grown-up? No. The mere thought filled me with shame. Nothing could possibly highlight how much of a mistake I was more than a new baby.

The bedroom door opened and Peter stood in the frame. 'Is everything okay? Can I come in?'

I tried to blink back my tears as we shuffled over, making room for him to sit next to Mum. He grabbed one of Mum's hands and the three of us sat side by side on my happy doona, my hand holding hers, hers holding his, and I wished the bed would just swallow me whole. No matter how hard I worked, no matter how perfect I made myself, I knew then and there that I would never fit in with their perfect new family.

With the news of the baby, the urgency to shed Renee and become Ruby became paramount. I was obsessed with becoming as perfect as I could be by the time the baby arrived. I suppose I thought that the more perfect I was, the more things I had going on in my own life, the less I would need Mum or Peter. I convinced myself that Ruby and the baby had the same gestation period. If I wasn't perfect by the time the baby arrived, then . . . well, it didn't matter what would happen because I had promised myself I *would* be perfect by then. I just had to work harder.

The one area of my life that I felt would affect my transformation the most was also the area that my mum had the least control over: my quest to be thin. I had been made very aware by Chantel and Justine how important it was to be thin, but, despite my efforts, I still didn't look like the other girls. Was I a terribly fat fourteen-year-old? No, but I was probably carrying a spare seven or eight kilos, which meant if I was going to be truly beautiful I needed to lose at least twenty. In my mind, being thin had become essential to my alter ego's success. I skipped more meals than ever before and I relied almost completely on my mother's earlier diet advice of only eating apples. Grandpa's constant desire to feed me chocolate éclairs and meat pies was now met with disdain: 'Stop trying to make me fat, Grandpa! We're not in Ireland, starving, like when you were a child. You don't always have to feed me!'

'But I love you, I want you to eat delicious things.'

'Food doesn't equal love, Grandpa!'

He looked wounded but the next time he came to visit his face was beaming as he presented me with a Cherry Ripe. 'Grandpa!'

I exclaimed. 'Don't you listen to me? I told you I'm trying to be thin, I can't eat this!'

'But you're beautiful the way you are and besides, I did listen to you! This is a Cherry Ripe, it's mostly fruit, look at the packaging!' He thrust it towards me. 'It says right here, "made with real cherries"!'

We each felt like we couldn't win. I didn't want to upset him, because every single weekend he travelled for an hour-and-a-half to come and see me, so as a peace offering I ate the Cherry Ripe and with every bite, he smiled and relaxed. 'Good girl! Now, I don't want to hear any more talk about you being fat, okay? You're perfect.'

'Okay, Grandpa,' I said and then I went straight to the bathroom and vomited the chocolate back up. At least this way we were both happy.

From then on I tried to make myself vomit at least once a day, usually after dinner, as it was the heaviest meal and the one that I could never get away with skipping. Often, after a day of skipping breakfast and trying to only eat apples, I would be unable to resist Mum's tuna mornay or Peter's chicken curry and I would gobble up everything on my plate, feeling guiltier and guiltier the closer my plate got to being clean. *Why can't you be more disciplined?* I thought, but it didn't really matter because I had found a way to get rid of it all. Every night after vomiting up my dinner, I went straight to my bedroom to start my exercises. I had recently bought an ab-cruncher and enslaved myself to a routine of sit-ups, push-ups, leg lifts and back raises, and I always finished off with two hundred and fifty Elle Macpherson 'pot belly crunches', which the magazines assured me would mean I was bikini ready in no time.

The more weight I lost, the more confident I began to feel. I started to get more attention from boys, particularly the ones across the road, and even my friends started noticing how different I looked.

Unfortunately, Mum also started noticing and it soon became the other thing we fought about. If it wasn't Peter, it was food.

'Where are you going?'

'To the bathroom.'

'No, you're not. Sit down.'

'I need to go to the bathroom.'

'I'm not stupid, Renee. Do you think I don't know what you're doing in there?'

'I just need to go to the bathroom.'

'Well, I'll come with you. From now on, if you need to go to the bathroom after dinner I will be standing outside the door.'

'Are you kidding me?'

'No, I am not. Peter and I work hard to put good food on your plate and you're in there vomiting it up.'

'You told me if I'm unhappy about my weight then I should do something about it, so I am.' I could tell I was frustrating her.

'I didn't say be a bloody bulimic! I said watch what you eat and do some exercise. Maybe instead of eating two helpings of pasta, you should just have one and not go and vomit it all up after!'

'So you think I eat too much, then? Well, that's even more of a reason for me to be thin. Now everyone thinks I'm fat, including my own mother!'

'I never said you're fat, Renee. I just think you should control your portions instead of overeating and then throwing up. You need to get outside in the fresh air and do some exercise.'

'I do lots of exercise! I play netball, I do an exercise routine every night, I ride my bike, I eat apples and I am still fat! Not everyone gets to look perfect from doing absolutely nothing like you do!'

'I am not perfect and this isn't about me. I am not allowing you to go to the bathroom to vomit up your food. Sit down.'

'No. If you're not letting me go to the bathroom then I'm going to go for a run.'

She looked pained.

'What? You just said you want me to exercise, so let me go!'

'Fine, go, but don't think I won't hear you if you go to the bathroom.'

From then on I had to be more careful. I started using little tricks to hide what I was doing, like telling Mum I was sweaty from exercise and having showers at night, quickly bringing up some of my dinner while the shower got warm, or vomiting in bushes when I went running at night. On days when Mum was watching me like a hawk, I took a handful of Ford Pills. Slowly the weight melted away, but it was never really enough.

At fourteen and nine months I was legally able to get a job, so I quit the cash-in-hand job at the local donut shop that I'd illegally been working at since I was twelve and started working at Kmart. I worked every shift they offered. Working at a large store allowed me to make a lot more friends of all different ages and from all walks of life. It was an opportunity to truly embrace my new identity. No one knew the old Renee, and I soon found a little gang of friends who seemed to really like Ruby. Working so much meant I could be out of the house *and* earning money, and with that came freedom. I never had to ask Mum or Peter for anything and the less I asked for, the more I felt like I didn't have to follow any of their rules.

For my fifteenth birthday I was given my first bikini, to show off my new slimmer physique, and, more importantly, a typewriter, so I could start writing books like R.L. Stine or my old favourites, *The Baby-Sitters Club*. The novels didn't get too far, but I did type up some flyers about my own babysitting services, which I dropped off around the neighbourhood. Soon enough I had a few regular families who enlisted my services on most Friday and Saturday nights, and before too long I was the most self-sufficient, cashed-up fifteen-year-old I knew.

—

As Mum's belly grew bigger and bigger, I started worrying incessantly about what it would be like when the baby came. Peter's family, Grandpa, even the next-door neighbours were excited about the baby being born, but I was worried about becoming more of an outsider. I thought about moving out, but I was too young and, looking at the price of rentals in the Saturday paper, I knew that, despite having a lot of money for my age, I couldn't afford it.

But then, like some sort of miracle problem solver, my French teacher came to class and encouraged any of us who were doing reasonably well to think about applying for the French immersion program. It was pretty reasonable if your family hosted a French student as a swap, but I knew Mum and Peter would never agree to that so I looked at the one-way program, which was almost ten thousand dollars for the year. But it was a year in France! *This* was what I needed to do; this was my opportunity to get away!

'Mum!' I burst in the door from school. 'There's this exchange program at school, you can live and go to school in France and immerse yourself totally in the life there so that you become fluent in French. I desperately, desperately want to do it, can you *please* look at the application?'

'A year in France? I don't know about that, Ren –'

'Please, Mum. It will be amazing.'

'I would miss you – wouldn't you miss me?'

'You'll have the baby by then, it can have my room – you won't miss me at all. Besides it's only a year!'

'How much does it cost?'

'Well, about eight-and-a-half thousand dollars but I have some money saved up and I can sell chocolate boxes at school to do some fundraising, plus I'll –'

'Eight-and-a-half thousand dollars? No, Ren, I can't. If you can pay for it, then go, but I won't do it.'

'I never ask you for anything! I pay for everything myself! Please can you just help me with this? Think about the opportunity, it would be life changing.'

'Ren, I'm not paying for you to go off to France when I haven't even been there myself, besides it's not just my money, it's Peter's too. Peter is the primary earner now, not me.'

'You could talk to him about it, I'm sure he would be happy if I was gone 'cause he could have you all to himself . . . you, Peter and your new little baby –'

'Don't start that crap again, Renee. You're fifteen! When you're older and you have your own money then you can do what you like with it.'

'It's so unfair! If Peter was my actual dad, then I'm sure you would both want me to have this type of experience, but of course you guys wouldn't want to spend that kind of money on me, because I'm not his child!'

'That's bullshit! Not all parents would just hand over that kind of money! If you're so convinced your *own* dad would pay for you then why don't you ring up and ask him? He hasn't contributed a single cent to your upbringing. No child support, no nothing. You know what? If you get your dad to pay for half, then I'll give you the other half, seeing as you have so much faith in a father you don't even know!'

'Really? Great, you'll pay half! Do you swear?'

'Your father won't give you the time of day! He's a criminal! He won't give you one bloody cent, I bet!'

I loved my mother for all that she was. In many ways I idolised her, her big smile, her pretty face, the way everyone seemed to just like her, and instinctively, I didn't want to do anything to displease her. Her immediate dismissal of France and her dare to get my father to pay for it got me thinking. Maybe he would pay for it? Maybe he had been thinking about me, wondering why he never heard from me or Nan anymore. Maybe he would be so happy to hear from me that he would want me to come and live with him when he finally got released.

Never in her wildest dreams would Mum have thought that I would take her words literally and try to track down my father, but if she knew her daughter at all, she would have known there is no more sure-fire way to get me to do something than to imply that I might not be capable of doing it.

# 18

Negotiating the prison system minefield was surprisingly easy. It had just taken a lot of trips to the payphone, a bag of silver coins and a fair bit of patience, but almost all of the prison guards were willing to bend the rules and transfer me though to other prisons and sections, until finally one guard asked me to wait on the line while they put me through to another area. And then a liquid, smooth voice came down the phone.

'Renee. My girl.'

———

I started speaking to my dad every couple of weeks, always calling from the payphone and never telling Mum. I didn't want to give her the satisfaction that she was right. Dad had said in our first phone call that there was no way he could give me even a dollar towards the exchange program to France, even though I gamely pointed out it was much cheaper than the years of paying child support that he had missed.

'I wish I had that kind of money, sweetheart, I really do, but I only earn eight dollars a week working in the carpentry shed here and that's more for luxuries like cigarettes, chocolate, phone cards, you know . . . not trips to France.'

'Eight dollars a week! God, I earn more in an hour and I'm only fifteen!'

He laughed. 'It's good you're earning your own money. You sound like such a smart girl. I'm sure you'll save up enough money for your trip one day.'

Why were all the grown-ups in my life so hopeless? I couldn't wait for a day when I didn't have to ask anyone for anything ever again, but until that day I decided that I kind of liked the idea of having a dad, a secret dad, who Mum and Peter didn't know was back in my life. It made me feel like I might have an out if things got too much, someone to talk to, plus he sounded genuinely pleased to hear from me. So I decided that I would keep calling him.

On 10 November 1997, I held my baby sister in my arms for the first time. Annie was a tiny bundle of perfection, already so loved and wanted by so many people that I swore to myself I wouldn't add my name to her list of fans, but in the end I couldn't help it. I loved her instantly. Her little nose, her sparkling eyes and above all the smell of her innocence. She was perfection personified, and I wished so very badly that I could be her instead of me. Everyone kept asking me how I felt now that I was a big sister, but I didn't want to be the big sister, I wished it was me being born to Mum again, with Peter as my dad, and that all the ogling aunties and uncles and grandparents were fussing over me now. I wanted so badly to have what she had that I could have cried. But how in the world could I have explained that to everyone? *Stop it! Stop thinking about that. You're fifteen years old, not a baby, you big sook! In three years you are out on your own, running your own life. There is no point wishing to be a baby again when you're practically a grown-up!*

Only a few weeks after Annie was born, the boy across the road, Sam, finally asked me out. The blond-haired, blue-eyed boy from a good family with a beautiful smile and a soft heart asked *me* out. From our first date everyone in the neighbourhood told me he was the type of boy I should marry and I pictured it clearly, because in my head, it aligned with my *Baby-Sitters Club* notion of perfection. As I dressed for our first date and then promptly changed because Annie spewed all down the front of me, I hoped with all my heart that this was it for me, that unlike Mum with her series of failed relationships, Sam and I would be together forever. Sam fit perfectly into my Ruby Tuesday fantasy life plan, because to me he was perfect.

⁓

Not long after getting together with Sam, I got accepted into the NRL Manly Warringah Sea Eagles cheerleading squad. Eight painstakingly long days after I auditioned, they called to tell me I made the cut. I could hardly believe it. I knew I wasn't perfect, still not thin enough, still not pretty enough and at best only questionably coordinated, but it didn't matter because I had successfully fooled the club into believing I was better than I was. Because hideously fat girls simply don't get picked to be Manly cheerleaders, right? Even I had to give myself that.

Two weeks later I was made captain of the school mock trial team, which meant representing my school in a renowned competition run by the Law Society of New South Wales. Births, Deaths & Marriages may as well have issued Ruby's birth certificate on the spot, because in my mind I had done it. I had pushed Renee and all her stained, dark imperfections so far down inside myself that only Ruby remained, which was a relief because everyone liked Ruby so much better. In fact, Sam's best friend liked Ruby so much that I ended up breaking up with Sam and started going out with him instead. Year 10 was going to be Ruby's year. My future was set – in a little over two years I would be out in the real world and a few years after that I would be standing on a stage dressed in black robes, mortarboard tilted elegantly on my head as I received my law degree. After that, well, naturally, I would be unstoppable.

# 19

A murderer, an armed robber and a Manly Sea Eagles cheer-leader are all standing on a country New South Wales train platform. It sounds like the set-up of a bad joke, but this was how my first unsupervised visit with my father and his new wife began.

It had been over a year since I'd tracked down my father and we'd made countless secret phone calls to each other before I was brave enough to approach Mum with the truth, inspired by Dad's idea of me going to his place for the weekend once he was approved for weekend release.

'He's not your bloody father, he's a fucking sperm donor! Why do you want to see him? It's me who's been your mother *and* your father your whole life – ME! Why are you doing this to me?'

'I'm not doing anything *to* you, Mum. He wants me to meet his wife and my half-brothers. If I don't go I'll always be wondering –'

'Fine, well you can just pack up all your stuff and leave for good then, go and live with your precious father and let's see what a great parent him and his jailbait wife turn out to be. You'll probably end up dead, you know!'

It was Friday, 6 March 1998, and about the same time as I was sneaking out of the school gates, my father was being marched out of Maitland Correctional Centre for weekend release, each of us anticipating our first face-to-face visit in six years.

The adventure began with a bus to the city and then the CountryLink train to Maitland. Plenty of time for me to think myself in circles. Weighing heavily on my mind was the fact that this would only be the sixth or seventh time that I had ever seen my father in the flesh. I had been so caught up in the novelty of pretending to be a 'normal' kid visiting my dad on the weekend that I had forgotten that nothing about this weekend was really normal. For starters, I wasn't even sure I would recognise him when I saw him. How ridiculous; who didn't know for sure what their dad looked like?

As I sat on the train, my stomach was knotting and fluttering. Oh God. A whole weekend with a man who watched the life of another slip away by the action of his own hand. What was I thinking? My mind raced through all the possible scenarios that the weekend might bring. Will I finally get to know the full story about what he did? What will my stepmother and little brothers be like? What if they don't like me?

I wanted so badly for them to like me, to feel like I belonged. I wanted a dad whose eyes sparkled when he looked at me, just like Peter's did when he looked at my baby sister. I wanted to feel normal.

The cityscape flattened out to farmlands and the sky faded from brilliant blues to wispy pinks and bruised purples. With my face pressed against the thick glass window, I watched fields of golden wheat change from canary to marigold and finally amber as the last rays of sun disappeared, tucking the farms away into the night's warm navy blanket. There was nothing to do but think. I remembered back to the phone call when my dad told me I was going to be a big sister. I had only just started processing Nadine's existence, and before I knew it, a baby was on the way too. Initially I had thought there must have been some mistake, and I was worried that I had been lied to again because even as a child I knew you couldn't have babies in jail!

'Dad, if you're really in jail, how can you be getting married and having a baby?'

He had gave a throaty, husky laugh. 'They have special visits here in jail: conjugal visits. They set up tents where you can have alone time with people you love, that you're married to. Do you know about the birds and the bees yet?'

'Um, yep.'

'Well, that's how we made your brother or sister. Nadine and me. You'll love Nadine. She can't wait to meet you.'

'So you met Nadine in jail too?'

'Yep and married her. You have to be married to have special tent visits. You shouldn't have sex if you're not married, okay?'

My nan had already told me a little about the birds and the bees but in no part of the story had she mentioned special baby-making tents. That had been another 'Dad' phone call that Nan had had to clean up after. Nan was a retired nurse who frequently claimed that she had seen and washed so many bits and bobs that she never got embarrassed by anything but I distinctly remember her cheeks turning a ruddy shade as she was forced to explain 'tent sex'. 'Well, dear, the way things work in jail is, the better behaved you are, the more privileges you get. And going on a good number of years now, your father has been what they call a model prisoner, so he has the freedom to enjoy certain comforts in life. With sex obviously being one of them.'

The train started to slow, forcing me back to the present, and I looked at my wrist: 8.03 p.m. *Shit! This must be my stop!* When the doors opened I flung my oversized school bag and myself out onto the starry platform without even glancing at a sign.

Looking around for a vaguely familiar man with a woman and two small children, I realised that these country stations were nothing like Central, no crowds to search through, in fact, no people to search through at all. If they had been waiting for me then I would have been looking at them, but there was no one except for a conductor in a miniature policeman-esque hat about to blow his whistle further down the platform. What should I do? Stay on the empty platform or get back on the train?

The train pulled away from the platform and made my decision for me and immediately I knew it was the wrong one.

'You right there, lovey?'

'I'm just looking for my dad, he's supposed to be picking me up. This is Maitland isn't it?'

'Nah, this is East Maitland, love. The next stop along the line is the main Maitland station. Perhaps your dad's there?' Looking at my blue-checked uniform, he said, 'That's not the Maitland uniform, are you not from around here, love?'

The guard came to my rescue, calling the next station and tracking down my dad. He would have to wait until I could get on the next train in half an hour. My face burned the colour of shame, eyes brimming with tears. What an idiot they would think I was, getting off at the wrong station.

It was almost nine o'clock when the next train pulled into Maitland and I spotted them straightaway: one arm around each other and their free arms stretched out to me. They had big smiles on their faces and so did the two little boys hovering near their legs.

'Hello, darlin', come over here!' my father said, pulling me to him. 'What a silly bugger y'are, getting off at the wrong stop! I told ya it was Maitland!'

My dad was by no means a big man but I was overwhelmed by the enormity of everything he represented. He had an impressive-looking mullet and was built like a Staffy, stocky and muscular and covered in tattoos; a typical meaty prison body just like I'd seen in the movies. One of his arms read like a roll call: Renee, Gemma, Nadine and Ryan, the eldest of my two little brothers. I didn't have time to find the baby's name because Dad wrapped his arms around me, crushing me to him, then pushing me back to arm's length.

He stood looking at me, searching my face as if in disbelief. 'God, look at you! You're not a little girl anymore, are ya?'

I shook my head, acknowledging that a whole lifetime had literally passed him by: mine. There was sadness in his big brown eyes, which were tired and soft looking, rimmed with regret – or maybe it was longing? I didn't know him well enough to be sure.

'I'm so happy you're here, Renee. Give your old man another hug.'

As we embraced, I thought how surreal it must have been for my dad; holding a teenage daughter in his arms, almost the same age my mother had been when she gave birth to his first child. A living, breathing reminder of a life that could have been theirs.

'All right, all right, get outta the way, Mick, and let me get a look at the girl.'

Dad's wife was the very definition of a butterball, no taller than five-foot-two and rounded in all the wrong places. Nadine wore a white lace-trim singlet over an ill-fitting black bra with one wayward strap that kept sliding off her shoulder, drawing my eyes to her heavily tattooed arms and chest every time she hiked it back into place. Her hair was lightning blonde with charred roots, styled in a mullet matching my father's. I allowed myself a small smirk, wondering whose idea it had been to have matching hairdos. Thank God Dad's was minus the peroxide.

Nadine's gravelly voice said, 'Well shit, Mick. Ya can't half tell the girl is yours, can ya. Look at her, she's the spitting image of your ugly mug, poor thing!' She winked at me and grinned. 'Now let's stop pissing about at the train station and get these kids home, ay, Mick!'

Nadine was already halfway down the platform, barking something or other at the boys when my dad draped his arm over my shoulder and half-whispered, 'Take no notice of her. You're beautiful. You look just like your mother the day I first saw her, except better fed.'

———

Waking up on Saturday morning, I didn't know what to do. Should I go out to the living room? Or stay in the room and wait? The house was quiet, so I sat and waited. *Tap, tap, tap. Tap, tap, tap.* A little giggle behind the door. 'I'm your brother, so open up or I'll huff and puff and blow your house down.' I opened the door to a gap-toothed grin. Ryan.

He must have been five or six, a cute little thing with big blue eyes, a shock of blond hair and a penchant for cuddling this big sister of his that he had never met before.

'Come on! I've got trucks!' Tiny hand, firm grip, Ryan pulled me from room to room searching for his cars. My little brother.

I took in my new surroundings. Peeling wallpaper penned with toddler art, thinning carpet stained and worn. The walls were bare, no paintings or photos, and every piece of furniture was old and brown. *Mission brown*, Mum would have said with a turned-up nose.

Hearing Ryan, Nadine was soon up, appearing bleary eyed with the baby on her terry towelling–robed hip. 'Morning, love. Coffee first then I can talk to you. Come into the kitchen.'

She set two steaming mugs of instant black coffee down on the plastic tablecloth and sat opposite me. I looked at Nadine and brought the mug to my lips, pretending I was grown up enough to like coffee.

She must have only been thirty but the deep lines on her face and smoker's jowls made her look older. My nan had told me years before that Nadine had served hard time for armed robbery and assault after she held up a bank at gunpoint. Nadine had been free for five years by the time I sat across from her in her kitchen, but I guess the damage had already been done, her face hardened by life, and the physical exhaustion of raising two young boys alone while waiting for my father to be released from jail.

'I want you to know you can trust me,' she said. 'We are going to be great friends, you and me. I have three boys, one older than you and these two, but now I finally have a girl in the family. I want you to know that you can tell me things that you can't tell anyone else, if you want to. Things you can't even tell your mum! That's what stepmothers and stepdaughters do.'

From the first day Nan, Mum and I learned about Nadine's existence, my nan and mum had hated her. Nadine was the one who had convinced my father to tell me about The Secret in the way he had, without Mum or Nan knowing it was coming, and therefore in their eyes she was evil, but maybe she wasn't actually that bad? I sort of liked her.

'What are my two girls talking about?'

'Nothing,' Nadine said.

'Ah, secret girl talk, ay? Well, let's make some grub. Who's up for pancakes? We've got a big day ahead of us.'

Dad had the weekend mapped out: we were going to spend the morning at home talking and getting to know each other and then after the baby's sleep we were going to the Maitland Bike and Hot Rod Show. Dad chewed with a slack mouth and his fork poised for action. With his elbows on the table and his body hunched over his food as if protecting it, he looked at me, not bothering to swallow before asking me the next in a long series of questions: 'What's your favourite food? Do you have a boyfriend? What's your best subject at school? Your best friend's name? What's mum's boyfriend like? Do you like living at home?'

And then it was my turn. 'Ask me anything you like,' he said, probably not realising I had been waiting a lifetime to hear those words. Nadine looked at me reassuringly as she led us to the lounge room. What did I have to lose?

'What's jail like?'

'You get used to it, I s'pose. There's some decent blokes . . . It's not so bad now 'cause I'm in sort of a share house with guys who are all about to get out like me.'

'Who were the men you killed? What did they do that was so bad?' I was like a starving child with a piled plate and no grown-up to warn me to start with small mouthfuls. I could see Dad was uncomfortable with my line of questioning, which made me feel smug for a reason I still can't quite put my finger on.

'Why don't we just keep getting to know each other, ay? Whaddya say? Keep it light.'

Did he really think I'd come all this way just to find out his favourite food was still fried chicken?

'Be honest with her, Mick.' Nadine prompted him to answer many of my questions, which no doubt rewarded me with more information than I ever would have extracted on my own. She seemed eager to hear what he had to say too, although I'm sure she'd heard it all before in their penpal letters to each other while they were still inside.

'Tell me what you already know first.'

*Why were all the grown-ups in my life always looking to tell me as little as possible?*

Like a bird humming fragments of a song heard on whispered winds, I began telling them what I knew. It was soon clear to all of us that I knew everything and nothing at the same time. Dad's brown eyes stared into my brown eyes, our olive-coloured arms and legs lost in their mission brown lounge. Everything was bland and brown except the conversation; expectation hung in the air.

'We were drunk.' He sighed. 'And we decided to rob the place of a man we knew, a teacher called Peter Parkes. We knew him from the streets, and he owed us a fair bit of money . . . for services rendered, you might say. And he did stuff to young boys . . . he wasn't a man, he was a coward, they both were.'

'What happened when you got there?'

'Things got out of control . . . Peter came home.'

'Why didn't you just leave when he came home?'

'We got into a fight. He owed me and Andrew money.'

'Why did he owe you money? What stuff did he do to young boys? Did he do stuff to you? Where was the second guy? Did they try to kill you guys?'

I likened myself to a weaver bird, collecting a twig of information here, another over there, before piling all the pieces together to admire my progress. Slowly I was bringing together the pieces of my beginnings – conjuring an image of the elaborate nest of lies I first took flight from. With every new discovery, I was awash with delight and disgust.

'Nan said you stabbed them with a kitchen knife. She said that after you stabbed them, you and Andrew sat in the kitchen peeling and eating apples with the same knife. Is that true?' I needed this bit not to be true. It didn't fit the 'steal from the rich and give to the poor' mould I was trying to squash him into.

'You can never understand the way it was . . . That first night with Peter we panicked, we didn't know what to do, I don't really remember how it happened or who did what . . . we both did it . . . With Con it was different though –'

'What do you mean it was different? Who's Con? Didn't it all happen at the same time?'

Lips and jaw tight, pupils round – he was annoyed. But after years of Mum's incomplete drunken confessions, I was too hungry for his sober details and truth to care.

'No,' he hissed, 'it didn't happen at the same time. Peter Parkes, the teacher was first, okay? The night with Con was a few weeks later.'

What? Two separate nights? Two separate murders?

The expanded truth hung in the air and I felt a shift inside me. It was becoming increasingly difficult to believe that my father was a moral crusader caught up in the heat of the moment. The evidence seemed to be mounting that the man who had breathed life into me might just plainly and simply be a cold-blooded murderer.

By the time we arrived at the show it was late afternoon. There were rides twirling, children squealing, neon bulbs illuminating the sweaty vendors who were working double-time to fill hungry hands with Pluto Pups, snow cones, hot chips and wands of fuchsia fairy floss.

Watching my father take in his surroundings at the show, I caught a glimpse of what he might have looked like as a young boy. Eyes squinting in the sun's diminishing rays, he seemed excited, gaze darting here and there, fingers pointing. His whole face was alight, brimming with possibility and life. Thinking about it now, it must have been so thrilling for him to wander anonymously through the crowd, shoulder to shoulder with the society he had left behind sixteen years earlier. No one watching him; he could break into a run and no one would follow – he was just one of the crowd. He briefly grabbed my wrist, steering me to the right, so we didn't get separated, and instinctively I pulled away, heart conflicted. Isn't this what I wanted, a father to love me, guide me? I wasn't sure what I wanted out of this trip anymore but I was absolutely certain that my father and I were not yet on familiar touching terms.

If he felt me recoil he didn't say, instead playing up the boring-dad role by telling me the history of the show: 'People come from all over the country to this show, you know, they pull more and more numbers every year, which means every year, there are rarer cars and flashier bikes. I read it in the brochure,' he said proudly.

I hated bikes and cars but even I had to admit that the Maitland Bike and Hot Rod Show had pulled a decent crowd. The show-ground was swarming with people, and hordes of forgettable faces passed us by until suddenly I was faced with the not-so-forgettable: gangs of men straddling big, gleaming motorcycles as far as the eye could see. An army of leather adorned with silver studs, each marked out by the name of a club emblazoned across their leathery arms and backs.

We stopped on The Gladiators turf. The ground was littered with crushed black bourbon cans and cigarette butts, discarded by callused, oil-stained hands. Each man wore the patch of a rotting skull with hollowed-out sockets and grim teeth, luminous against the shiny black leather. Nadine was kissing cheeks and Dad slapping backs as I stood behind them, trying hard not to gape. I had never seen bikers before, not in real life anyway, yet here I was submerged in a sea of bulging bellies hanging over blue jeans, long beards and stubbled jaws, pock-marked skin and blurry eyes, all of them different but somehow the same.

Dad had a surprise for me. Standing beside him was a beastly looking man as wide as he was high. His sunburnt face was flaking and his smile was dotted with black holes where teeth should have been. As Dad introduced us, I struggled to decide which was shinier: Kenny's bald head, his fist full of knuckle dusters or the gleam of the black bike he was resting against.

'Renee, Kenny. Kenny, my daughter, Renee. Kenny here is going to take you for a ride on his Harley. How about that?'

It seemed to be an instruction rather than an invitation, with no time or opportunity for me to say no.

Throwing his cigarette on the ground, Kenny swung his leg over the bike. 'Get on, darlin', whaddya waitin' for, a special invitation? C'mon, lovey, get ya arms around me tight and hold on.' I had never held a man before and this wasn't the one I'd imagined I'd start with. When Kenny kick-started the engine, the roar filled my ears with the sound of danger, but it also mercifully blocked out any last-minute instructions that were being barked at me by my dad, Kenny and Nadine, who was excitedly hopping from one foot to the other, clearly itching to swap places with me.

As we pulled away, all thoughts about not touching the beast evaporated and I gripped Kenny's leather vest tightly. When Kenny slowed down to turn out of the showground gates, I quickly let go of him to push the hair out of my face. I had no idea where we were going or for how long, but out on the road, the music, the lights, the festivities faded and everything was black. There were no streetlights or cars, just the sound of the throbbing bike and the wind whistling in my ears.

The whole time I was on the back of the bike I could hear my mother's voice: *Why do you want to go up there for the weekend? With him? They could kill you and I wouldn't even know about it until Sunday night when you don't arrive home.* I imagined my body in a ditch somewhere and wondered if my mother would hold it against me, seeing as she'd told me so. I was part way through mentally planning my funeral when Kenny pulled back into the showground and I was forced to acknowledge that perhaps I had not inherited only my mother's looks but also her tendency towards drama.

My father stood eagerly waiting to hear all about my first motorbike ride. 'I'm taking Renee on the Cha Cha for some father–daughter time,' he shouted to Nadine as he grabbed my arm to lead me through the crowd. Being afraid of Kenny seemed misguided when the imminent ride with my father clearly represented a far more terrifying reality: being alone with him.

I remember being conscious of two things as we lined up for our first father–daughter ride: my extreme aversion to spinning rides, and my father's careful words of warning that morning – 'No more talk of the bloody past, okay, girl? I'm almost a free man. I've done my time and I don't need you coming here and dredging up the past like some reporter. All of this is behind me, behind us!' But the weekend had resulted in more questions than answers and I couldn't let my opportunity slip away.

'Dad, why don't you want me to ask you any questions? Mum doesn't want to talk about it, you don't want to talk about it, but it's my life too . . . I just want to know the truth and then I won't ask again.'

He kept staring straight ahead as if he hadn't heard me.

'Tickets, please. Thank you. You can get on any carriage you like, sir. Heaviest person on the outside of the car.'

It was our turn to get on the ride. The sun had set and the music was blaring from huge black speakers at the sides of the stage, which our carriage was now facing. We sat looking ahead, and for the first time I noticed the girls on stage, dancing, gyrating, touching themselves, their breasts, naked bum cheeks, their crotches. My dad was watching too. The ride jerked into motion, spinning slowly at first. The girls on stage were shimmying their tops off, full round breasts exposed, squashed together.

My father put his arm around me and pulled me close, our thighs and sides touching. 'All you need to know is that I love you,' he whispered.

Round and round and round we went, the ride getting faster until eventually gravity denied me the ability to move out of his embrace. My head threatened to explode with my father's words, 'I love you, I love you, I love you', while at the same time The Communards' 'Don't Leave Me This Way' blared through the Cha Cha's dodgy speakers. I couldn't focus my eyes. We spun and spun, neon lights and jiggling breasts everywhere. The ride, the visit, this reality – I wanted to get off.

When the ride stopped, we sat waiting to be released by the attendant. I could see Nadine and the boys waiting near the exit, waving furiously, and I wondered if I might vomit. My dad's arm was still fixed around my shoulders, and he put his mouth to my ear. 'Did you hear what I said before? I love you.'

I felt like shouting, *Did you hear what I said before? I need answers!* But instead I whispered, 'Yes.'

'Well, aren't you going to tell your old dad you love him too?'

The attendant strode towards us to release the bar.

'Renee, don't you love me?'

*Clang.* The bar was up and I was out. Shoulders free from the weight of his arm, I ran down the steel ramp, but before I could even think about where to run, Nadine was upon me.

'It's okay,' she said, 'you're okay.'

My dad was at my back in seconds, hands on my shoulders. Everyone was too close to me – I couldn't get enough air.

'What's wrong with her? I just told her I loved her . . . What's wrong with her?' my dad kept shouting.

'Mick, just get your hands off her and give her some space.'

As I lay in the darkness that night, my cheeks burned with humiliation. I had let my emotions take control. I had failed myself, failed again at masking my emotions through the cool, calm and together facade of Ruby. Why did I do that? Why did I run? I had wanted him to love me, hadn't I? We could have been just a regular father and daughter riding the Cha Cha together if I hadn't run. Except that we weren't. We never would be. I now knew I didn't belong here with them, but I didn't feel like I really belonged at home either. Wide awake, I lay in my father's house counting down the minutes until I could leave for the train, and not for the first time in my life, I wondered why in the world my parents ever thought it would be a good idea to keep me.

———

Standing on the platform the next day, I let my father hold me longer and tighter than I really wanted as penance for the way I had behaved. We were back where the weekend had begun. As I pulled away to get on the train my father said, 'This isn't goodbye, it's just see you later. I really meant what I said last night . . . You don't have to say it back, but I want you to know, I do love you.'

I lowered my head to avoid meeting his gaze, the burden of responsibility weighing heavily on my conscience. I cleared my throat. 'I love you too, Dad.'

I wanted the words to be true, but they weren't. They were only a parting gift that I instantly wished I could take back.

The four of them waved and smiled from the platform, mouthing words that I could no longer hear through the thick glass window. As the train started pulling away from the station, I felt myself exhale for the first time that weekend. Maybe this was enough now. Maybe it was finally time to forget about The Secret for good.

# 20

After the trip to Maitland I told myself I knew enough now to just let it lie; I didn't need to know every detail about what had happened. But when it came to the idea of having a father I just couldn't let it go. I started to doubt myself. Maybe I had been too judgemental of my father, too immature about decisions and situations I could never understand. Maybe if I was more open-minded there could still be a way for me to build something with him. So I started calling him again, sporadically. Every time I did call, though, the pressure to visit intensified. But I couldn't go again. The very thought of being held close by him, kissed by him, still made me physically shrink from the phone. I kept making excuses about cheerleading a big game, babysitting, or working lots of shifts, but I couldn't stop myself from calling him.

Shortly after I turned sixteen, Mum and Peter announced they were expecting another baby. The pregnancy news was a shock and it instantly flung me further out onto the periphery of their perfect nuclear family. I just desperately wanted to get as far away from them as possible. I already spent as little time at home as I could, working every available shift and accepting every offer of a sleepover at friends' places that Mum permitted, but news of the baby meant I sought out these escapes even more. By now I had become the friend to invite on other people's family holidays – Forster, Port Macquarie, camping at The Basin. And then the golden invitation from a new best friend: two whole weeks in Fiji with her family. Amanda was pretty much the most normal person I had ever met: shy, conservative, sweet, and from a good family. She went to a private Christian school, but despite our obvious differences, we had become inseparable at work. I took the invitation as a testament to Ruby's success, proof of how good I was at pretending I was a normal teenager, a Northern Beaches sunshine kid who wasn't a murderer's daughter, wasn't an unwanted blight on her mother's new family and who wasn't constantly worrying that her Ruby facade would be exposed if she ever did or said the wrong thing. Looking back, I can't decide if I was more thrilled at the thought of going overseas or by how much Amanda and her family must have liked me to extend such a big invitation. But either way, I knew I never would have been invited if they had known the truth about me.

Mum agreed to let me go, with a few conditions. 'You have to pay for everything yourself, including your passport, and I'm not doing all the running around for the paperwork. And you have to try to get along better with Peter.'

'Okay! Whatever you say! Thank you, thank you, thank you!'

'I wouldn't get too excited, Ren. Both parents listed on your birth certificate need to sign the passport forms because you're not eighteen. I've tried to get this sorted out before. You need your father's permission to leave the country.' I could see the irritation on her face at the thought of having to ask my father's permission for anything.

'Don't worry, Mum. It will be fine. I can do it all. I'll just call him and then fax the forms to him; he can sign it all and fax it back. I don't think it will be a problem.'

'I should have listed your father as unknown. It was a mistake that I'm still bloody paying for!'

As I sifted through the paperwork Mum had dug out for the application, I read my birth certificate for the first time. Mother: Gemma Davidson, 16 years old, unemployed. Father: Michael Karl Caldwell, 20 years old, labourer. Child's name: Renee Joanne Caldwell.

Caldwell? That wasn't my name! My whole life I had been Renee Davidson.

'How come on my birth certificate it lists my last name as Caldwell, like Dad's, and not Davidson, like yours? Isn't Davidson my real name?'

'Of course it is, there's another certificate there somewhere that legally registers your change of name to Davidson . . . I was just trying to do the right thing by him, giving you his name, listing him as your father. Like I said, mistakes, all of it, that I'm still paying for.'

'But I thought he was arrested when you were still pregnant with me? Why did you want to do the right thing by him if he was already in jail for murder?'

'Oh Ren, I don't want to talk about any of that stuff, it's in the past, you wouldn't understand even if I did tell you.'

Locating the change of name form, I looked up at Mum, confused. 'This change of name form is from when I was four already. Why did you wait until I was four to change my name?'

'Does it really matter? Your name is Davidson. I said I don't want to talk about this stuff with you, just get your father to sign the forms and go on your bloody holiday.'

'Why can't you just tell me? It's okay for me to know certain bits of information or for us to talk about it all bloody night if Peter's out and you've had a few drinks, but it's not okay for me to ask any questions? Surely I can ask questions about my own bloody name, for God's sake? Everything always has to be on your terms and it sucks! I can never get a straight answer out of anyone about this stuff!'

'It's not important!'

'It's my NAME! My *past*. I think it's pretty important!'

'You're unrelenting! You'll be a fantastic lawyer one day, because you have no compassion; you're like a dog with a bone! Fine, I'll tell you. I was young and stupid, your age . . . I stayed with your father through the court case and then for a while after you were born. We were married – you were at the wedding actually – and then after a while I realised it was a mistake. I applied to have the marriage annulled and then I sought permission from your father to change your name, so we could be the same. That's it. Now you know.

'Here are all the forms, I've signed all my parts, now you just need to organise your sperm donor. You can use the home phone to call just this once.'

'Where did you get married? In the jail? Or was he allowed out? Did you wear a big white dress? Was I the flower girl? How long did you stay married for?'

'I'm not talking about it!' The look on Mum's face was thunderous, yet pained. 'I told you about your name and the rest has nothing to do with you. Now use the phone, before I change my mind and make you walk to the payphone.' Not often did I back away from an argument, but by now I had learned that some truths were better off being investigated when adults were lubricated with wine. This was one of them.

———

'Hold for the prisoner, please.'

I waited and then heard a click.

'Hey darlin', it's been a while since your last call. Before you came up you used to call every other week and now it's just every blue moon, that visit must have scared you off proper, ay?'

'Yeah, sorry, I'm mean no, it's not the visit, it's just that we've been really busy moving house and getting ready for Mum and Peter's new baby, and with school and stuff, I guess I just –'

Mum scowled at me and shook her head. 'Don't say anything about me! And hurry up!' she whispered. Annie's chubby baby legs were slung around Mum's growing belly, her head resting on Mum's shoulder, ready for her nap. With Mum supervising I felt nervous, almost certain I would fail at saying the right thing to please both ends of the call.

'Um, Dad, I can't stay long on the phone today, but my friend's family invited me to Fiji with them and I need you to sign my passport application. Would it be all right if Mum faxes . . . I mean, if I fax you the forms to sign? Mum said it's kind of urgent because it takes a while to process the forms –'

'Stop saying my name,' Mum mouthed at me.

'Is that your mother I can hear there in the background?'

'No, I don't think so, it's my little sister.'

'I can hear her, put her on.'

I mouthed to Mum, 'He wants to talk to you.'

She shook her head. 'No way.'

'I can hear her. Tell her I just want to have a quick talk to her. I just want to hear her voice.'

'Mum, he can hear you. He just wants to talk to you quickly, he said.'

'No. We have nothing to talk about. I don't want anything to do with him.' She moved towards the stairs with both her baby and her belly cradled protectively in her arms as if my father might jump through the phone and snatch away her happiness. 'I'm going upstairs, hurry up and get off the phone, Renee.'

'She won't talk to you, Dad. She says you have nothing to talk about. I think I better go. Can I send you the forms to sign?'

'I'm not signing anything or letting you go anywhere until I get to speak to your mother, she's right there, it's not much to ask.'

'She's not here anymore, she's gone upstairs! She won't come back down to speak to you.'

'You're lying. I know she's there!'

'I'm not lying. I swear she's gone upstairs. She doesn't want to speak to you and once Mum makes up her mind she never changes it!'

'Go and get her. You change it for her.'

'I can't, she won't talk to you.'

'Then I guess you won't be going on your trip.'

'Why do you want to talk to her so badly?'

'You can't just call when you want something and not expect to have to give me something in return. I'm going to hang up the phone. Don't bother calling me again unless your mother is willing to talk to me.'

The phone went dead in my ear. I tried to call back but the guard told me my father refused to accept my call.

I went upstairs to Mum. 'He isn't going to sign the forms,' I said. I wanted to cry but I didn't want her to see how disappointed I was.

'Well, I don't want to say I told you so but, there you go, that's your wonderful father for you! Remember the father you so badly wanted in your life? Now you have him to thank for not being able to go to Fiji.'

'Can you try not to look so pleased, Mum? And don't worry, it's not just Fiji he said no to, he said no to having anything to do with me too, he just wanted you the whole time, not me.'

I turned my back, leaving her and Annie to play. I couldn't believe she was trying to score points in this moment. I needed to be alone. On the sands of Collaroy Beach I sat and tried to let it all sink in. How was it that my own father, a convicted murderer who had virtually nothing and nobody to fill his days with, couldn't see the value of having a relationship with me? Why was I so disposable?

---

A few months later my father was a free man. I knew it was coming, because his weekend release had been part of a bigger plan to slowly prepare him for life back out in the community, but it was still a jolt to have our lives cross paths via the television.

My mother and I stood riveted to the TV, me dressed in my school uniform, bowl of Special K in hand, as the morning news-reader talked about the brutal Kings Cross murders of Peter Parkes and the Greek Consul General to Australia, Constantine Giannaris. Mum and I listened to a brief recap of the crimes, Andrew's suicide in jail and then about my father's good behaviour during his rehabilitation period which, 'in spite of the brutality of his crimes has resulted in Caldwell being released after serving just one of his original four life sentences.'

My mother had been worrying for months that they would mention her name or even mine in the reports of his release, but the mountain in our minds was just a molehill in the newsroom, and the report swiftly moved on to the well-documented push from some politicians for tougher policies on Australian prisoners, including the enforcement of original sentences handed down by judges, using my father's case as an example. The program then changed to something else, probably the weather, and slowly movement seeped back into the lounge room. I slopped my unfinished bowl of cereal into the sink, kissed Mum goodbye and ran to catch my bus. We never talked about his release again. Nor did I ever see his face again after it appeared on television that morning.

# 21

'Each student is to choose a well-publicised Australian crime and research the case. It can be any type of crime, but try and choose one that is well documented. Most of you will probably choose a fairly old crime, so I'd suggest taking a trip into the State Library, where you can access some of the old newspaper archives. You're senior students now and this is a major assignment, so I want to see evidence of bulk research time and a much higher standard of work than you have previously submitted in junior years. Questions?'

I had no questions but I held high hopes for answers. Surely if my father's release made the TV news, then his imprisonment would have at least made the papers? How did I not know that libraries kept old newspaper articles? For all of these years I could have gone and done my own research on my father's crimes instead of bothering with the adults.

I dressed for school the next day with absolutely no intention of going. I boarded an earlier bus than usual and stayed on with all the commuting suits over the Spit Bridge, over the Harbour Bridge and then by foot to the quiet calm of the State Library.

Having barely used a computer before, I had no idea how to use the newspaper cataloguing system and I desperately wanted to avoid asking for the librarian's help because I was convinced that when asked to find articles on murders committed by Michael Caldwell, she would know that I was his daughter and I would be shamed out of the library. But in the end I had to relent and the librarian was less interested in my detailed ramblings about the school assignment and more interested in expressing her utter disgust at my lack of library research skills. With a few keystrokes, the librarian had narrowed down the search to a hundred or so articles with the words 'Michael' or 'Caldwell'.

Heart racing, I began trawling through each article. The first few matches were just sports results and birth notices but within a few clicks I was engulfed by the murders as news headlines exploded with the possibility that a serial killer was on the loose in Kings Cross. An article in the *Sydney Morning Herald*, 17 November 1981, described the similarities between the two murders:

> A psychopathic murderer who has already killed a homosexual school teacher may have viciously stabbed to death the Greek Consul General ... [the] 41-year-old private school teacher had also been bound by hand and foot and gagged before being stabbed to death.

The front pages of Sydney's daily papers screamed about the 'Kings Cross Sex Murders' and the 'Hunt for Gay Blade Killers'. Quarter-page drawings showed the layouts of the victims' apartments, pointed out exactly where the lifeless bodies lay slumped when police arrived and detailed the murder weapon: a 20cm black-handled carving knife. For years I had collected drips and drops of information, slowly building up my well of knowledge, and now the floodgates opened thanks to black-and-white images I would never be able to erase from my mind. My father's crimes were suddenly more of a big deal than I had ever thought. Front-page-of-the-newspaper big deal.

And then the suspected culprits were found. *Sydney Morning Herald*, 1 December 1981:

A 19-year-old prostitute, Michael Caldwell, and a 16-year-old juvenile have been charged in the murders of Constantine Giannaris, Greek Consul General to Australia, and Peter Parkes, a gay activist and school teacher . . . Both men were found bound and gagged, and appeared to have engaged in sex shortly before their murders.

And also in the same edition:

A fifteen-year-old girl was also charged yesterday in the Children's Court with wilfully concealing knowledge of murder. The court heard that the girl, who was weeping in court, lived in a de facto relationship with Michael Karl Caldwell charged with the murder of Peter Parkes and Constantine Giannaris.

My heart sank as I realised the fifteen-year-old girl must have been my mother. Had she really known about the murders? Had she gone to jail too? Surely not, but I knew I could never ask. And my father! I had spent all these years believing that he was some sort of crusader and it turns out he was not only a murderer but a prostitute too! What was my nan thinking when she decided I needed this man as a father figure? My head was pounding. The library walls started closing in on me and it felt like everyone in the stacks had stopped to look at me. The words on the computer screen screamed at me.

*Who am I? What sort of blood is running through my veins?*

I continued clicking, trying to ignore the overwhelming fear that came with these new truths. When I got to the articles about the trials, my father's voice came alive as if I was watching him being tried for his crimes in the courtroom. In the *Sydney Morning Herald*, 4 November 1982, his statement to the jury was quoted:

'I went upstairs to pinch the stuff and . . . Andrew stabbed him twice in the throat. He was bleeding and struggling a lot and he kicked the table and made a lot of noise. He ended up on the floor and Andrew stabbed him in the back. I held the knife and Andrew hit it in.'

Was it really my dad who killed these men? Was he just trying to push the blame onto Andrew?

And then on 27 November 1982, the *Sydney Morning Herald* reported that my father was:

'convicted of the murder of Constantine Giannaris at Darling Point on November 14, 1981, and school teacher Peter Parkes at Potts Point on October 20, 1981. Caldwell was sentenced to life in prison, with Justice Lee telling Caldwell, 'You have shown yourself to be a vicious and cold-blooded killer.'

A vicious and cold-blooded killer.

If we are made up of half our mothers and half our fathers, how much of the vicious cold-blooded killer had trickled into my blood? What part of the woman who concealed two murders and went on to marry the culprit was in my DNA? It was too big to think about.

I put it aside for later and instead distracted myself with the dates. Something about the numbers had me transfixed, kept pulling me back to them. What was I missing?

The first murder took place on 20 October 1981. I was born on 20 July 1982. Maybe it was as simple as that? The twentieth held meaning because it is the same date I was born. But just in case, I counted the months from Peter's death to my birth. November, December, January, February, March, April, May, June, July. Nine months. Peter Parkes died on 20 October 1981 and nine months later to the day I was born. It seemed to me to be the most shocking revelation. I imagined myself as mere morula, burying into the lining of my mother's uterus, while at the exact same moment, streets away, Peter Parkes lay bleeding out from his stab wounds, gasping through his gag for his very last breath. In just a matter of days, my father had both created and extinguished a life. And for some reason I was overcome with guilt. It was as if Peter Parkes's life had in some way been exchanged for mine.

There were more and more articles to click through. In the latter years of my search results almost all of the articles were centred around my father's accomplice, Andrew, mainly because his family were protesting against the harsh sentencing imposed on someone so young. One article made reference to an interview renowned Australian reporter Mike Willesee conducted with Andrew while he was in jail, quoting Andrew as saying, 'Michael

Caldwell played the biggest part in my demise. I think if I had not met Michael Caldwell, I would not have committed those crimes.' Not long after Andrew's interview with Willesee, the papers wrote about Andrew's completion of an autobiography, *Between Dark and Daylight*. Three weeks after completing his book, Andrew hanged himself in his cell. *Oh God,* I thought, *more blood on my father's hands and a full-length book to remind me!* But, to my relief, when I checked with the librarian she told me that the book was out of print. I couldn't read it now even if I wanted to.

Faced with the prospect of going home to flesh out my hours of research into a school project, I realised there was no way I could ever willingly give over any of the information I had found about my father to anyone at school. I had thought I could submit the assignment as if it was just about some random murderer and of course no one would ever know but, faced with the task, I just couldn't. What if someone guessed I had a connection to the murderer, or asked why I had chosen this particular crime? With all that I now knew, there was no way I could sit down and colour in borders and do fancy bubble-writing headings to jazz up the pages that detailed my own father's horrific, bloody crimes. The thought was sickening. My mum and nan had been right all those years ago. No one would ever accept me or love me if they knew these awful things, knew what was in my blood. I would never be invited to sleepovers, or on wholesome family holidays with friends. I would be a social outcast. It was in that moment I knew I would probably have to play Ruby forever.

I hastily spent the last hour of my time researching another murderer, deciding that this time I truly had to be done with all of this secret stuff. Nothing good could come out of it, or out of

# 22

For all intents and purposes, the idea was that my Ruby persona should be perfect, but, like a normal teenager, I made bad decisions, experimented with drugs and alcohol and desperately tried to please my peers, which inevitably led to moments of vulnerability. In the predictable fallout, I judged myself harshly for exposing my true self, for making so many mistakes. I found it increasingly hard to balance my desire to be 'one of the gang' with maintaining my cool, calm and unaffected Ruby exterior, because, quite frankly, the two often collided in a heap. After a string of boyfriends, each lasting a few months, I began to think I had made a mistake breaking up with Sam. All of the boys I had been out with since had been great at the start but after a while they either liked me so much I found it suffocating or not quite enough for me to feel like they were worth the investment. It didn't help that I was paranoid that boys were only after one thing – a lesson I had learnt from my mother – and I was adamant I was too young for that. Being the result of a teenage pregnancy myself, people often expected me to follow suit or at the very least to be a massive tramp, and in silent protest I had set all of these rigid guidelines as to who and when and how would be the most appropriate scenario to lose my virginity. In true *Baby-Sitters Club* style, none of the scenarios in my head involved being on a sandy beach with some drunk guy I barely knew. It had to *mean* something. It had to be with someone I really loved.

So one night in the long Christmas break just before I officially started Year 11, I rang Sam to offer a long overdue apology for breaking up with him for his best friend and for parading it in his face for three agonising months. 'It's fine,' he said, 'it was a long time ago. How about I come and pick you up and we go for a drive?'

Within a few weeks we were inseparable. Completely and utterly immersed in each other's lives the way only sixteen- and seventeen-year-olds can be. If I wasn't at school or work, I was with Sam. We practically lived in his room or his car, just talking about our lives and listening to Red Hot Chili Peppers. Even though I would never have told Sam about my dad or how I really felt about most of the stuff going on at home, things were always easy between us, I was as much of myself with him as I could be without jeopardising what we had, because I knew he was never searching for imperfections in me.

———

In May 1999, my sister Ashleigh was born. Peter and I were each holding one of Mum's hands as Ashleigh took her very first breath in this world and I don't think I have ever quite been able to look at my mother the same way again. The hours of pain, the fierce determination on her face as she brought a life into this world . . . It was impossible not to think of her all those years ago, even younger than I was, pushing through the blood, sweat and tears with no one she loved holding her hand and then finally getting to hold me. I could almost see how she would have looked at me all those years ago, similar to the way she was looking at Ashleigh now, but even more mesmerised, because back then I was literally all she had. Seeing Mum in that moment made me feel bad about all the times I had told her she shouldn't have kept me, that she should have had an abortion and got on with her life, because in that moment, for the first time ever, I got it. I finally understood that she didn't keep me for my sake; she kept me for hers. At that time, Mum needed me to save her from the engulfing misery of her own life, she desperately needed someone to love, who would always love her in return. And I did.

—

By the time I turned seventeen I barely thought about 'playing' Ruby because, aside from keeping secrets about my family, I was living the 'Ruby' life I'd envisaged. Running on the confidence gained from superficial peer approval, the complete adoration of a doting boyfriend and a growing self-belief that maybe, just maybe, I might be working hard enough to get the marks for the life I so badly wanted, I had become the person I'd set out to be. Life seemed easier than it had ever been. I got my licence and bought myself the Freedom Mobile, a bright yellow Barina. I still struggled with my body image, but I was no longer vomiting every day and for the most part I was happy with who I was and how far I'd come.

Things at home were also calming down as I started finding my feet in this odd modern family I belonged to. The peace was in part thanks to my car. I was little more than a fleeting visitor at home. But it was also largely due to things becoming more strained between Mum and Peter. The worse things got between them, the more I was called in to be the impartial peacemaker. In a bid to help them renew the spark in their relationship, I volunteered to regularly babysit the girls so they could go out. Mum and I became closer again, often confiding in each other about what was going on in our lives, which for her was usually to do with trying to come to terms with how different her relationship with Peter was since they became parents. For me it was all about Sam and the HSC. Peter and I also forged a new bond, largely because I had something he did not: the ability to make Mum listen. He often came to me for advice on how to deal with Mum because, despite all their years together, only I could talk her down from the precipice of darkness and despair when she was in her most heightened emotional state. Peter tried his hand at navigating her out of the angry red hue of an argument many times but usually it only intensified, and frequently it ended with the contents of Mum's shoe cupboard being hurled at his back as he hastily made way for me to come in and do the emotional clean-up. It was in these periods of catastrophe that I became Peter's ally and, over time, an unlikely and steadfast friend.

As a teenager, any relationship that lasts more than a couple of weeks is fairly significant, so by the time I started Year 12, Sam and I were pretty set in stone. Sam was the most normal person in my life. He knew me better than most, but in the years since we had first met I had still only occasionally slipped and let my guard down with him about my insecurities. Sometimes, if we were out at a party and I got outrageously drunk, I would sit in the passenger seat of his car on the way home and cry with worry that if he knew the truth about me he wouldn't want to be with me, that I wouldn't be good enough. 'We are just so different, Sam; it's never going to work out between us.'

'Of course it's going to work. It is working, everything is great between us! Don't cry, I love you!'

'Just because you love someone doesn't mean it's going to work. There is still so much we don't know about each other and there is *so* much that is different about us.'

'Well, I'm pretty sure you know everything about me, what could I possibly not know about you? I know everything about you.' But of course he didn't, probably no one ever would. What would it be like to live my whole life and never have anyone truly *know* me?

On our first anniversary we finally slept together and it was exactly how a first time should be: tender, sweet and very awkward. I still can't imagine losing my virginity to a nicer person but it was bittersweet, because I already knew I wanted it to be over. It was hard to say goodbye to Sam because being with him was like being in a warm bath, it was just so easy to keep re-submerging myself. But I knew if I stayed much longer, the life I wanted to lead would pass me by. I was just about to turn eighteen and I had had enough of all the hand-holding *Baby-Sitters Club* stuff – I wanted to feel more than warm comfort. I wanted fire and passion.

We stayed together a few more months because I knew once I finally got around to ending it I would gain my freedom but instantly lose my best friend.

'We're both so young and so different. You're the type of guy girls like me should marry. I feel so . . . secure with you, but I'm only seventeen, I want to experience life, take risks. We just want different things. You're happy to live on the Northern Beaches forever and I can't wait to get out of this incestuous sinkhole. You finished school months ago and have no idea what you want out of life and I have clear plans to take over the world . . . right?'

We laughed at the last comment, knowing full well I was only half joking. And then I burst into tears and somehow it was left to Sam to comfort me while I persevered with busting up our high-school sweetheart love story.

# 23

Of course there were more boys after Sam, but no one worth jeopardising my exams over and no one nearly as important. I lived and breathed the impending HSC and took as many shifts at work as I could, certain I was going to need a lot of money to set up my new university life.

The night before my first exam, I cried to the point I could barely breathe with the pressure of it all. What if I failed? What if I didn't remember any *Othello* quotes? What if my calculator broke? 'They are just exams,' said Mum and Peter, trying to calm me down. 'You've done all you can do now, you just have to go and do the exams and whatever happens, happens.'

Peter tried particularly hard to reassure me. 'When you're my age you will wonder what all the fuss was about. No one even asks you for your HSC marks when you're older. The exams will pass just like everything else does.'

While I was in stress mode for the exams, Mum and Peter were in high-energy mode for their wedding. Peter had proposed the year before and despite not really getting along any better than they did then, the big day was planned anyway and somehow they could find no other day for it than three days into my HSC schedule. Mum spent much of the morning of the wedding being annoyed at me for trying to read my study notes, when, as her only bridesmaid, I should have been focused on the wedding. I suppose I could have set the study aside for just one day, but in all honesty I was still smarting over the fact that they couldn't have planned the wedding for any of the other eleven months that I didn't have to sit my HSC. They literally could not have cared less about the exams that I felt I'd been preparing for most of my life.

The day after the wedding, Mum, Peter and the girls flew out for a two-week family honeymoon to Fiji, leaving me to sit the rest of my exams alone. There had been many an argument about how selfish I thought it was for them to leave me in what were only the most important days of my life to date, but neither of them seemed to flinch as I viciously spouted teenage suicide statistics at them, hoping that they would change their minds and stay. They didn't.

In the endless summer days of limbo after the exams and before the results were released, I started going out with Ben. It was something to do. Ben was a friend of my good friend Luke who I had often seen around but never really bothered talking to much. Whenever I had seen him he seemed to be too drunk to talk, or happy to just stick with the boys. Ben was taller than all the other guys and he just seemed different, more serious, despite his baby face. Luke had told me Ben was the same age as us but had left school in Year 10 and had already been working for a few years. I guessed that's why he seemed more troubled than the rest of us – he was already a grown-up.

I invited Ben to my school formal and we officially became an item that night. My friends couldn't understand what I saw in him.

'His teeth are so crooked!'

'You can do way better than him, he didn't even finish school!'

'He's a wannabe thug who hangs out with all those Department of Housing kids who never move out of home, you know, the ones who rort Centrelink and get paid cash in hand. Why would you want to be with him?'

But the more people told me it wouldn't work, the more I was convinced it could. I didn't care what any of them said, they were all just superficial spoilt brats anyway, handed everything by their parents, but I could tell Ben wasn't like that. He was more like the me that I didn't let anyone else see. There was something in him that mirrored my own hidden imperfections, but he was obviously more honest than me, because at least his imperfections were laid bare. I loved him and his troubled boyish face almost immediately.

Even before I got my results back, Ben and I made a pact that we would give the long-distance thing a shot. He knew that all my first choices of uni were out of state, but we decided we had been brought together for a reason and we would try to make it work no matter which uni I was off to.

My exam results were available online at 6 a.m., Monday 18 December, in the year 2000. At 5 a.m. I heard Annie rustle. Sick with anticipation, I decided I might as well get up with her and let Mum and Peter sleep in, seeing as I had literally spent the night counting down the minutes until my future was decided. I took Annie downstairs, keeping her on my hip as I turned on our IBM dinosaur. Computers and I have always had a fraught relationship and this, coupled with the painstakingly slow dial-up connection we had, made me worry that I wouldn't be able to access my results at all. I wanted everything up and running with plenty of time to spare. While the computer whirred and the kettle boiled, I thought back to the first time I ever said I wanted to be a lawyer.

I was nine, dawdling out of the hairdresser's with one foot in the gutter and the other on the footpath, as Nan and I made our way to the club for prawn cocktails, my reward for suffering through yet another visit to Ludwig, Nan's hairdresser, who painstakingly perfected Nan's 'set' every pension day, even if it intruded on school holidays. I smiled at the memory.

'Do you think you might like to be a hairdresser when you grow up, Ren?'

'No way, Nan. I hate hair! I'm going to be a super-important lawyer who sends baddies to jail.'

'Are you nervous, Ren?' Mum appeared, taking Annie from me.

'Yep. I'm just waiting on the computer to start up.'

*Enter your student number and pin code*, the website instructed me. I wanted to have a practice go before it was time. I typed in my numbers and hit enter. The screen reset and the box came up with a ridiculously high grade.

*That's an unfairly high mark to use as the example*, I thought, and then I retyped my numbers once the clock ticked over.

The screen reset, but the stupidly high numbers stayed the same, again and again and again. I felt my heart pounding in my chest. My legs felt like they were about to cave under me. Could that really be my mark?

I whirled around to Mum, who looked uncertain as she tried to interpret the tears in my eyes. I was shaking.

Throwing my arms around her, I squeaked, 'I did it, I did it! I got the marks! I'm really going to be a lawyer now!'

# 24

Only weeks into my shiny new law-school life, my grand plans for world domination hit a slight hiccup: I couldn't find a job to pay for that life. With thousands of university students all descending on Canberra at the same time and most of them as desperate for cash as me, it was near impossible to find anywhere even accepting resumes, let alone one that was actually hiring.

Kimberley, a third-year student rooming in my on-campus house, said, 'If you want a casual job in Canberra you have to arrive at least a few weeks before the first semester starts, everyone knows that! You and every other student at UC wants a job, not to mention all the students at Australian National Uni too. You'll probably just have to wait until later in the year now when people drop out and move home or when the mid-year graduates finish. You could definitely get something then!'

'In the middle of the year?'

'Yeah, no one is actually *from* Canberra, you know, so everyone just moves away when they finish, which means they leave their jobs. Just ask your parents for money until then, that's what I do, although I'm third year now and I still haven't got around to getting a job.' I had already pegged her as one of 'those' kids whose parents did everything for her, but no job in three years? What a freeloader!

In the weeks before moving away I had worried incessantly about whether I would make friends, whether I would be smart enough to get through all the work after blabbing on to anyone who would listen about being a big-shot lawyer and, of course, I worried about what I was leaving behind: my friends, my family and Ben. Not once in all my worrying did I consider that I would find it hard to get a job! I had six years of work experience by then and had been financially independent – except for birthday money – since I was about fifteen, so I didn't like my chances of suddenly becoming parent-funded any time soon.

After a few weeks I got a small windfall: I started umpiring at the Monday night university netball competitions, which paid ten dollars a game. The trouble was that there were only two games, but it was a start. It turned out to be a great place to meet other uni students too and after a couple of weeks I got friendly with Sarah, one of the other umpires. One night we stayed back chatting after the last game and I asked her if she knew of anyone looking to hire someone. 'I don't care what the job is, I'll do anything,' I said.

'Anything?' She laughed at me, raising a well-plucked eyebrow. 'You really are desperate!'

'I'm actually beyond desperate so, yes, I will literally do anything.'

'Okay, well, first you should start looking further out of Belconnen, at other jobs, not just retail. I work at a fireworks outlet in Fyshwick and my roommate used to work at a brothel doing reception before she got a job at a bar in Civic. You can earn more money outside of retail because there are more hours, lots of places in Canberra are open twenty-four hours. Do you have your bar cert? I could ask my flatmate if her bar's got anything going?'

'No, not yet, I don't really have anything except my HSC!'

'Oh, that's right, you're a first year. Okay, so Fyshwick is your best bet then, and best of all, they'll pay you cash in the hand. Have you been to Fyshwick yet?'

'No.'

'You're in for a treat, then. Think freaks, fireworks and fucking and you'll have a pretty good idea what you're in for. But you'll definitely be able to earn some cash!'

———

The following Friday afternoon, after my morning classes, I drove to Fyshwick armed with my resumes. The night before my adventure someone had conveniently left the local paper in the common room of our house and I had cut out all the ads for every firework shop and adult store advertising their wares, so that I had a heap of addresses for my mission the next day. Lying in bed, I woke up suddenly, my heart racing – what if someone saw that just *those* ads had been cut out? In total darkness, I ran back out to the common area, thankfully finding the paper exactly where I had left it. I snatched it up and returned to my room with it, my secret safe.

Fyshwick is about a 25-minute drive from the University of Canberra, a little longer when you're unfamiliar with the streets and as bad with a street directory as I am. My plan was simply to drive around and drop the resumes in to all the fireworks shops and adult stores.

Several stops in, my pile of resumes was getting lower and none of the options looked favourable. The next place I went to was

Lilly's, a tiny sex shop that somehow managed to transport you to midnight the second you stepped over the threshold and set off the buzzer. The windows had been painted black, along with the walls inside, ensuring that the second the door closed behind you, the day and any sense of light and time was gone.

A guy who looked about forty was sitting on a stool behind the counter, eyes flicking between the screens positioned up on the walls. One screen was security footage, a view of the car park in which I could see my little Barina before the image flashed to a top shot of the counter and our heads. The other screens had an image of a blond-haired, all-American-type jock wearing only stark white running shoes and socks while thrusting into a naked girl bent over next to a sparkling pool.

I looked back to the guy behind the counter, hoping I hadn't been staring at the screen too long. 'Hi. I was wondering if the manager is in? I wanted to see if you guys might have any jobs available?'

'Oh. Not a customer then?'

'Um, no, not today. Are you the boss?'

'Sure am. What's your name? What can you do?'

'I'm Renee and I can pretty much do anything.'

'I'm Joe,' he said as he reached out his hand to shake mine. 'Convince me.'

Joe was looking for someone to do night shifts. He had a guy away and wasn't sure if it would be permanent. He also wasn't sure I was entirely right for the job.

'How old are you? Are you sure you can work long hours? They're pretty long.'

I felt like getting the job depended on my next answer so naturally I lied.

'I just turned twenty, and the longer the hours the better.'

He looked at me, his thick black brows furrowed in thought. 'Okay, I'll give you a go, but only as a trial, and only if you can start tonight.'

———

That first night at Lilly's I worked from 6 p.m. until 4.30 a.m. for eight dollars an hour. I was supposed to work until six but I was practically asleep on the counter, so Joe said, 'Go! Get some sleep. Come back at six and be ready to work the whole shift. Don't expect me to let you go early again!' He paid me eighty dollars cash from the register and I walked out from the blackness of the store into the crisp darkness of a starry Canberra night, warmed by the knowledge that now that I had a job, everything was going to be all right; my mapped-out life was safe. I got home and crawled into bed fully clothed, drifting off to sleep, thinking about vibrators, 'O' beads, ass-terbaters and handcuffs. Never mind the legal education I was trying to pay for, Lilly's was an education in itself.

I agreed to work Friday and Saturday nights as well as one or two other night shifts during the week. My job was to serve the customers who came in and make notes of everything that was sold so that Joe could reorder items. I also tidied up the shelves and the shop and had to make sure there was a constant loop of porn playing, something I failed to remember on my second night and I was almost fired on the spot. Aside from the continuous porn, there were a couple of other rules I had to follow: 'Never raise your eyebrows or judge the customer even if they ask for something totally fucking weird. If we don't have it, tell them we can order it. Don't get bullied by the girls from the brothel around the corner.

They'll try to convince you to let them take some lingerie or a costume or something without paying for all of it upfront; they'll swear blind that they'll be back with the money after their first client but the second they make any cash at all they conveniently forget about their debts and just shoot it all in their arm instead. Don't get me wrong, the girls are good customers, but unfortunately one lying cunt ruins it for the rest of them, okay, so no loans to any of them, got it?'

I raised my eyebrows in response and then, remembering the first rule, immediately furrowed them. 'Okay.'

When I worked with Joe, he either stayed out in the back office chain smoking and drinking coffee over paperwork, or he slept on the mattress he kept in there on the floor. His eyes were perpetually tired and he could be quite snappy, so while he had told me it was okay to wake him if it got really busy or I wasn't sure about anything, I felt nervous shaking his body to life when I got stuck on something.

The hours were exhausting but I quite enjoyed the spectacle of working in a sex shop. The best thing about it was that I could work thirty-plus hours a week, which meant that I would definitely be able to save up the seventeen hundred dollars I needed to keep living on campus by the end of term, but aside from that, I didn't mind the actual work either. I found it fascinating to analyse everyone who came into the shop and even more riveting to see what items they purchased. Before working at Lilly's, I'd never been in a sex shop, let alone taken the time to think about who might frequent them, but I was generally surprised by the customers walking through the door. Some were young and others really old, some came in groups, some as couples, but most were alone. For the first few shifts I did little else but watch the customers and how Joe interacted with them. Some nights I worked with a guy named Glen, who was also a student but at the other university. It was Glen who told me to bring my uni stuff with me and when it got quiet we could study. Glen was in his last year of his business degree, half of which he reckoned he had completed at Lilly's. It was almost the perfect job.

Just like Joe had warned, a lot of the girls from the nearby brothels came in frequently and at all different hours. I didn't necessarily know they were prostitutes until Joe or Glen pointed them out, but once they did I always recognised them when they came back in. A couple of the girls were fairly regular and all of them came in to buy vibrators to use on their clients or outfits to wear at work. I almost choked when I realised how much they were paying for such tiny scraps of material. 'How can they afford to pay so much for this stuff when they are so desperate for cash?' I asked Glen on my third shift after he had just finished flirting with one of the girls from around the corner.

'Desperate for cash? Are you serious? Some of these girls earn a fuck-load of money and they enjoy what they do. They aren't all *Pretty Woman* street whores living hand to mouth you know.'

No, I didn't know. I didn't have the vaguest idea.

———

After three weeks of glorious income, I got fired. It was a build-up of things, I guess. There was the night a customer asked me which vibrator I liked to use on myself while Joe was standing right next to me. Caught off guard, I knew I couldn't say that a few weeks ago I had never even seen a vibrator, so instead I answered, 'I don't really need a vibrator, because I, um, have a boyfriend.'

When the customer left, Joe shook his head and said, 'What were you thinking? You sounded like a frigid prude, it's not like the only people who use vibrators are desperate singles. If you don't know the products then just make up an answer, say something like, "Oh, there's this one I love over here, let me show you," and then just go and point at one and say, "Ahh this is it, the rabbit, it's a great seller." That's not so hard, is it?'

It wasn't, in theory, but once I started recommending products I found I was unable to do so without blushing and stammering and just generally cementing my inexperienced prudish status to Joe, who always seemed to be behind me rolling his eyes whenever I was put on the spot. The final nail in the coffin came on my three-week employment anniversary. A young guy with a shaved head came in dressed in gym gear. He looked at me but didn't speak, which wasn't uncommon with some customers. At any rate he looked like he could navigate the store pretty well himself, so I assumed he was a regular who probably knew where to find what he was after better than me. After a while I wondered where he was, so I checked the security camera. I could see him huddled up close to the shelves making jerking movements; his penis was visible out of the top of his sweat pants. I had never seen anyone masturbate before and I panicked. What if he comes around to the counter? What if someone else comes in? Should I let him finish or interrupt? I thought Joe would kill me if he found out I let someone jerk off all over his shelves so I called out, 'Excuse me, is everything all right back there? Can I help you find anything?' But the guy didn't answer.

I decided to wake Joe. I thought he would be pissed at the guy masturbating in his store but he was definitely more pissed at me for waking him. 'Oh for fuck's sake! Are you kidding me? Stay here.'

I watched on the camera as Joe effortlessly approached the man and dealt with the situation. When he came back he was clearly angry, but not at the customer. 'What's the fucking point of having you here if you can't deal with the customers? This sort of shit just doesn't fucking happen when there is a guy at the counter. Just get your stuff and go. I'll pay you for your whole shift, but tonight's your last night, it's just not working.'

———

I spent a week feeling angry, indignant and mortified. Who was Joe to fire me? And from a sex shop! Life just seemed harder in Canberra.

If it was just the money troubles I probably would have been okay, but my whole new life was crumbling. I wasn't enjoying any of my law subjects – in fact, I loathed them. I loved my sociology class, psychology was fascinating, but the law units were so dry and boring. I'm sure the moonlighting hours and lack of sleep didn't do me any favours in trying to stay focused on the hundreds of wordy legal texts I had to read and interpret each week, but the more I read, the more I started to wonder if law was really for me. I tried to tell myself that it would get better, that they were probably covering all the boring stuff first in an attempt to weed out the half-arsed uncommitted lawyers from the elite. I clung to this hope desperately, because if I didn't end up being a lawyer, what else could I possibly be? I'd never had a plan B. Plan Bs were for people who weren't one hundred per cent committed to plan A. In my mind, having a backup plan meant giving yourself an option to fail and that was just not in my nature. Besides, I couldn't change my mind about law now, not when I had just left my whole life on the Beaches behind. Being a lawyer was my destiny, my childhood dream, and it aligned with everything Ruby was supposed to be. Admitting to anyone, even myself, that maybe I had made a mistake was simply not an option.

Perhaps one of the hardest things to swallow in my new life was the fact that I was so incredibly homesick. After years of plotting and planning my great escape from home, I was genuinely shocked to discover how lonely I felt in my new grown-up life. I missed popping down the road for a swim with friends, I missed the proximity of Ben and, more than anything, I missed my mum. Before I had left for uni I had bought Mum her first mobile phone – a little prepaid brick that allowed us to talk to each other for free every night after 7 p.m. We talked most nights, both of us crying down the phone, uncertain of how long it would be until we saw each other again. I wanted Mum to come to Canberra, to see where I was studying, to just come and generally make me feel better about all the choices I was making. I wanted her to come and tell me that everything was going to be okay. I needed her. But she never came.

Mum and Peter were busy getting on with their own lives. They had decided to leave the Northern Beaches. With me finished school and out of home, they were looking to buy an old house up the coast and renovate it together. They were sick of the rat race and wanted to build a family home for the girls to grow up in, a place where they could hang pictures on the wall without having to get permission from the real estate. In the end they moved an hour and a half away from Sydney to Umina Beach, which made them four and a half hours from me. There was no way I could tell them I was drowning in my life in Canberra when everything was going so well for them. What could they have done about it?

Everything about my old life was ending, friendships were fading, old being replaced with new, and life on the Beaches was only kept alive through being with Ben. We had committed to doing the long-distance thing but without the convenience of living in neighbouring suburbs, we had begun to fight almost straightaway. It seemed ludicrous to fight with someone I hardly saw, but that's what ended up happening. Every other week we were breaking up and then I was driving back to Sydney so we could make up. Ben had never been a phone person and the physical distance was hard on both of us. Sometimes Ben just wouldn't take my calls for days at a time or he would call blind drunk from a party and say, 'It's over. You're too far away. I'm going to be with someone else.' As he hung up in my ear I would think, *Fuck him, good riddance.* But the bravado never lasted long. Alone in my room, with only a few new friends to call on, I would panic about losing the last of my old life.

Inevitably I would jump in the car and drive the three and a half hours to Ben's house to patch things up. Sometimes he was there; more often, though, I would have to drive around and find him. Other times I would be tucked up in bed and get texts from his mates telling me I should come and pick Ben up because he was getting out of hand. Often he had been in a fight, other times he had passed out or on occasion he had gotten 'blackout drunk' and flipped out on his mates. One such night I got a slurred call from Matt, a close friend of Ben's, saying, 'Ben just punched a brick wall. He's smashed his hand to pieces. Can you come and get him?'

'Why did he punch a wall?' I asked.

'He was trying to hit me but I moved and he hit the wall.'

It didn't matter what the drama was, whether it was with him, his friends or with us, I would always go. I loved him. And he wasn't like that with me — there was less bravado, more gentleness.

In many ways he was still a child, a scared little boy, who, unlike me, was unsure of how to control his temper or emotions. But it wasn't his fault. He had never had anyone to teach him. His mother had walked out on him when he was small, leaving him with a father who only knew how to talk with fists and anger. I'd been exactly where Ben was – before Ruby – struggling to distance myself from where I'd come from, and I was determined that, together, Ben and I would work out all these creases in ourselves and be happy. It was going to take time for both of us, but at least for the moment I was happy to be preoccupied with Ben's creases.

Once Mum and Peter officially moved away from the Beaches I was even more convinced that Ben was my last real tie to my old life. I was running myself ragged between Sydney and Canberra, trying to be present in my old life while forging a new one in Canberra. I didn't even realise that in trying to keep my Northern Beaches life alive, I had broken my very own golden rule of never having a plan B. Maybe if I had realised, I would have noticed that I wasn't doing a particularly good job of managing life A in Canberra *or* life B in Sydney.

# 25

Joe fired me from the sex shop on a Thursday night and by the following Saturday I was working as a receptionist at Canberra's self-awarded classiest brothel, The Palace.

Once again I had been interviewed and started work on the same day. Apparently this is very common across the sex industry, so that you don't go away to think things through and never come back. My official title was receptionist, which I imagined would involve answering phones and some sort of paperwork, but in reality I don't think I ever touched a phone, unless it was to clean it.

Jay and Gus ran the office. Jay was the boss who talked to the customers on the phone and booked the jobs, recommending the right girls to best satisfy the client's needs. Gus was the muscle for the building as well as the driver for the girls who did the outcalls, which Jay told me was when a girl provided a service in a client's home or a hotel room.

'An outcall is an extra service and each extra service costs more.'

I nodded. 'Okay, so what's a normal service?'

'Straight sex in one of the rooms on site. Fantasies, role play, greek, kissing, home delivery; they're all classed as extras and they all cost more.'

'A bit like ordering a pizza then, extra toppings and delivery cost more,' I said.

Jay broke into a loud laugh, his eyes twinkling. He translated what I said to Gus, who was obviously the younger of the two men but seemed to speak far less English; they were both from the same small European country and 'Jay' was an Anglicised nickname. Gus's lips twitched momentarily but I got the feeling that humour was not high on his list of employable qualities.

At first my job was simply to do the washing, general cleaning and preparation of the ten rooms that the working girls used to service the clients. I started at 5 p.m. every Tuesday, Friday and Saturday night, which was an hour before the night girls started, so that I had time to clean the rooms after the day shifts. Friday and Saturday nights were the most consistently busy nights, so it was my job to prepare for the onslaught. Each room had to have fresh sheets with an origami-inspired towel arrangement on top.

Once the beds were in order, I moved on to wiping down all the surfaces, paying extra attention to the showers and spas, which were not supposed to have any droplets left on them. 'It can't look like someone else has just had a shower here. The whole room has to look like new, like no man has ever been fucked in here, except the one walking in,' Penny, the Maori day receptionist, had told me quite seriously as she pointed out spots I'd missed. 'Men don't like to think they're just a dick.'

At the end of the spruce-up, I had to spray each room with vast amounts of Glen 20 in an attempt to disguise the 'used' smell, before moving on to restock the lubricant and condoms. Then I would repeat the process in the next room. Each was different to the last, with different-coloured walls and decor. One room, called 'The Party Room', had three beds in it and a really big spa, which I always cleaned last as Penny said it was usually only used in the wee hours of the morning, when the clubs closed and groups of guys came in wanting to keep the party going with their mates. 'They're usually coked out of their eyeballs and spend more time in the spa talking about what they're going to do to the girls than actually doing it.'

In between cleaning each room I diverted to the laundry, transferring armfuls of towels and sheets between the basket/washer/dryer, and then heaping them in the corner to fold later. No matter how fast I worked, the mound of folding always built up to improbable heights, as it was viewed as the least important job. After each job the girl using the room was expected to maintain its general cleanliness, which largely meant she wiped down the shower and then rolled everything up in the towels for me to sort out and clean. In my first few shifts, before I truly mastered the art of deconstructing a balled-up pile of sex-stained towels, I frequently found my hands coated in wetness, which I initially hoped was from the shower but became far less confident about after my second shift, when I delved my hand into the mountainous pile only to find my wrist decorated with a used condom and semen leaking down my arm.

———

When things were quiet, Jay and Gus usually sat around the office, chain smoking and arguing with each other about the state of Europe in a language I couldn't understand; they always sounded angry. Whenever I interrupted them to ask a question, Jay's tired, unshaven face would break into a smile, 'Come in, *krásný*, come,

come, thank God you have come to save me from the incessant ramblings about the Macedonian insurgency. What do you need?'

Jay preferred to show me how to do something himself rather than have Penny do it. He was quite particular about how his business was run, even down to the folding of the towels. He had nicknamed me *krásný* almost from the moment he supervised me folding my first load of emerald green lubricant-embalmed towels.

'Do you know what *krásný* means?'

'No.'

'It means "beautiful" in Czech.'

'Oh.'

'I think you're very beautiful.'

I didn't know what to say. I couldn't see how he would possibly think an awkward eighteen-year-old girl was beautiful when there were at least a dozen grown-up women sitting only a few rooms away, dressed to kill in spandex and leather, but my cheeks turned red anyway.

'I think you probably call me that 'cause you can't remember what my actual name is.' I smiled.

'Ah, cheeky and beautiful *Renee*. You know, you are wasting your time out here when you could be making *real* money out there on the floor. With your pretty face you could probably earn what I'm paying you for a whole night in less than an hour lying on your back.'

I kept folding. 'I have a boyfriend.'

He laughed. 'You and every other girl in there. Trust me, men are simple, he would never even know!'

'I think I just like doing this job.'

He shook his head. 'But it's no good, *krásný*. This job is for ugly girls.'

———

Once I had a handle on the washing and cleaning, I was allowed to start doing some reception work, which meant that when the doorbell buzzed I swapped my flats to heels and greeted clients at the door, showing them through to the lounge. 'Welcome to The Palace, have you been here before? No? Well, let me tell you about our services. We offer a full service as well as a range of fantasy options. For a regular service the cost is $110 for half an hour, $150 for forty-five minutes or our recommended service is an hour, which is $180. Beyond that you can extend if you want more time, or negotiate if you want any extras. Before the girls come out, can I get you a drink?'

The Palace had a complimentary bar service, so while I made the clients their drinks at the bar, one by one the girls would walk into the lounge and introduce themselves and any services they offered. It was an opportunity for the clients to ask the girls questions about what they would and wouldn't do. After all the girls had introduced themselves and gone back to their lounge room, the client would either tell me his choice or ask to see a few of the girls again. At some point a decision would be made and either cash or a credit card was handed over to me, which I would deliver to Jay in the office. Jay processed the payment while I went into the girls' lounge to let them know who had been chosen. Leaving the girls to retouch their make-up and adjust their outfits, I would race down the hall to get six fresh towels and then hand them over to the girl before she went in.

———

I usually only did the intros in the first half of the night when it was quiet, because in the early hours of the morning things would get really busy, sometimes with all ten rooms full for hours on end. Six towels for every job, in a full house, with back-to-back bookings and many a stained sheet, meant that I was mostly in the laundry, with Jay taking over the intros. He also preferred to do it if The Palace was really busy or if big groups of guys came in, because he didn't want customers staying in the lounge chatting to me for too long.

'They will take advantage of you, *krásný*. Drink the free drinks and sit in the lounge just looking, instead of buying.' Jay watched everything that happened in the lounge on the security video anyway, so if anything looked like it was getting out of hand, he would come in and take over. One night an old guy, probably about sixty, came in and, after meeting all the girls, asked to see the boss. Jay came in and the guy pointed at me and said, 'How much for an hour with her?'

'You can't afford her, she's a virgin that one,' Jay said, laughing.

'What's the price?'

'I'm just joking, brother, believe me I've tried to convince her, but she's not yet for sale. Which of our other lovely ladies can keep you company tonight?'

In the end the customer chose Sharon, a 49-year-old single mum of three who always called me 'love', and made herself endless cups of tea in between jobs. I never would have thought he would choose her, especially after propositioning me, but I was fast learning that it was hard to pick who got what jobs in this place.

The most intimidating part of working at the brothel was not actually interacting with the clients but interacting with the girls, trying to pretend that nothing fazed me, and that I'd seen it all before. I guess, like everyone else, I had a preconceived idea about what a prostitute would be like. For me, I had envisaged either a drug-addicted street whore or a big-busted porn star. In reality there were very few of these clichés at The Palace, but there was certainly a lot of everything else in between. There were about ten or fifteen women who worked at The Palace and these were the women I started to get to know a little. Some were young, some were beautiful, others had amazing bodies, and others were quite overweight. Some were friendly and others less so. Some girls, like Kate, scared the hell out of me. Kate was so confident and self-assured, and she would be genuinely annoyed when someone she thought of as less attractive got a job over her. Kate had the longest legs I had ever seen and always wore heels. She had a face that was model pretty and thick, glossy brown hair that framed her face perfectly. She made the brothel a lot of money, so she was allowed to come and go as she pleased but she often had run-ins with the other girls.

One night I was chatting to Sharon, who was having a slow night, when Kate snapped at me, 'What the fuck are you even doing in here, little girl? Aren't you supposed to be cleaning something? Here, take these cups to the kitchen. This room is for us working girls.'

'Don't worry about her,' Sharon said to me later. 'She hasn't had her fix yet.'

About a month into working at The Palace, Jay called me into the office. 'I have a favour to ask you. We don't have many girls on shift tonight and it's already really busy, Paige needs to see her dealer. But once she leaves, it could be hours or days before she comes back.

I want you to drive her there and wait. She just has to run inside and get what she needs. Then I want you to bring her straight back. She will pay you a taxi fee and petrol money. We never usually drive the girls anywhere, unless they have a job booked, but I really need her back here and ready to work tonight, she's always popular.'

Minutes later, Paige and I climbed into my little yellow Barina and set off. As we drove, Paige chattered away and flicked the corner of the street directory cover repeatedly. *Flick, flick, flick.*

'Sorry, hon, I'm a bit wired, thanks for driving, it's going to be a busy night I can just feel it.' *Flick, flick, flick.*

'That's okay, I don't mind getting out.'

'I bet you don't mind a bit of extra cash too, how much are they paying ya to be the door bitch?'

'Ten dollars an hour, cash in hand.'

She laughed. 'What the fuck! Is that all?'

'Yeah, but it's actually pretty good money for a uni student.'

'Really? You think that's good money?'

Paige was twenty-three. She had been working at The Palace for two years and she told me she wanted to do an arts/history degree one day. She asked me lots of questions about the university and how to apply.

'Here! It's here! Stop!'

I pulled up abruptly in front of a unit block in a dark street and Paige jumped out before I had even fully stopped the car.

'Don't worry, I'll be back soon.'

Sitting in the car with the heater blasting in an effort to combat the cold Canberra night, I looked at the clock. It was 11.30 p.m. I wondered how in the world I would find my way back if Paige didn't come back out, I was terrible at directions at the best of times. How long would I have to wait? Would she come back drugged out of her mind? What if her dealer came out too? I had always had this cocky belief that no matter what situation I found myself in, I would always be okay, but that luck had to end one day, right? Already in my short life I had hidden my judgement, beliefs, disgust and fear behind the always-smiling face of Ruby, but how long could I keep doing it for, when I was so very often out of my depth? I waited anxiously, mind ticking.

Ten minutes later I was overcome with relief when Paige ran towards the car. What had I been so worried about? Silly girl!

Paige was all bright eyes and smiles. 'Okay, let's go!'

As we were driving out of the street she took a little medical kit out of her bag and zipped it open on her lap. Inside was a clutter of empty sachets, needles and other bits and pieces. 'You don't mind if I get a fix while you drive do you?'

I looked at her. 'Um, what? Right now?'

Her watery blue eyes were like saucers in her deadpan face, glistening in the yellow glow of the streetlights. 'Is that a problem?'

I grimaced. I couldn't really stop her, could I?

Her lips peeled back into a wide smile. 'Look at your face. I'm just kidding, virgin, I'm not some hardcore fucking junkie or anything.'

She pulled some little bags out of her bra, stuffed them in the bag and zipped it back up. She had tears rolling down her cheeks, she was laughing at me so hard.

———

After that I became quite friendly with Paige, chatting to her when she was on shift and sometimes driving her to see her dealer to score. Paige wasn't a junkie, but many of the other girls couldn't or wouldn't work unless they were high or wasted. Jay preferred them high because high meant awake, whereas alcohol meant passed out and not working. It was a bit of an unspoken rule: drugs were okay so long as no one *looked* like a junkie, but alcohol was really frowned upon, because Jay thought the girls got too messy.

The exception to the alcohol rule was whenever Bella wanted to liven the place up. Bella was Jay's girlfriend and when she came in, the whole place centred around her.

Bella was as beautiful as she was lovely. She looked like Portia de Rossi with her long white-blonde hair and a peaches-and-cream complexion, but above all she had the most startling almond-shaped eyes that shone like two turquoise jewels on her face. Like Portia, Bella also had the charisma of a Hollywood star. You just couldn't help but be mesmerised by her whenever she was in the room. Bella flitted around The Palace like a butterfly. Sometimes she would answer the phones, other times she would chat and help fold towels in the laundry or she would just hang out in the office with Jay and watch TV with her feet up on the desk.

Every now and then she would come in on a Saturday night dressed in a tight bandage dress that showed off every curve of her enviable body. When Bella was dressed like this it meant she was going to Civic to party with her friends, but her pre-party preparations always began at The Palace and the whole place seemed to turn into some sort of strange sex-party-cum-nightclub under her influence. Bella would pop bottles of Champagne and many of the girls would come out of the lounge and chatter and drink in the vestibule nestled between the office and the exit that no one ever used.

On nights like these the clients almost seemed secondary to the girls' socialising, which made the energy of the place come alive.

Everyone relaxed a little, including Jay, who always smiled more when Bella was around and, on occasion at her request, he even swilled Champagne instead of scotch. Bella came in to see Jay, but whenever she was heading out with her friends she would also see a few clients and earn some quick cash before she left. She would pick and choose who she saw – she didn't like young guys and wouldn't see anyone drunk or drugged up. In between jobs I was amazed to see her duck into the office and be all over Jay, sitting on the desk, or on his lap, kissing him passionately.

I was making the beds in The Party Room on a Tuesday afternoon a few months after I first started. Apparently the room had been in use for the better part of the day by some businessmen escaping the Canberra frost and celebrating some big deal. The room was a mess. They had flooded the spa and then tried half-heartedly to clean it up by throwing every available towel on the floor. There were Champagne and beer bottles everywhere. Bella came into the room and surveyed the damage. 'Oh, I heard there was a bit of celebration in here, let me give you a hand, I have to talk to you anyway. Privately.' Bella closed the door as she entered and manoeuvred her lean dancer's body across the room, her turned-out feet carefully navigating the mess.

'I have a favour to ask,' she said as she bent down to help me stretch the fitted sheet tightly over the heaving mattress. 'I see this regular client of mine, privately at his house – no one else knows, especially not Jay, so keep this quiet. I usually go once a month with a friend of mine, but she can't make it and I need someone to fill in.'

I looked over the bed at her, smoothing the creases out of the olive sheet.

'He's really sweet, just a beautiful, beautiful man I have been seeing for ages. He just likes to pretend he's on a date with two girls. You wouldn't have to do anything with him and he'll pay you. What do you say? Do you think you could help me out?'

'Um, I don't know. I seriously would have no idea what to do.'

'You wouldn't have to do anything you don't want to, it's just dinner.'

'But I wouldn't even know what to say.'

'You just have to be yourself. He's a businessman, a lonely one. He lives to work. He has no family and he usually works really long hours. He's off overseas a lot, but uses Canberra as a base, so when he's in town, he just likes to have some company and unwind.'

'Do you have to sleep with him?'

'Sometimes I do, sometimes I don't. But I don't mind sleeping with him. *You* won't have to do anything though, you just have to come and be you.'

'Why do you need me? Can't you just go by yourself?'

'He always has me bring a friend and if he likes you and you feel like it, it could be a regular thing every month or so. Please. It's tomorrow and I don't want to cancel him. Plus you're not working so you can earn some extra money.'

'How much do you get paid?'

'It's different all the time. He gives me an envelope at the end of the night or the next morning, but he's generous. The least he's ever given me is two hundred dollars and I always have a great time.'

'Why me? Why don't you ask one of the other girls?'

'Gabriel just likes regular girls who can hold a conversation, not "hookers" who are on the clock, like all the girls who work here.

Plus Jay can't know, he likes all business to go through him so he gets his cut, and he would kill me if I took one of the girls off a shift to do a private job.'

Bella looked around the room, her eyes flitting over the spilled ashtrays and used condoms that I had just begun clearing, before she settled her gaze on me again. 'Come on, what have you got to lose, it's just one night, and it will be way more fun than what you're doing now, trust me!'

———

Wednesday's classes crawled by with barely a word penetrating my distracted thoughts. Torts and common law, Maslow's hierarchy of needs, psychology group work, all drowned out by my thudding heart and noisy head. *What should I wear? Should I just call and cancel? How much will I get paid?* I couldn't think straight. When it was finally time to go, I got dressed in jeans, heels and a black-and-white halterneck top, all the while telling myself the financial reasons I had to go, and ignoring all the moral reasons I shouldn't. It was just one night, I told myself. A performance. Just another one of those things about my life that I would never tell anyone about, another memory that I could smother with a Ruby Tuesday smile. Besides, was there really much difference between having one secret and ten? There didn't seem to be when my whole life was shaping up to be a masked performance.

Bella was waiting for me at our agreed meeting spot at 6.30 p.m., so that we could arrive at Gabriel's house together.

'I wasn't sure you would definitely come,' Bella said as she directed me to Gabriel's house.

'Neither was I.'

'You look different dressed up – good different. He'll like you.'

Gabriel lived in Manuka, a more affluent area of our nation's capital. It was dark when we arrived, but the glow of the front porch light was bright enough for me to see that the house was painted white, with lots of windows. It was beautiful.

The front door opened and suddenly Gabriel, the man who had been churning my stomach and occupying my thoughts for the last twenty-four hours, had a face.

'Good evening, girls. Come in, come in, it's freezing out here.'

He hung our jackets up on the hooks in the hallway and kissed us on the cheeks.

'Welcome, Renee, welcome. Bella, it is so lovely to see you again. Make yourselves at home, take off your shoes and follow me to the kitchen. I'm still preparing, so you can watch me work.'

Gabriel must have been in his mid-thirties; he had thick dark hair, olive skin and a short scruffy beard. He was wearing a crisp white shirt with the sleeves rolled up, cream chinos and an apron tied around a slight paunch. He was very attractive. Distractingly so.

The cream carpet was soft and thick beneath my bare feet as we walked down a long, wide hallway with colourful paintings hung evenly along the milky walls. The house smelled like fresh lilies and vanilla, the perfume made headier by the balmy temperature of the house compared to the infamous Canberra frost outside. Bella followed Gabriel and I followed Bella. We walked past a spacious living room on our right and kept walking to the back of the house, towards the smell of sautéing garlic and onions.

As we entered the kitchen and dining area, Gabriel sat us down on stools at the kitchen bench. Behind us was a large redwood dining table with three places already set. He obviously loved entertaining and was friendly and smooth, intent on settling us into the evening.

'Now, what will you have to drink? Red or white wine? I've started with white.' Setting down two glasses in front of Bella and me, Gabriel filled them with almost clear white wine and then moved back to the island in the middle of the kitchen, where his own glass of wine was. 'Let's have a toast. To good company and a lovely night.'

As Gabriel danced around the kitchen putting the finishing touches on his creations he made some small talk, before turning his bright, mischievous, green eyes to me. 'Enough of the chitter chatter. Tell me about yourself, Renee. How did you get to be sitting in my kitchen with the lovely Bella? What is your story?'

At first I was unsure if I should tell the truth or not. I didn't know if I should say anything about The Palace or how I knew Bella, because we hadn't really talked about it. Sensing my uncertainty, Bella touched my hand.

'Don't worry, he knows practically *everything* about me. He knows about Jay, everything, you can be honest.'

And so I was, I talked about university and living in Canberra, being fired from the sex shop and then getting the job at The Palace, and as I sat there, sipping delicious wine and speaking truthfully about my new life for the first time, I felt myself relax. I was having a good time.

When we sat at the table for dinner it was almost ten o'clock, and my cheeks were flushed from all the wine and the laughter. We were all talking over the top of each other as Gabriel set down steaming dishes to share on the table.

'This is *mansef*, the national dish of Jordan, where I'm from. This is sultana-and-almond pilaf, some salad and breads and these,' he paused, 'these are the best potatoes you will eat in your life!'

We ate, drank and talked. The wine changed from white to red and then Gabriel said, 'Let's have some port and a spa.'

Gabriel went to fill the spa and Bella turned to me. 'Are you okay to go in the spa?'

I nodded. 'Of course, but I don't have anything to wear.'

She laughed. 'You're joking, right?'

———

When Gabriel kissed me in the spa, I kissed him back, his rough jaw scratching my face but not in an unpleasant way; it felt manly. When he rubbed my shoulders with oil and traced his fingers down my back it felt so nice that my shoulders heaved and my eyes shut; they were heavy from both the wine and the nervous worry of the day. Later, when we had moved to the bed, I watched as Gabriel put a condom on himself and said, 'Are you sure this is okay?' and while it probably shouldn't have been, it was, it was more than okay. Gabriel was the fourth person I had ever slept with and the only person I had not been in a relationship with.

———

I woke up next to Bella. My mouth was dry and I knew that my head would ache when I sat up. I needed water.

'What time is it?' Bella asked.

'It's quarter to nine. I've got a tutorial at eleven. Oh my God, my mouth is so dry.'

'It's the red wine.'

We went out to the kitchen. There was a note from Gabriel with Panadol and two glasses of water next to it. The note said,

*Thanks for the great company last night, make yourselves something to eat and stay as long as you like. I'll be in touch, Gabriel.* Underneath the note there were two envelopes, one with Bella's name on it and one with mine, which we shoved in our bags as we left.

Driving home, Bella and I talked about Jay and Ben. I'd had a good time but in the light of day the reality of the situation started to set in. I had crossed a line. Not only had I cheated on my boyfriend, I had had sex with a man I didn't know and had been paid for it (assuming there was cash in the envelope in my bag). My aching head was making it difficult to decide how I felt about myself. Did this make me a prostitute? I knew I should feel bad but mostly I felt ambivalent and hungover. One night didn't define who I was, not that I really knew who I actually was anymore or even who I wanted to be. Working at The Palace, going to Gabriel's, none of this was consistent with my perfectly planned Ruby life, but it was a means to achieve it. The lines had all become so blurred. Was doing wrong things okay if it eventually resulted in good, like finishing my degree? I had no idea.

'What does Jay think about you having sex with clients? Doesn't he get jealous?'

'Not really, sex is sex and love is love. Plus, I don't care what Jay says, I do what I want.'

'How come you don't want him to know about Gabriel then?'

'Gabriel is different. He's not just a client, he's a friend, and Jay wouldn't understand that.'

'Ben wouldn't understand any of this. Actually I don't think anyone would. I haven't even told anyone about working at The Palace, because I know they'll think differently of me.'

'Really? But you're just a receptionist.'

'I clean semen-stained sheets and pour drinks for guys to sip while they decide which girl they're going to have sex with. Trust me, if anyone I went to school with knew what I did for a job, they would never be like, "Oh, she's just the receptionist at a brothel – no big deal!"'

'I suppose, I've never really thought about it. Where do you say you work then?'

'Ben and a few girls from uni still think I work at the sex shop. I don't know what everyone else thinks, they haven't asked and I haven't brought it up.'

'What about last night, what did you think of Gabriel?'

'I think I actually had a good time. He is so different to what I thought he would be like.'

'In what way?'

'He's so nice! I guess I thought he'd be a bit creepy.'

'Do you think you would see him again?'

'I don't know . . . maybe . . . I can't decide how I feel about last night yet. It feels a bit surreal, like it all happened to a different person, except I'm the one with the hangover. I guess, more than anything, I can't believe I actually slept with him.'

'Neither can I,' she said.

I ran the night over again in my mind – the dinner, the wine, the sex – Gabriel seemed to go to so much trouble, he had been more attentive than any date I had ever been on. 'Hmm, yeah, I guess I would see him again.'

When we reached the city, Bella and I kept talking until it was clear I was never going to get back to campus in time for class. The more we talked, the more the night before seemed like less of a big deal. Eventually we said our goodbyes, Bella shouting over her shoulder, 'Remember, don't say anything to Jay.'

When I got back to my room, I opened the envelope. In it was five hundred dollars and a note from Gabriel: *Fix your car, study hard and I hope I see you again very soon.*

I couldn't even remember mentioning that my car needed fixing.

———

After the evening with Gabriel I had a few nights off from The Palace to study for my final exams the following week. I wasn't particularly worried about the exams, but I knew I couldn't cram effectively with such sporadic sleep, and despite being uncertain about my future as a lawyer, I still wanted to do well. It was in this week I received a letter from the social sciences faculty, congratulating me on my outstanding results in sociology for the semester. As I stood in the quadrangle reading the letter, my heart filled with relief that this whole life I had envisioned for myself might actually be working out. The Palace was not the job I had pictured myself having at uni, but it had allowed me to accrue a thick pile of notes, which I stashed in an envelope under my bed, and which was paying for the career, the life, I so desperately wanted. None of this would matter once I was a lawyer, it would just be another thing I never told anyone about myself, but by then I'd be so successful no one would care anyway. I paid for my next semester's on-campus living fees and I put my car in for repair, which meant that once my exams finished I could go home to Ben for the uni break. On the surface, I felt like I was doing my best to make this life work and I took pride in the fact that I was doing it alone – I didn't need a handout from my parents, I didn't need anyone. I told myself it didn't matter how I achieved my goals, what I did to get there, as long as in the end I made sure that I did actually get there.

———

Ten days after the night with Gabriel, I went to The Palace for my weekend shifts as usual. It was one of those nights where no one stopped, every room was full and it seemed like every man in Canberra was having their needs serviced.

At 4 a.m. I hit the wall. I needed to sleep but all the rooms were still full, there were clients spilling out of the waiting room and the laundry situation was completely out of control.

'You can't leave,' Jay said. 'Go and get a few hours' sleep in the back rooms and then you can work a day shift to get things back in order. Penny will be in in the afternoon.'

'I'd rather just go and come back again later.'

'No, stay here, get a few hours' sleep and then you'll be fine.'

There were a few rooms out the back for the working girls to stay in. Usually only girls who were from out of the area or another state got to use them because they committed to working a few nights or sometimes even weeks back to back. The rooms were bare except for a bed. I chose the room furthest from the noise, pulled on a fresh sheet and closed the door as far as I could. The locks and handles had all been drilled out of the doors because one of the stay-in girls had apparently locked herself in and had an overdose a while back and they couldn't get in to help her.

As I lay down on the bed and pulled a sheet over me, I wondered how many people might have had sex on the sheets that I was gratefully wrapping myself up in. What a totally abnormal thing to ever have to think about, but then in the last few months the very concept of normal had become quite fluid to me.

*Inhale, exhale, inhale, exhale.*

Things that seemed inconceivable and beneath me only a few months ago were now less rigid in my mind. I was less judgemental, less naive – something I never would have thought possible.

*Inhale, exhale, inhale, exhale.*

My brain finally stopped and the windowless room became stale with the scent of my slumber.

———

*I'm drowning, I can't breathe.* It's one of those dreams that feels so real. *I can't breathe.* My eyes snap open, seeking relief in wakefulness. *It's just a dream, it's just a dream!*

But it's not.

Where am I?

'Shh, *krásný*, it's all right, it's all right, it's Jay.'

My nose fills with the pungent odour of nicotine as his fingers clamp down harder over my mouth.

I try to push him off me. *What are you doing?* I try to say, but my voice is muffled, inaudible through his cupped hand.

'Shh, shh, don't make a fuss, it's all right, don't struggle.'

'Get off me,' I say, trying to sit up.

I can feel his impatient sandpaper hands jerking at the sheet, pulling at my skirt and my underwear, yanking them down, to the side, anywhere, just out of the way. 'Fucking hell!'

And then I am bare.

I feel his hand briefly around my ankle, driving my knee upward so that the sole of my foot is touching my other calf, legs splayed. His right hand comes back up to my mouth while the other stays pressed into my thigh. Two pressure points on my body holding almost all of his weight. I feel like my jaw will break. 'It's been a while since I've had pussy as young as you, *krásný*. Let me feel you, I bet you have a nice tight little cunt, hey? Ahh, I thought you would. Relax! If you just relax, you might enjoy this.'

He thrusts into me, his breath heaving. He is in me and on me. I am riddled with him.

His words whispered in my ear are soaked with alcohol and cigarettes and I can feel myself withdrawing into my own head, into nothingness. *Be somewhere else, think of anything else. Everything ends, this will end, just try to think of something else!* My eyes are open or maybe they're shut, I can't remember, but everything is black. Ten minutes, twenty minutes, an hour? I don't know. Time has slipped away from me.

I have slipped away from me.

I feel his body sag on top of me and I know he is finished. He lifts his hand from my mouth and pushes his lips against mine, forcing his tongue between my teeth and rolling it around in my mouth, my face wet with his saliva.

Pushing himself off me, his silhouette rises above me on the bed and I can hear him fixing his pants. 'You could make some serious money with a pussy like that, *krásný*. Now you really should just try to get some sleep; the laundry is a mess.' He leaves the door ajar.

At some point I moved across the room and sat with my back against the door, trying to think what I should do. I think I cried, but maybe I didn't. I called Ben. I needed him.

'Something happened.' My voice cracked. 'I don't know how to say the words . . .'

'Try to breathe, I can't understand you, you sound hysterical.'

'I'm sorry, I'm sorry, I can't breathe, I just couldn't get him off, I couldn't stop it.'

'Come home, babe, just get in the car and come home. Everything will be okay.'

He's right, I thought. I needed to go home, get far, far away from this place. Somehow I was disappearing into the landscape of this life that I'd planned out. I had no idea who I was anymore. Every familiar part of me was gone. Are you even considered to be a person if there is nothing left inside of you? I sat and waited until the darkness of the night slipped away and as I waited, my high school scripture teacher's voice drummed rhythmically in my head.

*Oh, how the mighty have fallen.*

*Oh, how the mighty have fallen.*

# 26

I replayed my experiences in Canberra over and over in my mind a thousand times and more, but the ending was always the same. I realise now that I was a little girl playing in a very grown-up world, but the problem was that by the age of eighteen I hadn't seen myself as a little girl for well over a decade. Over time I tried to coach myself that being raped saved me from what might have quickly and easily slid into a more weighty career in a sex-soaked world. In the immediate aftermath it was hard to believe that Jay was anything other than the universe's way of tapping me on the shoulder and reminding me who I was. No matter how much I pretended to be 'normal' and 'perfect', no matter how many smiles I pasted on my face, I was still just a murderer's daughter with very questionable methods of achieving her overly ambitious goals. The rape served as a shocking lesson that threw me back down into my rightful place in the world.

Who did I think I was to assume that I could work where I was working, do what I was doing, and come out unscathed? Who did

I think I was to hide behind Ruby and pretend I was anything but the scum of my parents' mistakes? I was never going to be a fancy lawyer. Somehow, some way, it would have all fallen apart, because I was just like them. People end up being who they are born to be, they rarely escape the cycle; why did I ever think I could be the exception? Swept up in the bravado of being Ruby, I had become too confident. I had started believing my own lies, telling myself I was different, that I deserved more, and always assuming that I would land on my feet. I thought that nothing more could ever possibly happen to me. Until it did.

It would have been easy for me to blame my life's undoing solely on Jay and what happened that night, but there's not much point in lying to yourself, is there? I knew that every poor decision I made – and there'd been a few – had tightened the noose on the life I had been dreaming about since I was nine. And now the dream was dead. I blamed myself. Jay was my penance for indulging in the fantasy that I could ever break the mould I was born into.

—

I didn't need much convincing to return to the Northern Beaches, even though Mum, Peter and the girls had moved away. I knew their new house on the coast could never be my home and it would have hurt my pride too much to have run up there with nothing and no one but my mother for company. At least back on the Beaches I had some foundations and some options; and I had Grandpa to hang out with again, but he couldn't be the foundation on which I rebuilt my teenage life, so of course I relied on my relationship with Ben.

I had nowhere to stay when I first came back, so while I scouted out potential flatmates, I crashed at Ben's in his little annexed room off the side of his dad's place. The house was a lakeside shack in Narrabeen that had been inhabited solely by males for far too long – the sweat-stained mattress, the piles of paper and clothes embedded with pieces of old food, not to mention the mouldy bathroom with piles of used bandaids. It quickly became clear that Ben's dad's house could absolutely only be a temporary arrangement.

Whatever issues Ben and I had we ignored when I returned to the Beaches. Both of us had a renewed commitment to our relationship and somehow what happened with Jay seemed to bind us closer.

Neither of us really wanted to talk about Canberra. I was still trying to find the words for it all. What are the right words to describe my own rape, my own demise? They were proving hard to formulate. And Ben, who was usually a man of few words anyway, seemed eager to avoid any details between the broad brushstrokes. 'It happened at work,' I said, 'I was supposed to have a quick sleep before the next shift . . . I couldn't get him off me . . . he wouldn't get off me.' Saying it out loud made me gasp for air. My eyes spilled over, it was too much, too raw, there were no more words. I was gagged by shame.

Ben's jaw clenched, his arms weaving their way around me as he pulled me into his chest. 'It's okay, don't talk about it, it will just make you more upset.'

'I just feel so stupid. I should never have gone to Canberra.'

'Just tell me where to find this guy, where is this fucking sex shop? I'll go and smash all the windows and then I'll go inside and fucking kill him. I'll get Matty and a group of the boys together. We could drive down to Canberra tonight. I'll slit that fucking cunt's throat.'

I could practically see the anger pulsing through his veins. I had never seen Ben like this sober before. I wished I had the energy to be angry for myself but I was using everything I had just to keep it all together. I knew that if I wanted Ben to go to Canberra, he would, and I loved him for the sentiment and his hot-headed loyalty, but it was too easy for me to envisage myself trudging off to Long Bay Gaol again to visit yet another murderer. I was supposed to be making a new life for myself, not using my parents' mistakes as a blueprint.

'I don't want you to do anything to him; you'll end up in jail and your whole life will be ruined. And I definitely don't want any of your friends to know what happened. I don't want anyone to know. Ever. Let's just forget about it and get on with our life.'

'But I could talk to Matt about getting some guys to go down for me, just rough him up a little. He shouldn't just be able to get away with it.'

I knew what Jay did was wrong, but the violation of my body was too heavily soaked in my own failure and shame for me to see it as separate. The job at the sex shop, The Palace, the night with Gabriel – it was all tangled with my memory of Jay grinding himself into me. If I hadn't blurred the lines, then that night with Jay would never have happened. I had abandoned my moral compass and I had been punished for it. The guilt and self-loathing were all consuming. I never considered reporting Jay because it would only expose me further. I don't think it ever crossed my mind as an option, because if I'd learned anything by that age, it was to always hide the horrific and never speak of the ugly.

If I had told Ben the truth about where I had been working, and how the night with Jay had come about, then he probably wouldn't have been so hell bent on the idea of retribution; he probably wouldn't have wanted anything to do with me. In that moment the thought of being totally alone terrified me. No matter how imperfect things were with Ben, I had to make it work. I had already messed up so many things.

'I just need you to love me, not seek revenge for me,' I told him.

'But, babe –'

'Please don't, I don't want to talk about it anymore. Just stay here and hold me.'

And so he did.

Ben held me against him until the front of his T-shirt was thoroughly soaked through with my tears. When I finally calmed down and my breathing became steady, he hugged me to him and whispered in my ear, 'I think you've really ruined my good T-shirt, you know.'

A fiercely protective Ben and a desolate Renee worked well together. Ben was my lifeline, my justification for being back on the Beaches, and I threw myself into being the model girlfriend. It was a relief to have something, someone, to focus on other than myself and I was so very grateful, and guilt ridden, that I had Ben's open arms to run back to.

Within days I got one of my old part-time jobs back, and enrolled in a Bachelor of Education at the Australian Catholic University at Strathfield. I needed a new plan, a new life and, above all else, I needed to feel like I had my shit together, even if the inside of my head was a mess. In order to function, I needed to pretend that my whole life and sense of self had not just come crashing down around me; I needed Ruby. I needed to paste a smile on my face and try to pretend that I wasn't drowning in my own grief and guilt, because I knew that drowning wouldn't lead me anywhere except deeper into the dark hole I was in.

With only Ben knowing about the Jay incident, I was left to devise a story about my reappearance on the Northern Beaches for all of our friends. Of course, most of them had been privy to the many break-ups and make-ups of our relationship, so I largely centred my return around my commitment to making our relationship work, as well as the sterile nature of law being completely unsuited to a 'people person' such as myself. I rattled on to anyone who asked about how boring and dry law was and how much more personable and rewarding teaching was going to be.

The vigilance required to hide my misery was exhausting, pretending to be happy and excited when every fibre of my being was so full of shame and regret, weighted down by my failures. After the performance was over, I often sought comfort in self-destruction, sometimes slicing my flesh open so that I could allow myself to physically see some of the pain I was always trying so desperately to hide.

For me, teaching was a middle-of-the-road existence that could never compare to the gloss and shine of being a lawyer. I had always told myself that I wouldn't spend my life being a small cog in a big machine. I wanted to be important. I had fantasised about reading my story in the papers one day, 'Double murderer's daughter breaks the mould to be Australia's most successful family lawyer; QC application a shoo-in!' But I had let myself down. No matter which way I spun it, 'Murderer's daughter turns life around to become primary school teacher' would never quite have the same ring to it. I mourned the loss of my glamorous career, but even if it had been possible to transfer my law degree to Sydney, I knew that mentally I could never separate law, Canberra and Jay. If I was being totally honest with myself, I knew with the way I was feeling I was lucky to get my head around doing any degree at all.

A few weeks after my return, Ben took me out for dinner to celebrate my nineteenth birthday. We sat across from each other and Ben looked at me playfully with his puppy brown eyes and grinned. 'I have to say I really liked the idea of you being a lawyer because I thought if we ever got married I'd get to retire early, but I'm glad you're back from Canberra, even if it means you're just a crappy old teacher and I have to keep working forever.'

He put a small box on the table and said, 'Happy Birthday, Ren.' Inside the box was a chunky silver bracelet with a huge heart-shaped charm dangling off it. In the centre of the heart was a sparkling blue stone.

It was quite possibly the most hideous piece of jewellery that I had ever seen, but I smiled at him anyway, happy. I thought of how awkward he would have been just venturing into a jewellery shop, let alone trying to choose something. It was a big step for Ben and because it was genuine, I really didn't mind that the gift was awful – in fact, it was kind of endearing.

Ben tried to navigate his large tradie hands around the delicate clasp, to secure the bracelet to my wrist. At the same time he noticed the yellow gold bangle I had worn since I was sixteen already on there.

'Oh, you already have a bracelet? Can you wear two?'

'Yeah, it's fine.' And it was. My mother had always told me how useless men were at this kind of thing.

'The one you have is yellow, should I have got you yellow? I didn't know, I just let the girl choose.'

'It's fine, really.' I smiled.

'Let's move in together,' he said.

The duplex was across the road from Collaroy Beach, and the second I walked in I just knew I had to live there. The rooms were freshly painted in yolky yellows and brilliant whites and every room had a wall of windows that rattled with the constant sea breeze. The smell of new paint mixed with the salty air made me heady and hopeful that *this* was a place where I could truly start afresh. Maybe all of this had even happened for a reason, perhaps I was so focused on being extraordinary that I hadn't realised that ordinary could be pretty good too.

We moved in with two school friends: one of mine and one of Ben's, a guy called Chris. At the last minute an unlikely flatmate joined our crew: Ben's semi-estranged mother, Bernie, who had walked out on the family when Ben was still in primary school. She had just landed a job back on the Northern Beaches as the head chef of a restaurant in Manly.

The novelty of playing house together was exciting to Ben and me. We both carried chips on our shoulders from unconventional childhoods, and we were determined to play the adult game differently. We filled the place with matching furniture and while we unwrapped the plastic from the promptly delivered lounges and tables, we nutted out a little plan for our lives together. Ultimately we wanted to buy our own place, so we could avoid moving around like our damaged parents, but this was a pretty good start.

We decided to have an impromptu housewarming party the week after we moved in. It started small and got bigger and bigger as the night went on. Ben and Chris had their good mate Fitzy, a well-established drug dealer, come around to do business with the partygoers who, by this stage, were spilling down the stairs and into the driveway. By midnight the crowd was loved-up on ecstasy, speeding out of their brains or at the very least wasted on spirits. I'd barely seen Ben all night and was struggling to get into the vibe of the party. Even though the party was at my house I felt like a gatecrasher. I just didn't know how to fit in with these people anymore, couldn't work out how to make them like me. I felt like people could see straight through me, see the sullied piece of shit I'd become, and were sneering at me for intruding upon the good breeding of the Northern Beaches. I wanted to hide in the toilet like I had done all those years ago at school but there were too many people wanting to line up their drugs on the toilet lid for me to take refuge in there for long.

I found Ben in the driveway and pulled him across the road to the beach to talk. We were both pretty wasted. The alcohol and drugs made me extra anxious and talkative.

'What's up, babe?'

'I haven't really seen you tonight.'

'We moved in together, remember, you're going to see me all the time. It's a party, I just wanna hang out with my mates.'

'I know but I still want to talk to you too. I feel sort of awkward over there, none of them are really my friends anymore.'

'So? Who cares?'

'I do. I'm just worried it's not going to work between us if your friends don't even like me.'

'It's not like they hate you. They just don't care either way, plus I like you, so it shouldn't matter.'

'Maybe you wouldn't if you really knew me.'

'We've been together almost a year now; I think I know you pretty well, especially after the shit that went on in Canberra.'

'You don't even know the half of it.'

The speed, vodka and buried secrets were like a toxic cocktail being shaken up inside me. The pressure of everything was just too much, I had too many secrets trapped inside me and I needed to get one out, I needed reassurance that I wasn't awful, that the real me wasn't unlovable. My heart and mind were racing. I couldn't tell him about The Palace, so I decided to tell him about my dad.

'You know how I never really talk about my dad at all?'

'Yeah.'

'Well, I actually do know who he is, I've seen him a few times.'

'Really? Where does he live?'

'Near Maitland somewhere, well, at least he used to.'

'What's he do?'

'He's a murderer.'

'Bullshit.'

'No, seriously. I found out when I was six. I used to visit him in jail.'

'No fucking way, who did he kill?'

'It's sort of complicated. He killed two different guys.'

'How? Did he shoot them or something?'

'No, he stabbed them.'

'He stabbed them? That's fucking hectic! Why didn't you tell me?'

'I've never told anyone.'

'Fuck, I better not break up with you then, hey, or you'll get your dad onto me.' He laughed.

'It's not funny, Ben. Don't say that.'

'Sorry, fuck, I can't believe your dad killed someone though, and *stabbed* them, that's brutal.'

My eyes were filling with tears. 'Do you feel different about me?'

One of Ben's best mates, Matty, was stumbling across the road towards us. Matt was trouble, and troubled, but he was one of the few friends of Ben's I really liked. 'Hey, lovers, if you've finished fucking each other's brains out over here, then it's time to get back to the party.' He put an arm around each of us. 'I fucking love you guys. Ben you're like my fucking brother and Ren, I fucking love ya, but you're too good for this cocksucker.' He turned his head to Ben and slurred, 'Mate, that cunt Rebecca's just turned up and she wants to talk to you.'

'Who's Rebecca?'

'Just some slut that's hot for Ben, nothing to worry about. What are you guys doing over here anyways? Are you crying? Are you having a fight?'

'Nah, mate, just deep and meaningfuls – you know what chicks are like.'

'What's up?'

'We're just talking about fucked-up families, Ren's dad's a psycho, and she's worried I won't love her, but that doesn't mean shit, both my mum and dad are fucked too.'

I felt relieved to hear him say this, maybe he wouldn't break up with me because of *this* secret after all.

'Me too,' chimed in Matt. 'If you ever need me to sort someone out for ya, Ren, I *know* guys.'

I laughed. 'I know. Ben has already told me.'

'Hey, why don't you go talk to that chick and I'll stay here and talk to Ren. Gotta know my best mate's girl, you know.'

'No, come on, let's all go back,' I said.

'Nah, stay with Matty, and I'll come back in a sec with some more drinks. It's fine.'

'I thought you wanted to go back to the boys?'

'Nah, I'll just sort this chick out and get us some drinks and then we can keep talking about what you were saying. Stay here with Matty, I'll be back in a sec.'

Ben was gone ten minutes, twenty, a good half-hour, before I said to Matt, 'Let's just get our own drinks.' As Matt and I linked arms and crossed the street I could see Ben talking intently to a dark-haired girl who had her back up against the staircase to our house. She was wearing tight jeans and a yellow halter top which exposed her pale belly. Ben had his arm up on the wall, facing her, so I couldn't really see her face, instead my eyes were immediately drawn to the diamante chain around her belly.

'Bennie!' Matt called out. 'Time to wrap it up, bro.'

Ben took his arm off the wall and looked at Matt and I approaching. The brunette's face was now visible.

'Hi,' I said to her, 'I'm Renee.'

She narrowed her eyes. 'I know who you are, cunt.'

'Get the fuck out of our house,' Ben said.

Matt pulled me away. 'Let's go get the drinks. Fuck off, Rebecca, you dumb bitch.'

'Fuck you, Matt, who are you? Her best friend?' She turned to me. 'Just so you know, bitch, I fucked your boyfriend. A LOT. And he liked it.'

Matt dragged me inside. Out of the corner of my eye, I saw Ben push the girl up against the wall. Her head smacked against it and he held her there, her top bunched under her neck. 'Shut your fucking mouth, whore,' he yelled at her, but I couldn't hear what she said in reply because I was pushed back inside, embraced by the music. Matt quickly found Luke and dumped me with him. 'Keep her inside,' he said and turned straight back out to the fight.

'What the fuck's going on, Renny?' Luke said, putting his arm around me.

'Luke, who's Rebecca?'

'No one, she's just a psycho.'

'She says she slept with Ben.'

'Nah, no way, he wouldn't touch her.'

'Bullshit, Luke. Tell me the truth.'

'Okay, well maybe he did, but definitely way before you were on the scene.'

'Are you sure?'

'Yep, positive.'

'Ben lost his virginity to me.'

'Oh.'

'When did he sleep with her?'

'I don't know, ages ago?'

'How often?'

'I don't want to get involved. I love ya, Renny, but Ben will kill me if I tell you anything. Plus, I don't even really know.'

Ben came in the door with Matt, arms around each other. 'Silly bitch.'

The four of us stood looking at each other. Me and Luke, Ben and Matt. None of us said another word about Rebecca, but the memory of her hung in the air for the rest of the night. The image of Ben's bunched fist holding her by the cheap yellow material stuck in my mind. He would never have done that to her if she was telling the truth, would he? He was punishing her for lying. Either way, I decided to pretend I hadn't seen or heard anything. Things were good between us, and God knows I had my own secrets to hide.

# 27

We settled into a routine, Ben going off to work, me juggling uni and work, and trying to cope with the much more inconvenient commute to campus. Living with Ben was very different from how our relationship had been when I was at school. Partly because of the realities of day-to-day life, but a lot of it had to do with how different I was too.

I quickly began to realise that living with Ben actually meant less time together. Ben had always been a boys' boy, loving his nights out on the town, drinking and running amok with his mates. Before I went to Canberra we occasionally partied together, but mostly we didn't. I went out with my girlfriends, he went out with his mates and then we would usually meet up at the end of the night. Most of our time as a couple was separate from time with our friends. We often just hung out at the beach or went to the movies. This became hard for me when I came back from Canberra because I found it near impossible to put on my Ruby smile and pretend to be the same person I was before I left. I tried to go out with my school friends and be the same good-time girl I had always been, buying rounds of shots and dancing up a storm to Britney Spears at the same old incestuous clubs of the Northern Beaches, but the more I drank, the more I felt the alcohol seep into raw wounds, and the more I wanted to run away, either back to Ben or to being alone. I couldn't trust myself to go out partying because I knew after the initial numbing the alcohol might encourage the tears and truth to slip out of me and I just couldn't let that happen; I couldn't let any of these girls from school see the cracks in my carefully constructed Ruby mask. The air of arrogant confidence that wafted around me like a cloud of cheap Impulse spray throughout high school had vanished, and I didn't know how to get it back. Once I realised I couldn't trust myself I withdrew even more, staying home with my books where my tongue wouldn't have the opportunity to betray me.

Independent to a fault, I had always looked down on the type of girls who got boyfriends and dumped their friends. I couldn't understand why girls became so desperate and clingy and moved around with boyfriends like they were one unified human being, that wasn't me at all. It must have been hard for Ben to see me shrink away. I would have been happy never going to another party again, whereas Ben was still hell bent on going out drinking to the point of vomiting three times a week, which I just could no longer relate to. Why didn't he want to stay home and be with me? No matter how I framed the offer of a night in together, Ben chose to leave every time. Sometimes he was only out for a few drinks, but other nights ended up blurring into days. The more time I spent alone, the more my mind drifted to thoughts of Ben and Rebecca . . . surely there was no way Ben was out with the boys on all these nights? And if he was, why did he always have his phone off?

I was living inside my own head too much, driving myself crazy with possibilities, thinking constantly about how things could have been different. I knew I had to get out of this fog, this all-consuming depression, if I was ever going to be able to draw a line under it all. Somehow I needed to start getting over myself, over Canberra, and accept that whether I had planned it or not, Ben, teaching and the Beaches were going to be my future. I needed to get on with it, starting with making more of an effort with Ben. After all, he had stuck by me through all the Jay stuff and after I told him about my dad. He was really all that I had left of my pre-Canberra life.

I decided to surprise him with a romantic dinner. Three courses, wine and a date with the best version of Ruby that I could muster.

———

Ben stumbled in the door in the early hours of the morning. I was still sitting at our recently purchased dining table surrounded by the dinner I had made. For hours I'd envisaged myself dramatically throwing the food at him like you see in the movies, but I had spent so long cooking that, even in my fury, I couldn't bring myself to do it.

Ben had gone for a few drinks with the boys after work, swearing to me he would be home by six, which I instantly registered as seven. I didn't mind, as it gave me more time to prepare – I had rarely cooked more than pasta and sauce since leaving home.

After no sign of Ben at 7.30 p.m., I called. 'Ben, where are you? You know I have something planned!'

'Don't lose your mind,' he answered, 'I swear I'm like two minutes away, babe.' He hung up. I poured the wine.

At 8 p.m. he didn't answer his phone. I drank my glass of wine.

At 8.30 p.m., Matt answered Ben's phone. 'Um, Ben's left his phone at the pub, Ren, I have no idea where he is.' But I could hear Ben's voice in the background. I drank Ben's glass of wine.

At 9.30 p.m. the phone was off. I poured another glass.

I tried to put it out of my mind, to go to bed with my wine and read my book, but I couldn't. Anger boiled inside me. The old, confident me who first met Ben was outraged. *Who does he think he is to treat me like this? He should feel lucky to have a girlfriend like me – everyone has always said I was too good for him!*

*But you're not too good anymore, are you?* a little voice whispered in the back of my mind.

*Shut up*, I told the voice. I was too angry to be pulled down that path tonight.

By the time Ben rolled in, I was well and truly saddled up on my high horse. 'Where the fuck have you been? You said you were two minutes away!'

'Oh fucking hell, why aren't you asleep? I don't want to do this now.'

'Too fucking bad. You knew I was making us dinner. Where the hell have you been?'

'With the boys.'

'Why didn't you come home?'

'I didn't want to.'

'So why did you say you were two minutes away?'

'Because I didn't want to have a fight with you and ruin my night.'

'But you didn't think about ruining my night, did you? And what, you didn't think we would have a fight when you got home, after I've been sitting here waiting for you for hours?'

'Yeah, but I've already had my night out now.'

'You're un-fucking-believable. Were you even on your way home?'

'Nup, I was still at North Sydney.'

Ben's casual indifference only served to further infuriate me.

'And then where did you go?'

'Can't remember.'

'Were you with that girl?'

'What girl?'

'You know what fucking girl, that girl from the party, Rebecca?' I was practically screaming at him now.

'No. I don't think so. I don't know where I was. I told you, I can't remember.'

'Bullshit. I know you slept with her.'

'How do you know that? Because that's what she said? I swear I didn't sleep with her.'

'Don't fucking lie to me, I know you did.'

'So now 'cause I go out drinking with the boys, enjoying my life instead of being miserable here with you 'cause you're not going to be a fucking lawyer, you think I'm a cheat?'

'Stop trying to headfuck me. This isn't about me, it's about you. You've been with her tonight, haven't you?'

'You're seriously fucked in the head, Ren. You believe some drunk slut you don't even know over me, do you?'

'No, I don't believe her, or you, but I believe Luke.'

Ben's eyes betrayed him and I knew instantly that Luke had been telling me the truth.

'Well, what the fuck can you say about it? You've been with someone else.'

'What are you talking about?'

'That guy Jay.'

The words took my breath. He was punishing me. For being raped.

'I wasn't *with* him,' I whispered.

Ben's face was screwed up, emotions splashed across his face. Disgust? Anger? Or was he just drunk?

'You've still had another man's dick inside you. You think I don't think about that?'

I shoved past him. 'I don't want to talk about this anymore. You're drunk, you don't know what you're saying.'

'Oh, now you don't want to talk? Well, too fucking bad. You started this shit.' Ben grabbed my wrist hard and pulled me back into the dining room.

'Get off me, let me go! I'm going to bed.'

'No, you're not going to bed, you're going to fucking listen to what I'm saying. You think this is only hard for you?' Ben pushed me up against the wall, pinning my shoulders in place and lowering his head so his nose was almost touching mine. 'You're not even the same fucking person anymore, you're fucked.'

Out of the corner of my eye I saw our flatmate Chris's sleepy shadow fill the door frame.

'What the fuck, guys? It's the middle of the night. What's going on?' Seeing me against the wall, Chris's slight frame sprang forward. 'What the fuck, man? Get off her!'

'Stay out of it, Chris. It's none of your fucking business.' Ben pushed Chris back with his free arm.

'Ease up, Bennie, ease up. What's wrong?'

'She's a dumb fucking slut, that's what's wrong.'

'Okay, okay just let her go. How about we go get a beer? Let's just go and get out of here. Just take a breath, man.'

Just as the sun was lighting the sky, I stood at the bedroom window and watched Ben and Chris walk across to the beach, beers in hand. I didn't see either of them again for days.

# 28

I came out of the surf, dripping, thinking about the assignment I had to get done before I drove to uni for my afternoon tutorial. Out of nowhere, the thought popped into my head: *When was the last time I had my period?*

I sat down in the sand and tried to think. Watching the glistening beads of salt run down my arms, I mentally retraced my bathroom usage. I couldn't remember having it since we moved to Collaroy, so it must have been at Ben's dad's place? No, I would definitely have remembered having to endure a period in that filthy bathroom, so Canberra, then?

Fuck.

⁓

I locked the bathroom door even though no one else was home.

Sitting on the toilet, I peed on the stick and looked up at the walls, all of them painted the colour of happiness.

*Everything is going to be all right.*

There was nothing to do but wait. I stood up and examined myself in the bathroom mirror. My reflection was almost unchanged, clear tanned skin, big brown eyes, straight white teeth. It had been months since the two purple fingermarks on the inside of my thigh had faded and in that time both nothing and everything had changed.

I looked down at the urine-soaked stick, waiting for it to tell me if it was possible to fall even further from my own graces.

And then two pink lines. It was unmistakable.

My whole body shook. I wanted to scream at the injustice of it all; all these months of pretending that nothing had happened, willing myself not to think about Jay, and for what? My sewn-up secrets were bursting at the seams.

Six months earlier I had my whole successful lawyer life mapped out and now it seemed inevitable that I would never be anything but a failure. I was my parents' child, everything I'd sworn I'd never be – and worse. My life was over when it was supposed to be just beginning.

I stared hard at my face in the mirror and felt enraged. *How can I look so fucking normal when everything is ruined, when I am so thoroughly fucking ruined?*

I couldn't stand it, couldn't bear to look at myself and all that I had become, or maybe it was harder seeing all that I would never become.

Raising my hands to my face, I watched closely as my fingers bore down, fingernails on flesh, gouging and ripping until my face was bloodied and raw. I looked like I had fallen prey to the claws of a savage animal; the outside of me now as ugly as the inside. And I was filled with relief.

I was days away from the foetus clinically becoming a baby, in the very final moments of even being eligible for the procedure. My lucky break. The clinic was full, but they squeezed me in at the insistence of my GP. Another stroke of luck.

'Listen, I need you to get this girl in in the next few days, we don't have a lot of time based on her LMP dates . . . She's a smart young girl with her whole future ahead of her –' He paused as the person on the other end of the phone responded. He looked at me before angling his swivel chair away from me. 'She's a rape victim,' he said in a lower tone down the receiver.

It felt like he was talking about someone else. But whoever he was talking about was obviously worthy of an appointment because I was immediately scheduled in.

My mother borrowed the new automatic car from Peter and drove down from the Central Coast to be with me. I had hoped to avoid telling her about the abortion and the rape, partly because I wasn't sure if I could find the words to tell her just how royally I had fucked up my life and partly because I knew that no matter what words I found they would always be considered small fry compared to what she had been through herself at my age. Besides, in choosing to give birth to me, she had made her stance on abortion very clear.

I called the clinic to double-check if it was at all possible that I could drive myself home, but they insisted that I would be a drugged-out hazard to both myself and others on the road after such a procedure. By this stage Mum was very close to initiating a divorce from Peter, so the timing of my problems was less than convenient. I worried about putting unnecessary pressure on her, but in the end, after I had exhausted all my other options, I had no choice and, to her credit, she came.

Too tall to sit between my little sisters' car seats in the back seat, Ben had to sit in the front with my mother and make agonising small talk. It was a relief for me, because it meant I could just gaze out the window and avoid looking either of them in the eye. If only Ben had his licence, we could have kept both the mothers out of it and avoided the scene that had unravelled just before we left.

Ben's mum thought I had gotten pregnant on purpose and was trying to trap her son. 'It's how Ben's father got me to stay with him. He told me not to worry about a condom, it was just one time, he said, but I knew the second it was over, I was pregnant. I had just been given a pastry apprenticeship in Paris.' She was lost in her own memory, still bitter about what could have been. When she finally came back to the moment she spat, 'My son is too young to be tied down to your daughter!'

'My daughter never forced herself on your son. She's too good for him anyway, why would she want to trap him? She would be the one trapped. It's just a fling.'

Ben's mum and my mum must have been roughly the same age, but Bernie wore every hardship she'd ever endured on her face, whereas my mother looked like she had been kissed by the angel of time, a payoff perhaps for her shitty life. Watching them fight was like watching a gazelle fight with a feral cat, my mother flouncing her air of physical superiority while Bernie snarled behind her long grey hair, her nose constantly twitching with the desire to sniff out her next line of speed.

Ben's mum insisted she wanted to come with us, to make sure I went through with it. My mother was adamant that such a vile woman was not getting in her car. The car she drove her babies around in! They'd gone on and on, until there was no more time and we had to leave.

Bernie could never have even imagined the truth, and there seemed to be no point even trying to convince her that, at nineteen, I had no interest in being tied to Ben, or anyone, in such an irreversible way. Besides, the blood tests and the corresponding dates made it clear that the only person this pregnancy would be tying me to was Jay.

———

I woke up in the stark white room feeling unsure. Was it over? The nurse stood at the foot of my bed, rearranging instruments on a metal trolley.

'Am I okay? Is everything okay?'

'Oh sweetheart, you're awake! Don't get up, you're pretty out of it. We had to knock you right out because you were very distressed. Poor poppet.'

I vaguely remember my desperate voice asking, 'How badly is it going to hurt?'

'Just start counting backwards from ten and you won't feel a thing,' I was told.

'Ten, nine, eight, seven –' And then nothing. A black hole in my consciousness.

Opening my eyes wider, I tried to sit up and felt confused. Was I still riddled with him?

'You're fine, sweetheart. Everything went fine. It's all done. We'll just keep you here for a little while longer, and then we'll take you through to recovery.'

I let out a long breath and burst into tears.

The nurse came to me immediately. 'Oh sweetheart, it's a big day for you.'

I threw my arms around her and sobbed. 'I'm just so relieved it's all over. It's really all over.'

'Honey, the drugs are going to make you feel even more emotional than normal. Everything is okay, it's all over now. You will leave here and just get on with your life.'

Lying in recovery, I thought of the only other girl I had ever known to have an abortion. We were sixteen at the time, and in Year 10. Beth had told someone, who in turn told someone else, who then told everyone in our year exactly why Beth wasn't going to be at school that day. We all knew before she had even returned home from the clinic that she had killed her baby. It's the way things happened at a girls school. The following week, Beth was back. As she walked through the quadrangle she looked pale and lonely. She must have known everyone had found out because we were all looking at her. She lifted her head to look in the direction of where I was standing with a group of other girls. *What a slut*, I thought, *I would never have an abortion.*

Maybe it was a coping mechanism, distracting myself with thoughts of Beth instead of focusing on what was happening to me and my body, but as I lay there, having just been through what Beth went through all those years ago, I was overcome by the realisation of what a thoroughly shit person I could be sometimes.

The days after the abortion were bleak. Ben and I fought constantly, over everything and nothing. A part of me wished he would hurry up and break up with me so that everything in my life just flatlined. Surely it was inevitable?

The nurse had said I would be able to leave the clinic and get on with my life, but it was impossible. My own thoughts about the morality of abortion plagued me. I wasn't against it, but it was something for other girls to do in the right circumstances, not me. It wasn't something I should have done. I had taken a life. I could have chosen not to but, despite everything, I was still my own first priority. Buried inside me were the embers of a notion that I could have an extraordinary life, but I knew that that would be impossible if I took any more baggage with me. I had tried to think about what it would be like to look into the face of a child every day and see Jay staring back at me, but it just wasn't conceivable. I wasn't that noble a person. As it was, the recurring nightmares I'd started having ensured that Jay and I were seeing more than enough of each other anyway.

'Stop being such a miserable fucking bitch! You never go anywhere anymore. If you're not at uni you're here with your head stuck in your books, oblivious to the fact that you're just getting fatter and frumpier. Get up and look at yourself in the mirror, it's disgusting!'

But I didn't need to – it was true. I'd put on at least ten kilos since I'd been back on the Beaches and that didn't look to be slowing down anytime soon, especially with Grandpa arriving almost daily on the L90 bus from the city to feed my sadness with Cherry Ripes. He didn't know why I was sad, but he knew I was and he had no idea what to do. It was like I was a twelve-year-old girl again, burying myself in food and *Baby-Sitters Club* books, just like after my nan died.

'Are you listening to me?' Ben continued. 'Get up and look at yourself in the mirror.'

Oh yes. The fight. What were we even fighting about this time? I couldn't think.

I got up and looked in the mirror. I looked at myself and then, unable to keep looking, I locked eyes with Ben's reflection. I started to cry.

'I'm sorry. I just feel so terrible. It's probably all the hormones, I'm sure I'll be okay in a few days.' My face was wet with snot and tears while my permanently red-rimmed eyes swelled once more.

Ben stepped forward and put his arms around me. 'Is it weird that you turn me on when you cry? Fuck, it's been so long. Come on, turn around and let's make up, all we've been doing is fighting.'

'I can't *make up*, Ben. The clinic said no sex for four weeks, you know that.'

'I know but it will be fine, those sorts of people are always over the top with that stuff, and it's been a couple of weeks now.'

'I don't want to, I'm still bleeding, plus I don't really feel like it. We've been fighting. Just go to the party.'

'Make-up sex is what couples do, for fuck's sake! You should be happy I still want you after all this shit that's been going on. You're a mess! Ever since you came home, everything's about you. Well, what about me? What about what I need? What's the point of having a girlfriend if you never have sex?'

'It's not like we *never* have sex, but it's been hard for me lately. I'm just not ready. The clinic said *any* penetration could cause permanent scarring – it could affect my chances of falling pregnant later and I really want to have kids some day. It's just not worth the risk.'

'Fuck that shit, seriously! Some other guy fucked you when he wanted to, but me, the guy who loves you and puts up with all your shit and tears, can't even get near you, this is fucked! You're fucked!'

And he was right, I was fucked. Every word he said felt true.

I had been avoiding him since I'd got back from Canberra, finding excuses not to have sex, and when they'd all run out I'd practised my newly honed trick of being physically present but mentally absent. Ben didn't deserve it. Any of it.

'You're right, I am a mess, my head's a mess. I'm sorry, I'm just . . . I'm trying to work on it. I just need a little bit more time.'

Ben wrapped his arms around me. 'No more time! Come on, babe, I need you, plus it's not even my fault. You're actually kinda hot when you cry.'

I let Ben kiss me backwards onto the bed.

It didn't matter. None of it mattered.

# 29

When we were served the eviction notice at Collaroy Street, everyone was distraught at being forced to leave our beach-side pad in the peak of summer, but I was relieved. I couldn't go to the bathroom anymore without visualising the bruised finger prints on my thigh, which when I sat down immediately metamorphosed into the two pink lines forever scorched into my conscience. Yes. I would be glad to leave. Another fresh start.

In the serving of the eviction notice I felt I had also been given the opportunity to be completely honest with Ben. If the next move really was to be a fresh start, then there couldn't be any untold secrets, not even one, because I was drowning in them; drowning in all that I had to hide. I needed just one person to be real with. I had to tell Ben about The Palace and Gabriel because if I didn't I would never be able to trust my own worth in the relationship. I needed to be loved for all of me. Or not loved. Whatever the outcome, I had to tell the truth, because always being someone else was exhausting. If Ben wanted to break up with me, then we would all be moving anyway, and if he didn't the next place would truly be a new beginning. I felt sick with anticipation at what he might say, but also wondered what it would feel like to set it all free.

I heard Ben being dropped off, van door slamming, and then whistling as he walked up the drive. He was in a good mood. His key wasn't even out of the door before I started.

'I have to tell you something.'

'Hey, babe, how was uni?'

'Fine. I have something I need to tell you. I know I've told you all these secrets lately but there's one more. It's eating me up and I just need all this shitness to be done. I don't want any secrets or lies between us. If you want to break up with me, you can.'

'What are you talking about?'

I took a deep breath and looked him in the eye, 'I slept with someone else in Canberra, a man called Gabriel. It's a bit of a long story.'

———

The following two weeks were a miserable existence, full of anger, silence and snide slut-shaming remarks. I couldn't decide which hurt the most, but in the end it was the uncertainty that got to me. I assumed I was moving alone, but I wasn't totally sure, because we were still sleeping in the same bed and no one in the house seemed to know we were over. I tried to approach Ben for a decision either way, but he was too angry, shoving my arm away as I pleaded with him to just tell me what he wanted to do. 'Don't fucking talk to me,' he spat. 'I'll tell you if and when it's over but only when I'm good and fucking ready.'

'I know you're angry, but surely you've decided by now if you want to be with me or not? We're supposed to fly to Thailand in ten days, so at the very least I need to know what you're doing with that.' I had bought Ben surprise tickets to Thailand for his birthday a few months before and I'd planned out the whole trip for us. 'The ticket is obviously yours if you still want it, but if you don't, I don't want to waste it. I'll change the passenger name over and give it to someone else.'

'If I'm on the plane, I'm on the plane, you'll have to wait and see. Why? Aren't you going if I don't?'

'Of course I'm still going. I'm on uni holidays, what else am I going to do? I've been planning this for months. Besides, if we're over I'd rather be as far away from here as possible.'

The thought of going alone made me nervous but every day that passed seemed to make a solo trip more of a reality. If I did end up alone I knew I had to use the trip as an opportunity to pull myself out of this misery, but if Ben came, if he stayed with me, it meant I still had *something* left.

As departure day grew closer I started to worry that, if push came to shove, I wouldn't have the guts to go alone. But my worries were wasted because interest in the spare ticket was mounting – both Mum and Shelly, a friend I'd made in Canberra, offered to go with me. I fantasised about it, about being in another country, free from all the drama and chaos of the last year. But as much as I wished I could, I knew I wouldn't say yes to taking either of them, not while there was still hope that things might work out with Ben. He really was the only person who truly *knew* me now, no mask, no pretences, all of my secrets laid bare, and if there was a chance that he was willing to stay with me in spite of it all, I had to take it.

Three days before we were all supposed to be out of the duplex, I was boxing up the contents of the bookshelf in our room. Over the noise of the masking tape gun, I heard Ben come in the door from work. He walked into the room and slung his backpack onto our bed, sending a cloud of worksite particles into the air. He turned to face me. 'I'll stay with you,' he said.

Ben and I peered out the window as the plane took us up into the cloudless sky. Unlike me, Ben had never been on a plane before and his long legs bounced, full of nervous energy. I shifted my gaze from the view to watch his animated face taking it all in while the plane curved around the city skyline. A month in Thailand, just the two of us; no secrets. This was going to be a good year for us, I could feel it.

Using Bangkok as a base, we would bus it up to Chiang Mai to go elephant trekking, then make our way back down to Koh Samui, Phuket and Phi Phi Island. Our last three or four days would be back in Bangkok to do some shopping.

The trip was going so well that, on the bus down south, I looked up from my well-thumbed *Lonely Planet* and said to Ben, 'Let's just keep doing this! Let's not go back home. Do you know you can do a flying course in Bangkok? Maybe I'll be a pilot, that's way cooler than teaching.'

'Why? Why would you want to stay here? It's so fucking hot and poor,' he said.

'Because there's so much to see! We could get jobs and just keep travelling . . .'

'I don't really like all this travelling around, I'd rather have just stayed in one hotel and can you stop talking about being pilots, it's stupid! You're not going to be a pilot!'

'What would be the point in coming to Thailand if we just stayed inside a hotel? We could be at home doing that.'

'I would have been quite happy staying home. I'm not even the one who wanted to come to Thailand, you're the one who planned this trip.'

'Aren't you having a good time?'

'Yeah, but I would've had a good time having a few weeks off at home too.'

⁓

The air was wet from the heat of the day, made worse by the sheer number of bodies trying to occupy the same space. The music was thumping in my chest, the base acting like a heart, beating for the whole crowd. Ben and I were still red faced from the day canoeing around the ancient limestone caves in Phang Nga Bay. It had been one of those days where everything just felt right. We finished the tour by posing for a photo in front of a sunset-lit James Bond Island. Ben's arms were wrapped so tightly around me that only my head was visible. When I think of that photo, a personalised postcard is etched in my mind. If I shut my eyes I can still smell the sea breeze, still feel the warmth in my cheeks from too much sun and smiling. After the tour ended, the guide dropped all of us *farangs* at one of the beachside bars in Phuket. Everyone stayed for a few Singhas before the group dispersed back to their hotels or out to dinner. Ben and I were staying in a pretty basic room, with a shared bathroom, in the backstreets of Phuket so neither of us were in a hurry to head back to its four bare walls. We moved onto another bar and then another and then later a club where we could no longer talk over the music. I was trying to pull Ben up to the dance floor: 'Come on, just one dance! Please!' But he was unwilling. 'I hate this music, almost as much as I hate dancing, I'm going to get another jug of beer.'

I sat down at the table with Ben and tried to talk to him. We were both drunk and probably ready to go home.

'How about we just head back?'

'I haven't finished my beer yet. I'm not ready to go.'

'Let's go get something to eat then, we've been drinking for ages.'

'Stop nagging me, I'll drink until I want to stop. You're not my fucking mother.'

'I'm just saying let's go somewhere quieter, you don't even like the music, so let's just leave.'

'Do you mean to say you're finished prick-teasing on the dance floor then?'

'What do you mean? I'm just dancing! It's called fun, Ben.'

'Yeah, if you call dancing like a slut fun.'

Things were heading down a well-trodden path: Ben had gone way past happy drunk and was now meandering towards confront-ational drunk. I was desperate not to ruin the happiness of the day, so I reached over to him and stroked his sun-streaked hair. 'Come on, babe, we've had such a good day, let's just go back to our room.'

'I'm staying and drinking my beer. Why don't *you* go back to the room? My beer will be more enjoyable without your nagging about dancing anyway.'

'I think we should stay together. We've both been drinking and we're staying in a pretty dodgy backstreet.'

Ben drank two more jugs of beer, and then stood up abruptly. 'I need to take a piss.'

I waited for him at the table for five minutes, then ten. *He must have gone to the bar again*, I thought. After fifteen minutes I went looking for him around the club. I started to get worried; maybe he had passed out in the bathroom? I got one of the guys coming out of the bathroom to call out for Ben and to check the stalls, but he wasn't in there. After another ten minutes the DJ climbed down from his box and made his way over to me. 'If you're looking for the guy you were with, I saw him walk out the front door a while ago – he's gone.'

'Really? Are you sure?'

'Positive. I thought you must have had a fight 'cause you were just sitting at the table.'

'Oh, okay, thanks. I'll go and have a look for him.'

'Be careful out there by yourself.'

I stood out the front of the club and looked as far as I could see up and down the street. Which way would he have gone? He was so drunk, maybe he had gone back to the room and thought I would just follow? I walked quickly back towards the guesthouse, the street lights fading from flashing neon to sporadic lamp posts the further from the beach I got. At the guesthouse, I realised Ben was not there and that he was the one who had the keys to our room, along with the bumbag with all our money in it. The reception office was locked up and I didn't know what to do.

I sat on the gutter under a street lamp and waited. It was 1 a.m. After half an hour I decided to walk back to the club – maybe he had become confused and gone back to find me. But he wasn't there, and the DJ said he hadn't seen him again. 'Go look down at the beach, lots of drunk Aussies go there to pass out.'

At the beach a friendly looking man in his thirties approached me. 'Lovey, it's really not safe for you to be hanging around down here by yourself. All sorts of crazy shenanigans go on down here, and what's a beautiful girl like you doing on your own anyway?'

'I'm looking for my boyfriend,' I explained. 'He's pretty drunk and he has our keys and all our money with him. I can't get into our room. I've looked everywhere.'

'What's he look like?'

'He's about six-foot-two, brown hair that's sort of long and shaggy, and a pretty long face. He was wearing a Singha singlet but that doesn't really narrow it down around here, does it?'

'You're probably not going to believe me, but I reckon I saw your man stumbling out of one of the pubs not long ago.'

'Really?'

'Yeah, do you want me to help you look?'

Sean, my new Irish counterpart, and I walked the streets of Phuket for an hour and a half, scouring the beach, checking with the security at pubs and clubs to ask if anyone had seen someone like Ben. Finally, I gave in. 'I think I'm just going to head back to the guesthouse and check again. If he's not there, I'll wait at reception until they open, surely they'll have another key.'

'Where are you staying?'

'Siam Guesthouse.'

'My hotel is near you, I'll walk you back.'

We were minutes away from Siam when I saw a figure staggering down an adjacent street that I knew was Ben.

'Ben, Ben,' I called out. 'It's me.'

We walked towards each other until we were all face to face.

'Where the hell have you been? You just left me in the club. You have all the keys —'

Ben looked at Sean. 'Who the fuck is this?'

'Hey there, matey, your girl's been pretty worried about you. I've been helping her look for you, it's pretty unsafe for her to just be wandering around here on her own at this hour.'

'Have you been keeping her safe, then, have you?'

'I've been helping her look for you, I didn't want her to have to sleep on the street.'

'Well, thanks for your *help*. Now you can just fuck off.'

'Ben! I've been walking the streets for hours looking for you, you're the one who went off without saying anything, Sean has just been walking with me.'

'Yeah and now he can fuck off. FUCK OFF!'

I turned to look at Sean. 'Thanks for all your help. I'm really sorry about him.'

He looked uncertain. 'Are you going to be okay?'

'Yeah, yeah, I'll be fine, really, thank you.'

'Okay, well, if you're not okay, I'm just at the Paradise Inn, down the road there . . . Are you sure you two will be all right?'

'Just fucking go!' Ben shouted at him.

Sean began walking in the opposite direction from Ben and me.

'So did you fuck him too?'

'Ben, what are you saying? I've been trawling the streets looking for you. Where did you go?'

'To get away from you.'

'Obviously you've been drinking a lot more.'

'What has that got to do with you? You can't tell me what I can and can't do, you fucking whore. You're lucky I'm still with you at all.'

'Don't say that; let's just go back to the room.'

A few locals had started to come out into the streets to see what the two *farangs* were fighting about. I kept trying to walk towards the guesthouse to calm things down, but Ben kept pulling me back.

'Don't walk away from me, you slut.'

'I'm going back to the room.'

Ben pulled me by the shoulders so hard that I fell to the ground. He came and bent over me, his eye catching the leather necklace around my neck that was threaded with white beads spelling out his name in black ink.

'You fuck some guy in Canberra, then you walk around the streets of Thailand with some strange Irish guy. Tell me, were you really raped, or were you begging for it? I think I can guess. Did you enjoy pretending not to like it?'

Ben had me pinned with his whole weight. Every time I tried to sit up, he pushed me back down so my head smacked against the pavement.

'Ben, please can you let me up, everybody is looking.' I was crying, shaking. 'Please.'

'You are piss weak. Stay on your back where you belong.'

'Stop saying that! Just get off me.'

'Stay down! You make me sick, you don't fucking deserve to wear my name around your neck.' He pulled at the leather string until it snapped, the beads flying into the street, little plastic balls bouncing everywhere and then, finally, still.

I pushed him off and tried to get up, but he pushed me back down. I tried to crawl towards the Thai men watching across the road, shouting, 'Please help me, please help me stop him.'

The men stood around smoking and looking on with interest while Ben's rage gained momentum, his foot connecting with my ribs, stomach and legs over, and over, and over again.

Every time I tried to get up and move a few steps towards the guesthouse, Ben shoved me back down, my palms shredding against the bitumen. Back up, a few more steps, then back down. Finally, I ran the few metres to the guesthouse and all the way up the stairs. I sat with my back against the door and waited momentarily for Ben to make his way up the stairs. He opened the door, and we moved our fight inside, and the shoving continued.

'Just stop, Ben. STOP! What are you even doing?'

Grabbing my arms, Ben threw me backwards onto the bed and pinned my arms over my head. 'What am I doing? What am I doing? I am teaching you a lesson. You don't tell me what to do, who the fuck are you? You're no one. You think you're too good for me but you're lucky I'm even with you. No one will ever want you if they know what a slut you are. Do you want me to tell everyone?'

'No.'

'No, that's right. You're just a dumb slut, aren't you?'

'No, I'm not.'

Ben leaned down and gritted his teeth. 'Yes, you are. Say it, say, "I'm a worthless fucking whore".'

'I'm not saying it.'

Ben let go of my left wrist and drew one hand back. 'If you don't say it, I'll fucking punch you. Don't make me fucking punch you.'

'As if punching me is any worse than what you've already done. You just kicked me like a dog in the street.'

'That's because you are a dog. Now say it!'

'You're not in control of me, Ben. I won't say it. I'll never say it.' Everybody has a threshold and in this moment, after everything, I'd found mine. It was all I could muster, but I felt determined not to give in on this, certain that if I did I would lose myself completely.

I stared defiantly up at Ben, our eyes locked, and for a second my confidence faltered. I thought he might actually punch me. I shut my eyes.

*Thwack.*

*Thwack.*

*Thwack.*

The sound of flesh splitting flesh.

My flesh.

My face opened like an overripe watermelon, juices bursting onto every surface. 'Oh my God, oh my God,' I heard Ben say, so I opened my eyes to see what he saw. My thick red blood had saturated the starched white sheets and splattered high up onto the walls. Ben looked instantly sober and surprised. Surprised to see my face bloodied? Surprised, like me, that he actually followed through? Or perhaps it was shock as he took in the sight of my blood dripping down his fist. I couldn't tell.

Sweet metallic blood. It was all I could smell, all I could taste and all I could see. It was everywhere.

*Why is there so much blood?*

Ben's voice crashed through my thoughts, hysterical: 'What the fuck is wrong with you? What *the fuck* is wrong with you?'

I looked at him, waiting for more. I didn't understand.

'Why the fuck did you make me do that? Why? Why did you make me do that?'

———

I slept fitfully on the blood-soaked sheets next to a comatose Ben, my heart racing. *What am I going to do? What am I going to do?* I tried to think of a plan, but my face was throbbing so much it was hard to focus on anything but the beat. I kept thinking about how much the guesthouse was going to charge us for destroying the sheets; they'd possibly never get all the blood out. I still had no idea what I looked like, because there was no mirror in our budget room, but I could feel that my face was encrusted with dried, flaking blood. The smell and taste had become pungent, like off meat. I had to clean myself up, clear my head, quickly make this past, not present. Ben didn't move as I rustled around in our backpacks for the toiletries bag and a towel, before heading to the shared bathroom down the hall. I locked the door and turned to the small mirror over the basin. I could barely see myself, my eyes were so swollen, both from crying and the force of Ben's closed fist, but I didn't need perfect vision to know that the person staring back at me couldn't possibly be me. The girl in the mirror had hollow, defeated eyes and an inflated nose decorated in hues of purple, black and yellow; it made my eyes water just to look. But it was the girl's cheeks and neck that I couldn't stop looking at. The blood had faded from a brilliant red to an expired rust colour and it had begun to crack on my skin like day-old face paint. It would need to be forcefully scrubbed away. Turning from the mirror, I peeled my clothes off and stepped under the warm water of the shower. The spray hit my body and trickled down over bruised arms and tender hips. Each drop turned watermelon pink before pooling at my feet. With my face angled down to avoid the direct spray, I watched while the drain tried to swallow the pain of the wee hours of the morning. Down, down, down, like Alice through the rabbit hole. I wished I could go back to yesterday, when I was a different person.

Sitting at the end of the bed, I waited for Ben to wake. By lunchtime he still hadn't made motions to rise, so, pulling on a hat and sunglasses, I ventured out to get him some food and more bottled water. There was no way he would talk in the hungover state he was in if there wasn't food.

'Ben, sit up, drink some water, we need to talk about last night.'

Smelling the food, he sat up and began to rifle through the plastic bags, assessing what he should eat.

'I don't know what there is to discuss. I feel like shit. I need to eat and then I need more sleep. Go away for a few hours and we'll talk later.'

'Ben, look at my face, do you really not know what we have to discuss?'

'Fuck! I'm too sick. Just go!'

———

I retraced my steps from the night before down the winding streets to Patong Beach. *He's right*, I thought, *it will be good for me to get out in the sunshine and the salt water will be good for my face.*

Belly down in the sand, I propped myself up on my elbows and looked out at the glistening water. The sound of the ocean and laughter filled my ears. Everywhere I looked there were couples holding hands, strolling up and down the beach, enjoying their holidays. Everyone seemed so happy. There was a whole big sunny world outside those blood-splattered walls, and I was desperate to be part of it.

I walked into the ocean, and the coolness of the water made me feel alive. I slowly edged my way up to my knees, then a little bit further, until finally my tender hips and ribs were submerged.

Falling forward, weightlessly, I ducked down deep beneath the surface; the laughing from the shoreline became silent. I stayed under until I had no more bubbles to release and my lungs and face were screaming for relief.

Ben's voice played in my head over and over again: *Why did you make me do this?*

I didn't have an answer.

Salty water; salty tears; stiff, stinging body. Pounding face.

Why? Why did I make him do it? Why did I push him? I could have just said the words: *I'm a dog, I'm a whore, a worthless fucking whore.* See? They're just words. But they're not.

If I had said them, I would have had to let go of myself completely. No amount of punching or kicking could possibly be more demoralising than that. The physical wounds would heal, but if I said those words it could make them real, and if that's all I was then I might as well just keep swimming out into the sea and end it all right now.

I felt trapped.

Leave? Stay? Leave?

I imagined myself marching into the room and telling Ben, 'What you have done is unacceptable and unforgivable; we're over.' I could see myself throwing all my stuff in the pack, turning on my heel and marching right out the door, out on the street to . . . But where would I go? Would I stay in Thailand? Or go home? What would Ben do? Would we be flying home on the same plane? Either way, we would have to see each other at home. I couldn't just leave, it wasn't that simple. *Who cares!* I argued with myself. *You can't stay with him – look at your face!*

I knew that any rational person would leave, but I just didn't know how I could turn that knowledge from a thought to reality.

I didn't have it in me. Maybe it *was* my fault? I had put Ben through a lot lately and while I knew he'd always had a temper, this wasn't who Ben really was.

*Besides, maybe after this things will be even? Surely if I forgive him for this, he will forgive me for Gabriel?*

In less than an hour, I had given myself permission to stay.

We spent the remainder of the trip licking the gaping wounds of who we had each become. Ben promised it wouldn't happen again, swore it had only got so bad because he was drunk and still hurt by all that I'd put him through. He barely remembered the details, didn't think it was anywhere near as bad as I'd made out – except for the blood, that is. So we swapped rooms and forgot about the blood. We both wanted to move on, put the night behind us. We were both sorry for the things we had said and done. We were sure it would never happen again.

We weren't really *that* kind of people.

# 30

Five days before Ben and I had flown to Thailand, Mum, Grandpa and I lugged every lounge, bookcase and plate that Ben and I had accrued down the twenty-four narrow steps of Collaroy Street and into the back of the shift-stick rent-a-truck, closing the door on Collaroy Street behind us. Sitting three abreast in the cabin, Grandpa spent the entire fifteen-minute drive telling my mother how clever I was being able to drive a truck, 'and a manual too, Gemma. Just look at her, will you? Remember the day she was born and she was so small she fit into the palm of my hand? And now look at her, driving us around in this big truck!' He examined his hand and then me in wonder. No matter how bad I felt about myself, Grandpa's rose-coloured glasses always made me smile.

The semi in North Manly wasn't much to look at – grey walls, grey tiled floors and almost no natural light – but Mum and I had done what we could to arrange it so it was homely and ready for Ben and me to return to after our trip.

A few hours after we touched down in Sydney, I set about unpacking the samurai swords, paintings and batiks from the oversized striped bag we had filled in Bangkok. As I pondered over which wall to nail a picture hook into, Ben went outside to call his boss to check the site details for work the next day. I could see him through the lounge room window, phone pressed to his ear as he paced up and down the overgrown path in the small backyard. The backyard was perhaps the only redeeming feature of the semi, and I hoped to cut it back a bit and maybe put some tables and chairs out there, so we could escape the darkness of inside.

The back door slammed, interrupting my thoughts of home decor, and Ben materialised, his neck and face alight with his 'angry rash'.

'I can't fucking believe it! I just can't fucking believe it.'

'What's wrong? What's happened?'

Ben paced like a caged lion. 'Fuck! Fuck! Fuck!'

'What? What's going on?'

'I've just lost my fucking job because of you, that's what's going on!'

'What do you mean?'

'It's pretty clear, isn't it? I don't have a fucking job anymore. What bit don't you understand?'

'But *why* don't you have a job? What happened?'

'They got another apprentice while I was away. I told you I didn't want to go to fucking Thailand!'

'Ben! It's hardly my fault. People take holidays all the time and don't lose their jobs. You just took annual leave.'

'I would never have lost my job if you didn't buy me that stupid ticket to Thailand. Everything you touch literally turns to shit, you're just fucked. I hope you're fucking happy!'

With no work to front up to the next day, Ben took off, stumbling home only a few hours before I was due to leave for my first day back at uni. I'd barely slept, waiting for him to come home, unable to believe that we were already in this situation again.

We were both ready for a fight when he walked in the door. Our first fight since that night in Phuket, and even though we swore it wouldn't happen again, Phuket had set the new benchmark for our arguments. Yelling, pushing, threats, then inevitably the follow-through. As long as there was no blood this time then it wasn't that bad, right?

Despite the significant height difference between us, we were eye to eye, my body held in place against the cool bedroom wall by Ben's hands encircled tightly around my neck. My feet dangled.

Kicking and swiping, I choked out, 'Put me down, I can't breathe, let me go!' I couldn't break free. There had to be a victory soon.

'Stop kicking at me!' Ben said, his hands tightening around my neck. 'You will never fucking beat me, do you understand? Do you understand?'

Eyes bulging, my throat begging for air, I moved my head as much as I could, nodding, and stilled my legs as instructed. I understood.

'Should I let you breathe now?'

I nodded again.

I didn't make it to uni that day. Or any day after that.

———

With Ben not working, we really needed cash. Despite working countless part-time jobs to make ends meet, I finally accepted that I was no longer destined to get a degree. I needed to grow up and get a full-time job. I scoured the *Manly Daily* and finally found an ad that spoke to me: 'High-End Real Estate requires enthusiastic Property Officer. No experience necessary.'

Leaving the interview, I knew the job was mine, having beguiled the panel with my story of seeing their ad and immediately wanting to put my law degree on hold to test out a career in my other great passion, real estate. It was the sort of bullshit story only a real-estate agent would believe, but it worked, and two weeks later I started my first ever nine-to-five job at Northern Beaches Realty, Manly.

Working six days a week and going to TAFE two nights a week to complete my Real Estate Certificate meant that there was some much-needed space put between Ben and me, but the resentment Ben had towards me over losing his job seemed to intensify with every hour I was away from the house. There was little I could do right. I searched employment websites every day for jobs that Ben could apply for, sending off the resume I had compiled for him to anything and everything that might be suitable. With every unsuccessful application, Ben's frustration and anger grew. He began to spend his days hanging out with other jobless mates, getting stoned and drunk, funding his own needs by selling small bags of speed for ridiculous amounts of money on behalf of his dealer mate, Fitzy. At night we came home and very quickly slid into a cycle of misery, blame and resentment.

When the arguing had finished and I had finally heard the last of all the terrible things I had become, I hoped that at the very least the physical exhaustion of going round for round with Ben might result in a dreamless sleep. But when I shut my eyes that payoff was rarely granted.

Most nights I exchanged physical rounds with Ben for the rehashed emotional terror of Jay. The dream was always the same.

Me watching the scene from overhead as if looking over the top of a maze. Unable to stop the 'film', I watch on time after time as Jay got up from his desk and walked down the long hall of The Palace and looked both ways before pushing open the door to the room where I lay. When the door closed, the view narrowed and I could only see inside the room. As I peered down into the dark, waiting, I could see my sleeping figure illuminated on the bed. I knew what was going to happen, I'd lived it a thousand times or more, but still I tried to yell out to myself, 'Get up, wake up.' No matter how hard I screamed at myself, there was no sound, only silence. Like an old movie, the dream was always in black and white, maybe that's why there was no sound. Looking down, I watched myself be raped, over and over, my own eyes looking back at me, questioning, *Why aren't you doing anything to help?* I watched as Jay got up and adjusted himself. It was over. As he left the movie reel cut, and the last thing I saw was the door ajar. My mind flickered static and then the 'film' started again. If I watched closely, I could almost pinpoint the moment that the fight, the life, the unwavering confidence that I would always be all right, slipped away from me for good. I could actually see my whole self-worth haemorrhaging out of my body, until there was nothing left but hollow darkness. It's shameful to stand by and watch the very essence of yourself disappear. But every night I did. Everything in me was forever broken that night. At some point the dream cycle was interrupted, sometimes by the sounds of my own tears but often by Ben's furious hands shaking me awake. 'You're having one of those dreams again! Every friggin' night you do this! What's wrong with you?'

I wanted to die.

I couldn't see how it would ever possibly end unless I died.

Work, Ben, Jay, work, Ben, Jay. My whole life was on a film roll, being wound tighter and tighter, and I didn't know how to change the reel before it snapped.

I knew it was me who had to change, somehow I had to make things different. Maybe if I wasn't so argumentative, things wouldn't get so bad? Maybe if I could just find Ben a job then we would be happier? For a period it became so bad that Ben told me it was over nearly every weekend. It didn't matter what happened during the week, by the weekend we were in the black hole of hatred. Ben would always go, and in various states of broken I would hear myself begging him not to leave me, not to be with someone else, to please give me another chance, because by this stage I knew in my bones what Ben had known for a long time: no one in the whole world would love me for who I was.

In the hours, nights and days alone with my thoughts and memories, I found various ways to numb the pain of the life I had come to lead and the disappointment of who I had become. In these moments I teetered dangerously between my intrinsic desire to pull myself free and succeed at all costs, and the ever-present genetic tendency to give in to self-destruction. In the darkness, total self-destruction seemed more achievable. On these nights I allowed myself to give in to the idea that I was nothing. That perhaps I had always been nothing. I let every single wall of defence I'd worked hard to build up over the years come crashing down around me, freeing all the horrible thoughts that I had spent a lifetime training myself to block out to simply run riot in my mind. I allowed myself to replay over and over and over every misery, every rejection and every failure that had led me to this moment, until I finally felt the hot tears run down my face, even though I had told myself I wouldn't let myself cry anymore. And then to numb the pain I would go to the freezer and swipe a finger of Ben's carefully weighed and bagged drugs around the inside of my mouth, or drink heavily until the pain was so thoroughly numbed that I could slash angrily at my own flesh and barely feel a thing as I tried in vain to shred away the shame and pain that I had allowed in. Other nights I left the house and tried to destroy myself in other ways: drinking, clubs, sometimes meaningless sex where I hoped to be demeaned in the way I thought I now deserved, but it wasn't to be. It always seemed on these nights there was a gallant 'daddy'-type knight wanting to save me, to take me home and love me in the way a beautiful girl like me should be loved. But I've never been the type of girl who wanted to be saved by anyone other than myself. I would never trust anyone else with the task. Sometimes, in moments like these, it was apparent that I was barely able to even trust myself.

Come Sunday, Ben would be home, promising change and wanting to 'make up', and I found myself resigned to the fact that sex would probably never be anything more than a dutiful currency in my life with him. The only way to make amends with Ben and start over.

I think we both wanted it to end – the fights, the violence, the relationship – but we didn't know how to stop it. For my part, the magnitude of leaving, packing everything up and being totally alone, seemed inconceivable, especially when I could barely look at myself in a mirror. But staying was also inconceivable. I started to welcome the violence, hoping that the next time, the next weekend, Ben would be so drunk, so angry, that he just wouldn't stop. He would just keep going, and going, and going until he strangled or beat the life right out of me and then I wouldn't have to work out a way to end it all.

Because it would be done for me and we would both be free.

The small amount of people who were still in my life started to notice things weren't quite right with me. The self-hatred, the lack of energy and, perhaps most obviously, the physical evidence of the fights, were all getting harder to hide, even with my Ruby mask firmly fitted each day. I saw Grandpa more than I saw anyone else; he visited me a few times a week either at home or for lunch at work, and we spoke on the phone every night. He started incorporating a wellbeing check into our usual conversation routine: 'Did you eat something for breakfast? You have to start the day properly, you know,' and, 'I hope you're not working too hard, you do too much for such a young girl.' And then he'd ask, 'I'm not being nosy or anything, but what's that mark on your arm from? Why can't you turn your neck properly? Have you been crying?'

'It's nothing, Grandpa. I'm fine. You really don't need to worry about me.'

'It's my job to worry about you, Rennie. At least until you get married and then you're someone else's problem,' he would chuckle. It was a joke he had been making since I was about four – whenever I was in trouble or being a pest, he would sigh dramatically and say, 'Can you hurry up and bloody get married so I don't have to deal with these problems anymore?'

One lunchtime, in the middle of Manly Corso, Grandpa looked at me with watery eyes. Putting his giant hand gently around my wrist, he said, 'Promise me, Ren, if Ben ever does anything to you, anything at all, you will tell me. I'll look after you. Give him a good bunch of Irish fives, I will, that good-for-nothing.'

I laughed in spite of myself as my eyes began to fill just like his. 'I promise, but really, everything is fine.' It seemed absurd to hide behind Ruby to Grandpa, when it was him who'd actually created her, but how could I ever possibly explain it all? I would break his heart with all that I had become.

———

One day six weeks into my job at Northern Beaches Realty I arrived at work with a souvenir from home for the first time; a crossover between Renee's home life and the charade of Ruby's world. On paper it was Renee who got the job, but in my mind it was actually Ruby who went to work every day. Ruby had been many things to me in my life: a nickname, a scapegoat for texta murals on Nan's wall, a little sarcastic voice in my head, a secret persona I created to safeguard my shortcomings; but during this time of self-loathing and despair, Ruby was so much more. Ruby was my cloak, my costume. A mindset and character that I needed to mentally inhabit in order to function outside of the emotional torment I was living in. Being Ruby in this time was like being a widow at a funeral, meticulously dressed for the occasion of living, brimming with determination to get through the day, but nonetheless broken into a million pieces on the inside. I did my best not to let people see, but I'm sure they must have. It's hard to hide all that you are.

On this particular day, though, I knew my Ruby mask wasn't going to be enough to get me through. As I unlocked the door and slid it across, the little bell over it jingled. Knowing I was usually first in, the owner, James, continued working as he said, 'Morning, Renee. How was your weekend?' He looked up from his work, in search of my answer, and his face changed instantly, 'Oh my God! What the hell happened to your eye? Are you okay?'

'Oh, um, yeah, it's actually kind of funny, I was playing tennis on the weekend with my mum and I swung for the ball, and, well, I totally misjudged it. The ball literally landed in the socket of my eye, at full speed. It looks bad, doesn't it? But it's actually fine. Sorry.'

James looked at me, unsure. 'Okay, well, yes, it does look really bad. You can't sit here at the front desk or near the window with your eye looking like that, people are coming in with multimillion dollar homes for us to manage. Come and sit back at this desk, that way, for your sake, people won't be staring at you all day.'

Everyone in both the Property Management and the Sales office three doors down heard about my eye and I spent the day fielding questions from my colleagues. Rachel, who was only a couple of years older than me and my only real friend at work, pulled me aside. 'You know you can always come and stay at my place anytime you want . . . if you need to. I used to be in a hard relationship and I know what it's like.'

'I just got hit with a tennis ball, seriously.'

'I know, but if you just want to come and stay anyway, have a girls night or something? My door is always open.'

'Thanks, Rach.'

I went home that night and for the first time in a long time I instigated the fight with Ben. 'You can't keep doing this to me, Ben, look at my face! I've been moved to the hot desk out the back at work because my eye looks so offensive to clients! People *know* I didn't get hit with a tennis ball, they all know it was you! You have a problem –'

'I have a problem? The only problem I have is *you* and all of *your* problems. You would drive any man to beat the crap out of you, to strangle the absolute life out of you, given half the chance! I'm sure if your work friends *really* knew you, and what I have had to put up with, then they wouldn't be so concerned about your stupid eye.'

I thought of the shocked and worried faces of all the middle-aged marrieds in my office and I knew that if they did know my secrets there would definitely be judgement in their hearts, but I strongly doubted that any of them in the same situation would be driven to violence. The suffocating pity in their eyes told me that.

'I just don't believe what you're saying anymore. I know I've made mistakes, I know I'm not perfect, God knows you never let me forget it, but I can't keep going on like this. If it's so hard for you to put up with me, then don't! Leave! Break up with me! GO!'

I started to cry uncontrollably. 'I just can't take it anymore! This isn't normal. At least I take responsibility for the mistakes I've made, but you, you just blame everything on me. But it's not just me, it's you too! It's not normal to hit your girlfriend!' I buried my face in my hands. *How will I ever get out of this? I have got to get out of this!*

I felt Ben's hands on my shoulders and then around me, turning me towards him so my face was buried in his chest. 'Babe,' his voice was soft, 'I said I was sorry on Saturday night, I swear I'm not going to do it again, you just make me so angry sometimes . . . But it's in the past okay? It's *all* in the past.'

———

I celebrated my twentieth birthday and we limped our way past our two-year anniversary.

Ben was finally working again, but we were getting further and further into debt. One Friday after work I arrived home to find

Ben's mobile bill in the mail and, with Ben away for the weekend working on a job site up the coast, I opened it and went to pay it over the phone. I almost vomited when I saw that the bill was for eight hundred dollars. There was no way we could possibly pay this bill. It had to be a mistake! I looked through the bill, searching for an obvious error, a call to Greece or something that looked amiss. I trailed through the numbers: mine, the restaurant where his mum worked, his boss's and then this one other number almost daily, sometimes multiple times a day for twenty minutes, an hour. Who could he possibly be calling?

I called the number and a girl answered. I hung up. My heart was racing. I tried to call Ben but his phone was off. Was he really away working up the coast again? Ben had been gone most week-ends since he got the job working overtime, but to date there had been no extra pay. Ben swore his boss was going to pay him soon, he was just waiting on payment from the site bosses, but he didn't want to ask him again because he was still technically the new guy.

I took a deep breath and called the number again.

'Hi, my name is Renee, I'm Ben's girlfriend. This number is on Ben's frequently dialled, and I –'

'Hi Renee, I'm Jasmine, Ben's friend. I've heard all about you –'

'Oh, that's funny, 'cause I don't think I've heard anything about you. Where are you friends from?'

The girl laughed. 'Ben's boss Basha introduced us when he started working with him. We're good friends now.'

'Yeah, I can see that from how often you talk to each other. What type of friends are you?'

'Just friends for now, but I guess you should speak to Ben about that.'

'Is he with you now?'

# 31

There were still a few months left on our lease, time that I now knew I had to use to harden my heart against Ben, pull myself out of this rut, and change everything. Again. I started with the self-destruction: the obvious kinds had to stop. But still it was hard; I slipped up, fell apart, and I wasn't always able to stick to the strict expectations I had held for Ruby.

I was happiest at work, but Northern Beaches Realty had been sullied. I had taken too many days off trying to avoid another hot desk sentence and I knew that I would probably never amount to anything more than the general dogsbody of the office. I still dreamed of doing something great with my life, I just needed to get a start, find my passion again.

I began looking for a new job. I didn't want just any job, though – it needed to be a career move. I was certain that once I was happy with work, then I could truly focus on fixing all the other areas of my life. There was only one job that I applied for, one that screamed at me from the computer, *This is the job for you!*

> Client Services Officer/Property Manager required for a growing
> community services organisation. Must have extensive property
> management experience and/or case management skills to manage
> a complex needs portfolio of community housing clients.

I don't know why community services work had never occurred to me before. I had aced 3 Unit Society and Culture at high school and only got mediocre achievements in Legal Studies, but no one, including me and our school careers advisor, had ever really thought much about that. It occurred to me that perhaps I had been on the wrong path all along.

The role was most definitely above my on-paper skill level, but in my heart I was sure I would be perfect for it. I just needed to get a face-to-face interview and then I knew Ruby could win them over.

I beefed up my resume considerably from eight months of dogsbody experience to a year and a half of integral team leader experience. I applied to do a Bachelor of Social Science degree via correspondence so that I could technically say in the interview (when I got one) that I was currently undertaking my degree, therefore having both property experience and social work skills. Prepared, I lodged my application for the position and waited.

Phone interviews were the first round. Then what I had hoped for: the offer of a face-to-face interview. I felt confident leaving the interview but, for the first time ever, a little desperate too. I really wanted this job. I could already see myself in the small terrace house in Bondi Junction where the organisation was based, working alongside the incredibly passionate people who had just interviewed me. Even more than that, I desperately wanted to work with disadvantaged clients to help them get their lives back together. This was important work! I handed in my resignation at

Northern Beaches Realty the next day, giving them three weeks' notice. Regardless of the outcome of the interview, I had to work somewhere I *felt* something about.

A week after the interview I still hadn't heard anything about the job. I called to see if there had been a decision. 'I'm sorry we haven't gotten back to you yet. There are two of you we're still deciding between – you each offer different things that we would value greatly at the organisation – but we're just awaiting some news from our funding body and we'll get back to you as soon as we can with an answer either way.'

They checked my references and, from where I sat at my desk, I heard Rachel from the sales department give me an absolutely glowing reference. But then I heard nothing.

Another week went by, and I had to sit on my hands to stop myself seeming pathetic and calling again. I was leaving Northern Beaches Realty in only a week's time and I still hadn't applied for any other jobs because I was pinning all my hopes on this one.

When my mobile finally rang I just knew it would be the call delivering my fate.

'Hello?'

'Hi, Renee, it's Kerryn from Eastern Suburbs Housing Association. I'm sorry it's taken me so long to get back to you but we have been waiting on some big news here and we didn't want to make a decision before we knew. As you know, we have been splitting hairs over you and another candidate, but we have just had a sizeable chunk of new funding confirmed, which means that we are now in a position to grow the organisation's capacity. This means that we can now offer both you and the other candidate, John, a position at the organisation. Welcome to the team!'

When Kerryn and I hung up, I jumped up and down on the spot, squealing with delight. This was it, the first step towards reclaiming my future.

———

I started at Eastern Suburbs Rental Housing Association (ESRHA) on 2 December 2002, when I was twenty years old. The organisation managed social housing tenancies across the Eastern Suburbs, and worked on the ethos of providing services to those who truly needed them most: clients with mental health issues and HIV/AIDS, women and children escaping domestic violence, and young single mothers. Every client on the books had, like me, weathered a storm in life. File after file revealed the story of yet another vulnerable person whose path had taken an unexpected turn for the worse. People who for one reason or another needed a helping hand to get their lives back on the right track. With every passing minute I spent at work, the passion inside me grew. *This* is what I was meant to do with my life. Because if there was anyone in this world who knew how easy it was to get stuck up to your eyeballs on a mucky path and have to face the consequences alone, it was me. And I didn't want that for anyone else.

I couldn't wait to get up and go to work each day, I would have worked twenty-four hours a day if they had let me. From the very beginning I was there early and working late, never wanting to leave anything unfinished on my desk. The team, the clients, the feeling of being passionate about something again filled me with hope, hope that maybe *everything* hadn't been in vain, because at the very least it had brought me to this moment, where I felt like I had a greater purpose again.

Within weeks of starting work at ESRHA it was like I had worked there forever, like I had found a little niche where I belonged. My direct manager, Guy, took me under his wing and became like my fairy godfather, constantly sprinkling my day with wisdom and endless excursions to get coffee so he could tell me what a wonderful job I was doing. 'I've got big plans for you and your career, missy,' he would sometimes say. I don't know what it was Guy saw in me, but he was steadfast in his belief that everything I touched sparkled, and his blatant favouritism towards me became a bit of a joke between me and my new office mate, John, who was also managed by Guy but was yet to be touched with the sparkle wand.

John had started a week after me; his big rugby-player frame had filled the door of our tiny shared office space before he launched over the threshold to shake my hand. 'Hi! I'm John,' he said, his friendly tanned face breaking into an infectious smile. 'You must be Renee! I've heard so much about you!'

John was so full of enthusiasm and warmth that he reminded me of a Labrador, a loyal best friend, but with a distractingly sun-kissed face. I caught myself thinking that if John and I were to ever have children, they would surely have the most olive-coloured skin of any white children alive, because despite living by the beach my whole life, this Western Suburbs boy was even more tanned than me! My cheeks burned when I caught myself; why was I thinking about coffee-coloured children with a guy who hadn't even been in the same room as me for more than a minute?

For some reason I had thought John would be so much older than me, given all his years of experience in real estate, but it turned out he had left school a few years earlier than me and we were the same age: turning twenty-one the following year. Despite thinking of John as my competitor, I quickly came to enjoy seeing him every morning almost as much as I enjoyed the job itself. We were instant comrades.

---

Ben and I had been living separately under the same roof since the fallout of the Jasmine phone call, each of us awkwardly waiting for the lease to end. Now that Mum was divorced and only had custody of the girls during the week, she had lots of spare time to hang out with me. I often spent my weekends up the coast with her, or going down the M5 to hang out with Shelly in Canberra. For the first time in a long time I realised that even though I had almost no friends left, it might still be possible for me to make some sort of enjoyable life without Ben and that I might even start to feel like I did at work all the time.

As the end of our lease drew closer, John and I started talking about the possibility of me taking over one of the rooms in his share house because, by chance, one of his flatmates was moving back to New Zealand. We spent our lunchtimes talking about whether it might ruin our budding friendship if we lived *and* worked together, but either way I had decided I wanted to be as far from the Northern Beaches as possible.

One Friday the whole ESRHA team went out for drinks and dinner, and John and I sat next to each other, thighs touching under the table. We sipped our drinks and tried to ignore the growing electricity between us. My phone rang and for the first time in weeks, it was Ben. Unable to ignore the call, I moved my leg away from John's and answered.

'Hey.'

'Hey. It's me, where are you?'

'Out with work friends, why?'

'I miss you. I've been thinking a lot over the past few weeks and I don't want us to be over. You seem really different lately when I see you at home, happier maybe? When the lease ends I want to move with you. I want us to give it another go.'

I got up from the table. 'Where is this coming from? Why now? We've been avoiding each other at the house for weeks, we've barely spoken a word. What's suddenly made you feel differently?'

'I guess I don't *really* want to be without you. I mean the first few weeks were fun to be single, but I actually miss you. I want to work things out and I know you still love me.'

'I do still love you, Ben, but I feel like I've just done the hardest bit of the break-up: actually deciding to break up. Things haven't been good between us for a long time.'

'I know, but let's try again. Now that you're happier, things will be like they used to be, things will be better between us.'

'How?'

'I'll move away from the Beaches with you. I know you hate it, so let's leave, let's get away from everyone here and do all the things we used to say we were going to do, like save for a house.'

I wanted to make it work with Ben; I had no one else in my life except for Grandpa, Mum and Shelly, and I did still love him. Or at least I loved the idea of what I thought we could be: two underdogs triumphing over adversity. I didn't want to fail at this, didn't want to throw away all the years I'd put into being with Ben and, above all, I still felt grateful that after *everything* Ben still wanted me. I could see how difficult it must have been to be with me at times and I didn't want to be the type of girl who drove a man to the point of violence or into someone else's arms. But like Ben said, now that I was feeling a little happier I would surely be easier to be with, easier to love. And away from the Northern Beaches, across the Harbour Bridge, how could we not be happy?

'Come on, Rennie, we've been together more than two years now, don't just throw it all away! Don't quit on me!'

And so I didn't because, in my heart of hearts, I have never been a quitter.

———

We moved to a big apartment in the centre of the city with Ed, one of Ben's friends from work, and his girlfriend, Zara. We moved under the agreement that our reunion was only a trial, a final attempt to see if we could make a life together, because, in spite of everything, we really did love each other.

From the moment we moved to the city, Ben was true to his word, and things were different between us. The arguments stopped and we started going to concerts and out to dinner again. One night after I had been away for a few days at a conference, I came home to a path of tealights, dinner in the oven and Ben standing by the dining table with a tea towel over his arm like a waiter, pouring wine. 'I really missed you,' he said, flashing his crooked boyish grin at me before throwing the tea towel into the air and swirling me around the lounge room. We danced, my small feet on top of his big feet, just like I used to dance with my Grandpa as a little girl.

It was these shiny moments that I hoped would spill into forever. They kept us going. Ben still went missing for nights or weekend jaunts back to the Northern Beaches but I didn't care, I just tried to keep my mind busy instead of worrying about who he was with or when he would be home. On occasion I even went out on the town myself, usually with Shelly or Mum or sometimes even John.

Things were the easiest they had been between Ben and me since we had first moved in together. I was also slowly winning the battle of pushing everything that had happened in Canberra and beyond deep down inside me. It was only ever at night that my subconscious continued to betray me. Night after night, I awoke to my own thrashing after another sweat-soaked reunion with Jay. The difference now, though, was that it was accompanied by a recovery routine. Ben often woke me and said, 'Babe, wake up, you're just dreaming again. Go back to sleep.' Or often, because we were awake anyway, Ben suggested we have sex to help us get back to sleep. I usually agreed because not only did I want to make amends for waking him up, it also meant I wasn't left awake in the dark with only my memories of Jay to keep me company until daylight.

The more time I spent at work, the more I felt myself evening out. Very slowly my world was opening up to include a few more friends, and there were daily compliments from John, which I always took to be insincere as he was clearly a smooth talker, but they coloured my cheeks and quickened my heart rate all the same. My heightened anxiety about not being good enough sometimes slipped from the forefront of my mind and I found myself going hours or even a whole day without consciously being on guard or hiding behind Ruby; I was just me. Most of all, my growing confidence fed off the praise that was heaped upon me for my work. Not only did I love my job, I was good at it, and the harder I worked, the more free I felt from the past. I was so grateful that in the midst of so much chaos, I had stumbled across a career path that I felt passionate about.

John had very quickly become my second favourite reason to go to work. Sitting only metres apart, we peppered the day with fragments of our lives: jokes, bickering, flirting, advice-seeking and laughter. Too much laughter for a workplace. Eight hours a day, five days a week, month after month, we soon knew each other's looks, tone and moods instinctively and there was an easiness about our friendship that I had never experienced before. We were chalk and cheese. He hated to be alone; I felt like I was always alone. He liked to work with the radio blasting while tapping his fingers on the desk incessantly to the drumbeat and I liked to work in silence, quietly focused on the task. John worked as if there was no such thing as a deadline, whereas I often refused to leave the office if there was even the smallest task left to do. But somehow it just worked. In less than six months, this larger-than-life man with his loud, ugly shirts and twinkling denim eyes that were always gently mocking me had become one of the closest friends I had ever had.

Sometimes when Ben was at work or back on the Beaches, John and I met up on weekends to do stuff together. I had hoped John and Ben might be friends, but after one very awkward trip to the beach, Ben made his utter dislike of John very clear.

'He's a fucking cocky prick – he doesn't want to be your friend, he just wants to fuck you!'

'It's not like that, we're just friends. We sit side by side in a tiny office, so of course we're friends!'

'I don't want you to be friends with him, just go to work and do your job.'

'You can't tell me who to be friends with. I'm friends with everyone from work, but you don't seem to have a problem with anyone else, just John.'

'No, because HIV faggots like Guy and non-showering vegan hippies aren't trying to fuck you, but John is –'

'You're so narrow minded, it's disgusting. I don't know how we are even together sometimes. John and I are just friends, the same as everyone else at work. But you don't want me to have any friends, do you? You want to be able to go out and do whatever you like and just have me here waiting for you! That's not who I am! At least, it's not who I used to be before you!'

'So go out with Shelly, go and see your mum, I don't want you to go out with anyone from work anymore!'

I sighed. I was so tired of it all, so tired of walking such a controlled line all the time. 'This is all a mistake, Ben, you and me living here. We shouldn't have stayed together. I should have moved alone.'

'This is because of him, isn't it? You want to fuck him too, don't you? Or have you already? Tell me, have you fucked him already? Did you do it here in our bed? Or at your office?'

'No! It's not like that! We just work together!'

'You're fucking lying, tell the truth.' Ben shoved me across the lounge room and I fell backward on my bum from the force. He moved towards me, squatting over me on the ground, his hand tight around my neck. 'Tell me why you suddenly don't want to be with me,' he said, his eyes wild. How can eyes be so loving one moment and so full of loathing the next?

I used my hands to prise his fingers away from my neck and shouted up at him, overcome with misery, 'It's not because of John that I wish I never moved here, it's because of this, because of you! It's because of that night in Thailand and all the other nights that end like this. I don't want to be here. I don't want to be with you.' I wished I could just pack my things and leave, but I felt so weighed down by everything. I felt trapped.

Then there was quietness.

'Tell me honestly, do you not want to be with me because you have feelings for John?' Ben looked at me from underneath the hair falling across his eyes, waiting for my answer.

'No, it's not about feelings for anyone else, it's about my feelings for *you*, my feelings about how you treat me. I don't know anyone who treats their girlfriend like you do, but if we're talking about John, then yeah, I know for sure he wouldn't treat a dog the way you treat me.'

'So it is because of him! This is bullshit! What if he knew what a fucking whore you are? That you are the daughter of a psychopathic animal? What would everyone at your precious job think of that? They don't know you! But I know you!'

'None of that stuff is even relevant to my job, it wouldn't matter! I am good at what I do and even you can't take that away from me!'

But something in my expression must have betrayed me. He knew I would never want anyone, especially people at work, to know about my past. What if he told them? What if he told everyone? I needed to keep my secrets safe; locked away forever.

Ben's face looked calm now, controlled. 'And what would your beloved friend John think of you? Do you think he'd still be bothered with you if he really knew you?'

'Probably not,' I whispered. 'But what I also know is that no one at my work would think it was okay to hit someone either, no matter what they've done. Especially John!'

'That's fucking bullshit – you would drive anyone to it! Anyway, you're full of shit, have I even hit you tonight? No. I've barely fucking touched you. I said things would be different between us, and they have been, haven't they? Not every guy would stay with you after what you've put me through, but I have, because, for some fucking crazy reason, I love you.'

I felt torn. I loved many things about him, but I wished that I didn't. And even more than that, I was so scared of being totally alone. I wanted someone to come in and make it easy for me, take Ben away or force me to leave. I wished someone would pull rank on me, swoop in and separate us so that I didn't have to. I needed help. It should have been easy – all I had to do was walk into the bedroom, pack my things and go, but it was impossible. Where would I even go? I had to work in the morning, I had to stay. The longer I sat there, the more caged I felt. Why had no one ever told me that you can never escape the choices of yesterday?

———

On my twenty-first birthday, Ben surprised me with a ludicrous pile of presents. Twenty-one of them. A white cashmere coat, perfume, matching underwear sets, a dress to wear out that night after work because he had arranged for a night of dinner and dancing just for us. I was overwhelmed, my eyes filling with tears at the display of love and the effort he had gone to. It was out of character and extravagant, but I knew it was less about my birthday and more about making up for the previous few weeks; making amends for two incidents in particular: the bruise and the family dinner. If only I hadn't reacted so physically when Mum hugged me tightly, hadn't yelped in surprise at the agony of her touch, perhaps things wouldn't have erupted so badly. I replayed the scene from a few weeks ago in my mind, wishing I could undo it.

'What's wrong with your back?' Mum asked.

'Nothing, it's fine, just a little sore.'

'That's rubbish, you're too young to have a sore back, let me have a look.'

'No, Mum, it's fine, you just hugged me too tight.'

A look crossed her face and she pulled me around roughly and lifted the back of my top.

She gasped. 'What the hell happened to your back? It's purple and black!'

I hadn't seen what it looked like yet as we didn't have a full-length mirror at home, but it was pretty painful, so I had guessed it must be quite bruised. 'It's fine, Mum, just an accident.'

'There is no way this was an accident, how would you fall and hurt the middle of your back like that? Unless someone pushed you or punched you.'

'No one punched me, Mum. Just forget about it, we're supposed to be having a fun night together.'

'Ben did this to you, didn't he?'

'No.'

Later that night, after I'd had too much wine, Mum asked again. Despite knowing that I shouldn't, I admitted that yes, Ben had done it, but it wasn't what she thought. 'It all just got out of hand. A silly fight and I ran into the shower to get away, I forgot to lock the bathroom door. Anyway it was just a slight shove and I landed against the shower taps. You know I bruise easily.'

It was mostly the truth except that I *had* locked the bathroom door and Ben had busted it right off its hinges. And the bruise had come about not so much from a slight push but repeated forceful shoves against the tiled wall, my back and head connecting with the taps and tiles. The confession wasn't about Ben though, it was about me. I needed Mum to know that it was me who had caused all this to begin with.

'It's not Ben's fault, Mum, it's mine. When I was in Canberra I worked at a brothel –'

She looked horrified. 'Were you a prostitute?'

'No, but I could have been.'

'What did you do there? How could you work there and not sleep with anyone?'

'I was a receptionist. Well, more of a hostess, a cleaner, I guess, but I did sleep with one person but not at the brothel . . . it's hard to explain exactly. But it all started with that, with working there. If I hadn't worked there, my life wouldn't be like this now. It's my karma.' I was drunk and rambling, not piecing together a full story but unable to stop the wave of grief engulfing me as I confided the state of my life. Maybe she could fix it? That's what mums do, right?

Mum put her arm around me as I sobbed. 'If I hadn't worked there I would never have met Bella, never slept with Gabriel. I wouldn't have met Jay, would never have fallen asleep in that room . . . the rape, the abortion, it's all my fault.' I was gasping for breath. 'It's my fault that things with Ben have ended up like this, it's because of me. The bruise is nothing compared to what I deserve. Nothing compared to what I have done to myself!'

'Oh, Ren,' she said.

'I'm sorry,' I sobbed. 'Sorry I'm such a disappointment.'

'You're not a disappointment, Ren. Everyone makes bad decisions. But I don't want you working anywhere like that again, okay? And you shouldn't tell anyone about it. You haven't told anyone else, have you?'

'Just Ben, I told him everything. About my dad, about Canberra, about everything . . . I'm sorry.'

'Ren! What were you thinking? He could tell anyone, everyone! Why did you do that? Telling him about your dad especially doesn't affect just you! He could ruin your whole life! And mine.'

I burst into fresh tears. 'I don't know what I was thinking, I needed to talk to someone! I know it was a mistake. I'm sorry!'

'If you want to talk to someone, talk to me. I've been telling you your whole life that you should never talk about these things to anyone, okay? And the Canberra stuff too, what were you thinking? Promise me you won't tell anyone anything about this stuff again. It will come back to haunt you!'

Not for the first time I wondered what it would be like to always have to hide all these secrets inside me. What if I was like my nan and died with so many secrets hiding in my heart and mind? Just like her, I would never know what it would be like to be loved unconditionally, to be free.

The weekend after my confessions to Mum, Ben and I had gone out for dinner with his dad and my mum, an early birthday celebration. Ben's dad, a balding tradesman, had a 1950s view of a woman's place in the world that clashed with my mother's views and immediately returned her to her default stance of defiant teenage runaway. Stan – who rarely left the Northern Beaches, preferring to unwind from the working week by blowing all his money on a few large punts on the horses and a Chinese takeaway – was intent on goading my mother about her upcoming holiday, which she was desperately saving for. 'Why would you want to go to Asia, Gemma? I reckon about the only good thing to come from those chinks is a good Szechuan beef, and you can get that right here in Australia.'

It was only a matter of time before Mum betrayed my confidence to point score. 'I can see where your son gets his piggish behaviour from. I suppose it was you that taught him it's okay to hit women too? I guess you think it's okay that my daughter's back is bruised to all buggery because your son thinks it's okay to lay his hands on her? Tell me, Stan, did he get that bravado from watching you hit that witch of a woman he calls his mother?'

I thought Ben's dad was going to reach over the table and punch my mother right in the face. Everyone in The Crab Shack was watching and waiting to see what was going to happen at our table next.

'Mum! Stop it, stop talking! You're drunk! She doesn't know what she's saying –'

'I'm not drunk!' she slurred. 'I just thought that Stan should know that the apple clearly hasn't fallen far from the tree. Another racist brute. What a proud father he should be.'

———

Ben's voice brought me back to my birthday. 'And don't think this is it! Tomorrow, I have an even bigger surprise for you. We're going for a long drive.'

The presents, the night out in a fancy hotel and now the anticipation of another surprise; all of it should have made me feel happy, but it didn't. At twenty-one, I was completely laden down with life. I should have felt grateful that Ben had gone to so much effort for my birthday but the highs and lows were exhausting. I didn't want extravagant peaks to balance out the troughs; I just wanted an equilibrium I could rely on.

The whole drive south, Ben kept glancing over at me and asking, 'Are you happy? You don't seem that happy? Why aren't you excited about everything I have done? Come on, don't ruin your own birthday by being a stroppy bitch!'

'I'm sorry, it's just that I can't stop thinking about the last few weeks. I love all the effort you've gone to today, I really do, but you know what? Instead of all these presents and surprises, I wish everything was normal between us. The highs don't counteract the lows, they just make me feel crazy!'

'Get out of the car,' Ben said, pulling over.

As the passenger door slammed, I wondered if Ben was going to come and pick me up again, or if I was really going to have to make my own way home this time. I spent the next half-hour walking along the side of the freeway. It wasn't the best birthday I'd ever had. Eventually our silver car slid up on the gravel beside me, the passenger door opened and I got in silently. Ben turned the car around and continued to drive south as if nothing had happened. There was no need to talk. What could be said that hadn't already been said?

———

As we reached fifteen thousand feet, Ben and I edged to the rear of the plane. Around us other jumpers were anxious, a few jokingly kissed each other goodbye just in case they didn't make it, but as Ben and I stood on the edge waiting for our countdown, I felt no fear. I heard Ben shout to me as we bent our knees to jump, 'Happy birthday, Ren!' Falling forwards, I plummeted towards the ground and still felt nothing, except for shock at how cold the air was on my face for such a beautiful sunny day.

# 32

Out of nowhere my fairy godfather, Guy, resigned from work. Overcome with shock, I couldn't even begin to imagine anyone who could possibly replace him, his odd sense of humour, crinkly-eyed smile and penchant for gossiping with the receptionist, Angela, while sneaking a cigarette out in the car park.

'What do you mean you don't want me to leave?' he said to me in his office that afternoon. 'I thought you would be thrilled to get rid of this old fuddy duddy.'

'Why would I be thrilled? God knows who will end up in your chair now – they might be awful!'

He grinned. 'I don't think you'll mind them too much, actually.'

'What do you mean? Do you already know who's replacing you?'

'Well,' he leaned towards me over his large L-shaped desk, 'it's all very hush-hush for the moment, but if everything goes according to my plan, little miss –' he paused for effect '– then it will be you who inherits all this.' He waved his arms flamboyantly around his freshly painted purple office and the heaped piles of paperwork strewn over his desk and winked. It seemed he really had had a plan for my career all along.

———

Not long after Guy left, I cleared my desk in anticipation of my freshly recruited replacement's arrival. I spent the afternoon hauling all my bits and pieces upstairs and arranging them in my new office. John and I were the last to leave, finishing the day in our little shared office for the last time.

'Don't think because you're technically my boss now that I'm going to do everything you say,' John said.

I smiled at him, but already I felt the tears springing to my eyes. 'I can't believe we're not going to share an office anymore! I'm going to miss you!'

'Oh my God,' John said, 'are you seriously about to cry when you just got promoted and you're getting your own office?'

'I think so,' I said, starting to laugh at the same time as the tears began spilling down my cheeks. 'I know it's silly but I really am going to miss you!'

'Come here, you big goose! You're only moving upstairs! We're still going to see each other every day!' I could hear John smiling as he pulled me into one of his big bear hugs. 'Seriously, you are the only girl I know who would cry after getting promoted because she doesn't want to move to her own office, with a door! You crack me up, Ren.'

I laughed and cried into his hideous purple shirt as we held each other and laughed for longer than we should have, longer than Ben would have liked, but neither of us let go.

'I mean, personally I still can't see why they gave the job to you over me, but seriously, babe, you should be happy. You deserve this!'

We pulled back, still touching. 'I'll tell you what,' John said, 'I promise to make the effort to come upstairs and visit you every day, would that make your promotion easier on you?'

I smiled. 'Yes, it would.' And even though he was making fun of me, I already felt better.

'Okay, should we go home now, boss? Do you feel like you can face coming to work on Monday?'

'Shut up,' I said and shoved him away. 'Let's go.'

———

Shortly after my move upstairs at work, our flatmates, Ed and Zara, skipped out on our apartment. Unable to pay the exorbitant city rent alone, Ben and I hastily moved to a sunny, but noisy, apartment in Coogee. Just the two of us, even though we were seeing less and less of each other, with Ben spending a lot more time back on the Northern Beaches with his mates and me spending most nights working late or studying. Rarely did I spend time with anyone except Mum, Grandpa, Ben or John and the more time I spent alone, the more I realised that while I had pulled myself out of the rut work- and study-wise, there was still more to do. I needed more than a career path and the promise of a degree in social sciences in a few years when I finally finished, I had to work on how I felt right now.

I started running and swimming and doing boxing classes with John before work. John had to leave his place at five in the morning to get to my new gym in time for the boxing classes and he did this two or three times a week, both of us on a 'get fit' mission. We routinely left the gym and headed straight to the beach for a swim before we headed back to my place to get ready for work. As a tradie, Ben was always long gone by the time we got there. The three hours John and I spent alone with each other before work eased the twelve-stair distance that my promotion had put between us. All of the jokes, bickering and life stories moved from the office to the gym.

Even though John and I *were* just friends, the more time we spent together, the greater the possibility that there could one day be more to 'us'. The way we laughed together, looked at each other, knew each other, it was impossible to ignore. The tension was palpable, practically visible to the naked eye, but no matter how hard John pressed me on it, I would never admit it. I couldn't risk saying it out loud, because once the words were said the line would be crossed and I would probably end up losing both John and Ben.

'Why are you still bothering with Ben, when you are so clearly going to end up marrying me?' John grinned at me in the park at lunch one day. It had been a running joke between us since a month or two into our friendship. He was joking but I could see he was frustrated with me, frustrated to be saying these exact same words again.

He had a way of making me laugh in spite of myself. 'Ugh, not this again, another marriage proposal?' I was smiling back at him, resisting the urge to stroke the side of his face.

We had got to this point several times in our friendship already – the more time we spent together, the closer we got. The tension kept building until it reached a climax.

'Seriously, Ren. You know there is something between us. Why won't you give it a chance?'

'Trust me, John, you just like the idea of me. If you were actually with me, you'd soon change your mind. We're better off as friends. I like you too much to ruin it.'

'Don't tell me how I would feel if we were together!' His eyes were brimming with tears. 'I know how *I* feel and I don't want to just be your friend anymore. I know you feel the same way.'

'I do like you, but I'm with someone – you know I'm with Ben. It's complicated . . . it's hard to explain.'

'So what if you're with Ben? Just because you've been together for years doesn't mean you're supposed to be with him forever. He's had his time and treats you like shit! Complicated isn't good! I don't know what goes on between you guys at home, but I'm not an idiot, no one in the office is. You come to work with marks on your arm, you had that black eye a while back and I don't care what you say, I know that it wasn't a remote control that accidentally hit you!'

'It was a remote! Ben threw it to me and I didn't catch it. It was an accident! Plus it's none of your business, John. I don't know why you have to do this! You are my best friend, but that's all we can be because I'm with someone else!'

'But I know you want to be with me! Argh! You are so frustrating. Your loyalties are to the wrong person. You say I'm your best friend but you give me no credit, you keep this whole section of your life a big secret . . . Why do you want to stay with Ben? You're not happy! You can talk to me –'

'I know I can, but there is nothing to talk about!'

———

'I've sort of started seeing this girl, Emily,' John announced a few Mondays later as the two of us stood in the reception area, pulling out files we needed.

'Oh. That's good.'

'I can't just sit around and wait for you for the rest of my life,' he said.

'I never said you should! I'm glad you're seeing someone. I'm really happy for you.'

'Your face doesn't look that happy.' John laughed.

I attempted to rearrange my expression, forcing a bright look. 'Of course I'm happy for you. What's she like?'

'She's a great chick, I reckon you'll really like her! My band is playing a gig next week. You should come and meet her.'

'I'm not sure about next week, but I'll try,' I promised, already knowing that I wouldn't go, and even more certain that there was no way in hell I would ever be friends with Emily.

Although it pained me to hear of John and Emily's romps, him having a girlfriend instantly relieved the pressure on our friendship and we resumed our own blurred relationship with just as much intensity as before, but with fewer marriage jokes.

———

When things were good with Ben, I could clearly picture how our life would roll out together: the house, the children; all the things we had talked about. But when it was bad, I wondered how I was ever going to get out. I often asked my mother, 'How did you know when it was time to break up with David all those years ago? Was it hard when you decided to leave Peter? Do you ever wonder if you made a mistake?'

She always replied, 'Ren, one day you will just wake up and know you can't stay anymore and you will pack up your things and go.'

I couldn't imagine it, but I believed her, and hoped that she was right, that soon I would feel strong in my convictions, one way or the other.

———

The team at work was disbanding. Kerryn had resigned to go travelling and she had invited us all to a big farewell party at her place. The theme was angels and devils, and as I got ready in front of the mirror at home I felt happy with what was looking back at me. I was slowly but surely winning my battle with the twenty-plus kilos of post-Canberra weight that had crept on. I still had a way to go but I looked good in my floaty white dress and fluffy halo. Ben was dressed all in black with red glittery devil horns. I was excited to be the one taking Ben to a party instead of the other way around for once. Before we left the house we posed in the lounge room, cheeks smushed together and smiling for the camera, which Ben was angling towards us to capture our fancy dress. It was going to be a good night.

We picked Angela up on the way to Kerryn's. Things were already in full swing by the time we arrived, music blaring, the living room a sea of white-chiffon angels and red-and-black devils. Ben sat between me and Angela, tucking into the bottle of Jim Beam he had brought to the party. About a quarter of a way through the bottle, John arrived and joined our little gang. He kissed me and Angela hello, and shook Ben's hand half-heartedly. 'How are you going, mate?' John and Ben made no secret of their dislike for each other, but they always did a reasonable job of being civil in person. They chatted until eventually Ben broke away to get more mixer for his drink. Angela, who was always trying to leave John and me alone in the hope that we would declare our undying love for each other, immediately left us to go to the bathroom. The music was getting louder and louder, and after about twenty minutes John said, 'I can barely hear you, come outside for a second so we can talk.'

In the unit block hallway, John and I stood resting against the wall, our shoulders touching.

'What's wrong?' I said.

'Something happened with Emily.' It was a long story, they were out somewhere and they went back to her place and . . . any second now Ben was going to come looking for me, and I couldn't help wondering if John was ever going to get to the point of the story.

'So we were in bed together, we'd just finished, you know, and don't get me wrong, the sex is great between us, she is a really awesome chick, seriously up for anything, but then she said she loved me and I just sort of found myself looking at her and I thought, NO! I mean I like having sex with her, but I definitely don't love her.'

'Maybe it's too early to love her, maybe you haven't given it enough of a chance.'

'No. It's not too early, I just *can't* love her. It's impossible!'

'You are so dramatic. Why is it impossible?'

'Because I love someone else.'

We looked at each other and I grimaced. *Why does he always make this so hard?* I grabbed his hand, torn, as I tried to think of the right thing to say.

I heard the door to Kerryn's apartment open and instinctively I dropped John's hand. Ben stormed out, glaring at me, with Angela seconds behind him. Still clutching the almost-empty bottle of Jim Beam, Ben said, 'Say your goodbyes, we're going. I'll wait for you in the car.'

I shut my eyes and took a deep breath. When I opened them, Angela and John were staring at me. 'I've got to go,' I said, not meeting their eyes.

'Don't,' they both said. 'Just stay.'

'I can't.'

'Well, I'm coming too then,' said Angela, 'You promised to drop me home. I want to make sure you're okay.'

Angela and I got our stuff from inside and I hugged John goodbye.

'You can still stay,' he said, willing me with his eyes.

I shook my head. 'I'll call you tomorrow.'

The tension in the car was sickening but Ben refused to say a word to me or Angela the whole way back to Rose Bay. I pulled up at Angela's house and got out of the car to say goodbye.

'Call me if you need me,' she said, her flushed face wrinkled with concern.

'Don't worry,' I said, pasting a big smile on my face, 'it's just a misunderstanding. Ben will be fine, I'll be fine.'

From Rose Bay to Coogee, Ben's rage flared. 'You are a cheating fucking whore! You are a cunt of a human being!'

Somewhere around Bondi Junction, he extended his arm and I felt his palm hit the side of my head, forcing it into the window and causing the car to swerve.

'Ben, you're going to make me crash the car!'

'I don't give a fuck, you fucking bitch!' Ben hit the dashboard, his fist pounding into the radio and air-con vents.

'Please, let's just talk about it when we get home. You're not listening to me.'

The screaming and punching continued. The rear-vision mirror flew off its hinge and I struggled to maintain a steady hand on the wheel. My eyes were torn between the road and the passenger seat, trying to see what was coming next. As we reached the top of Coogee Bay Road, the old-fashioned headstones in the cemetery were illuminated by the headlights of our car. We were only five minutes from home now, almost safe. We rounded the bend onto

Malabar Road and then suddenly the wheel was heavy under my grip before being wrenched completely out of my control. Ben had leaned over and grabbed the wheel, angling the car towards the headstones. We crossed the white line onto the other side of the road and then just as suddenly, I felt my head jolt away from my neck as the wheels screamed and tipped us the opposite way and directly into the line of a telegraph pole on the corner of an adjacent street. I could hear Ben saying, 'I don't care if you die, I don't care if we both fucking die, you fucking bitch.'

I braked as hard as I could and pulled the wheel as far to the right as it would go, and when I opened my eyes, I realised that somehow we had managed to miss the pole. Panting and gasping for breath, I shouted at Ben, 'I could have died! What the hell is wrong with you? You almost killed us both!'

We were only a few kilometres from our driveway, so with my jaw set I put the car in reverse and launched backwards off the gutter onto the road. 'Don't even fucking think about touching the wheel again,' I said as I put the car in drive and edged slowly along the street, my eyes staying on Ben rather than the road. I could tell the fight wasn't over.

In the driveway Ben got out of the car and I immediately locked the doors. I could just sit in the car and wait it out, wait until he went upstairs and passed out, but Ben had other ideas.

He started pushing the car, rocking it back and forth. 'Get the fuck out of the car!' As he came around the back of the car to my side, he kicked the panels, metal crumpling, before he appeared at my window. 'Open the fucking door or I will open it for you.' His fist began slamming against the window repeatedly, *bang, bang, bang*. 'Open the fucking door!'

How long would the thick tinted windows hold up?

The next-door neighbour appeared behind Ben in the drive. 'Mate, if you don't stop what you're doing, I'm calling the police. I've got kids asleep inside and all I can hear is you screaming and swearing your head off, not to mention you're ruining your car! You need to go inside and sober up.'

'Mind your own fucking business, mate!' Ben shouted, now facing away from my window, his back to me.

'You're making this my business because you're disturbing the entire street. You're lucky I even bothered coming out to warn you before I call the cops, I'm sure some of the other neighbours have already put in a call. If you keep carrying on the way you are they'll arrest you for sure!'

I got out of the car. 'Sorry about all this,' I said. 'He's just had too much to drink, there's no need to call the police, I'll take him inside.'

I made my way around the car and up the stairs to our unit. Behind me I could hear Ben telling the neighbour, 'I'll do what I like to my own fucking car, mind your own business.' I couldn't see where his final blows of contempt landed as he showed the neighbour who was boss, but I heard them and I knew the damage to me and the car was going to be costly, if not irreparable. It seemed inevitable.

———

Two weeks after Kerryn's party, unable to face the neighbours, we moved again.

And then we had another party to go to.

If it had been anyone else's party I wouldn't have gone, but Nat and I had been friends since high school and I guess in spite of everything a small part of me hoped that I might just be able to slip back in with the Northern Beaches crowd, the way Ruby had fitted in a lifetime ago. The last time I had seen most of the girls who would be at the party was the day we got our HSC results. A part of me wanted to have that old familiarity again, be with people that sort of knew me, 'friends' I had grown up with. I guess I also thought it might be a way to close the distance separating me and Ben. At the very least, a fun night together might prevent it from widening.

I wore a simple black dress with a low back that I knew looked flattering on my slimmed-down frame. 'Are you sure I look okay? I don't look too fat? I haven't seen any of these people for so long. I'm actually nervous.'

'You've asked me a hundred times already! Yes, you look good. It's your best dress, your legs look hot. Now stop asking me! Drink some vodka.'

The old me would have swanned into the party expecting a great night, but I was so nervous I could have been sick. The pressure to look just right and make sure things between Ben and me appeared harmonious was overwhelming.

Walking into the drive, I clutched Ben's hand. 'Please don't just go straight off and leave me!' I begged through my smile just before we said hello to three girls I used to go to school with.

We stopped so Ben could say hi to some of his old schoolmates, so I turned back to the three girls to have a quick chat. Two I recognised, but the third I couldn't place at first. 'Hey girls, how are you? It's been ages.'

'Hey,' said Lacey and Lauren.

I turned to the girl who I couldn't quite place. 'Hi, I'm Renee, I think we might have met before?'

'I know who you are, you dog, we went to primary and high school together.' She took a short drag on her cigarette, the smoke billowing in her face as she exhaled.

I searched her clouded face; it *was* familiar but not entirely recognisable. I scanned my brain and then *click*: Alana Stevens, but with a very different nose to the last time I had seen her.

'Oh my god, Alana, I'm sorry, you look so different, your face –'

'Oh fuck off! As if you didn't recognise me, just turn around, I'm not interested in talking to you anyway.'

The party probably couldn't have got off to a worse start. My heart was thumping and I wanted to burst into tears but I knew I couldn't. I couldn't lose face, couldn't let these girls walk all over me, so instead of crying I clenched my jaw and looked her in the eye. 'You haven't changed a bit since high school then, have you? Same bitch, new nose! I'll see you later, Lacey, Lauren.' I spun quickly back to the group of boys, smiling as confidently as I could, but shaking.

As the boys chatted I could hear Alana and the girls behind me.

'I heard she isn't at uni anymore, she dropped out.'

'Yeah, but the real question you want to ask me is how did she even pay for uni to begin with?' Alana said.

'What do you mean?'

'I heard she used to get paid for it.'

'For what?'

'*It!* Sex, you dipshit!'

'Bullshit!'

'It's true, Ben told Matt, who told Brooke, who told, well, everyone. I can't believe you've never heard this! And then she supposedly got raped, that's why she's so messed up, why she dropped out, I reckon.'

The party disappeared as I registered their words. There had to be a mistake. Ben would never betray my trust like that. Not after everything we had been through together. Not after I had already paid my debt to him.

'You'd have to be truly fucking desperate to rape her.'

'I thought you had to be hot to be paid for sex.'

'Hmm, guess not then. Look at her.'

The girls' voices fell away. None of their words mattered. My heart was thumping, ears ringing, the whole party seemed to spin in a way that wasn't due to the vodka, and I had still barely made it past the driveway. I looked up at Ben's smiling face, laughing with his mates. He was relaxed and happy, we could have had a great night out, but somehow without even touching me, without even knowing, he had just delivered the biggest blow of all.

# 33

The physical abuse with Ben had always seemed forgivable compared to the emotional damage I had caused myself. I knew the violence wasn't normal but in my mind it was almost a payoff for the burden I'd placed on Ben to keep my secrets. Now I knew he hadn't kept them.

After Nat's party my mind was plagued with thoughts of Ben on one of his many drunken jaunts gleefully regaling the whole of the Northern Beaches with skewed and exaggerated versions of me at a time that still made my heart throb with pain. All of Ben's physical and emotional betrayals finally bled together in my mind, two separate streams joining together to make one haemorrhaging river of grief. What was I doing with him? With my life? For the first time I saw with absolute clarity that I was nothing to Ben, completely replaceable. Whether he was with me or another girl, his life would be the same – but mine didn't have to be. I was responsible for what happened next and I knew that if I stayed I would drown in my own misery.

There was little point confronting Ben about what he'd done, because I didn't want to hear the explanation or lies that he would tell me in an attempt to undo the betrayal. I didn't want him to undo it – I wanted it raw and fresh in my mind because I had finally run out of forgiveness.

On the day I turned twenty-two nothing could bring a smile to my lips. The brightly packaged parcels of clothes, tickets to *The Lion King*, the purebred white Persian cat – none of Ben's offerings could distract me from the fact that I was starting another year feeling the exact same way that I had begun the last. I was too young to feel so old. All of this time I had told myself that the violence had stemmed from the rape, which had only happened because of my wayward decision to work at The Palace, but for the first time I contemplated the idea that maybe even if Canberra had never happened, Ben's violence would have come anyway. It was in him. In his soul, and it was there long before I came into his life.

I also tried to think objectively about my time at The Palace, think about what I had actually done versus how badly I was punishing myself. A small, rational part of me knew that it was probably time to give myself a break, try to accept that back then, at eighteen, I was still a child; sure, a child who had stubbornly refused to give up on a dream no matter what the cost, but a child all the same. Did valuing success over common sense and morals really equate to me deserving to be raped? And did the rape really warrant the continual punishment from Ben? Though my head was still clouded with self-blame, I knew in my heart that I had more than paid the price. I felt resolved enough to know that no matter how much of the blame rested with me, I certainly didn't need Ben or the whole of the Northern Beaches to act as my judge and jury anymore, because no one would ever judge me harder than I'd already judged and punished myself.

I spent the months following Nat's party mentally trying to process it all, sifting through all the decisions I had made that had led me to now. What had kept me with Ben for so long in the first place? Maybe it was Ruby's fault? Maybe hiding so much of myself behind a mask of smiles made me the perfect candidate to hide the violence? And Ben? What made him play his role in all of this? What did *he* see when he looked at himself in the mirror? I knew he didn't hate himself like I did. At best, we were both products of our childhood. He grew up in a violent household with a poor view of women and I was taught to keep secrets, never wanting to fail or quit at anything. We were the antithesis of each other's needs – destined for disaster.

I started separating myself from him; slowly taking more and more of myself back from him. With staffing changes at work I gained two good friends, Abbie and Naomi, and I started spending a lot of time with them, staying over at Naomi's house, going out for dinner or to see John's band. I spent every morning and evening at the gym and I started spending more time with John, not just before work but after work too. If we weren't together then we were on the phone for hours talking about quitting our jobs and buying a pub together in some random corner of the world and never coming back.

The more time I spent away from Ben, the looser the bind became. I felt loved by people in a way that I hadn't been loved before and it proved to me that what I had with Ben couldn't possibly be love. I felt my self-worth creeping back, but I still didn't want him to know I was leaving yet. Even after all the soul searching and certainty in my mind I was still unable to say the words until

I was totally prepared, totally sure I would not fail in leaving this time. It was incredibly frustrating – what was the point in mentally breaking up with someone if I was still physically in the relationship?

Staring in the mirror one morning I examined my reflection, imploring myself to explain what I was still doing here. I had so much going for me, so much life waiting for me, and I was still inherently a good person. In fact, when I thought about it, I knew I was a better person than when I had first set out for Canberra: a more raw, softer, more human version of myself, much more than any shallow mask I had ever presented. Perhaps I didn't need Ruby anymore because I was finally beginning to understand that life happened, and that sometimes no matter how hard people tried, they still failed. Ultimately, perfection of any kind was an illusion. For the first time in years I realised that I didn't hate who I saw in the mirror, maybe I even liked her a bit, liked who I was becoming, truth and all. But most importantly, after all the blood and betrayal, what I now knew for certain was that I finally liked myself more than I liked Ben. My life was more important to me than he was. The realisation was shocking, straightforward and monumental. But, most importantly, it allowed me to see that leaving was no longer impossible, it was inevitable. After all, I had my whole life to live.

———

Four years and three months into our relationship, I finally sat Ben down and said the words, 'We just can't do this anymore, *I* can't do this anymore.' All this time I had thought I couldn't end the relationship because I would have failed and wasted four whole years of my life, but in saying just one sentence I realised how close

I'd come to wasting *all* of my life with this person. I expected a huge fight, braced myself for the back-handed blows, but there was nothing.

I could see in his face that he didn't believe me, didn't think this time would be any different to all the other times. He engaged only half-heartedly as he stomped out the door. 'Fuck off then, you bitch. Good riddance! I don't need you, but you, you'll regret this, we both know it. You'll come crawling back. You need me.'

But as I heard Ben drive off in his work van, I knew that this time was different. It didn't matter how long he was gone, I knew I would see it through.

The next time I saw him he was moving his things into the spare room. 'Just until I'm out of the doghouse again,' he said, his face beaded with sweat as he dumped a pile of his clothes into a heap and grinned at me.

———

At work I was asked to act in the role of Executive Officer while the existing EO, James, took a sabbatical. I couldn't believe that James and the board of directors would have the confidence in me to manage the organisation and that soon I would be left in charge of a multimillion-dollar budget and team of staff. My heart swelled. Not only did I know I would do a great job, I knew I had earned it, and I was thrilled at how great it would look on my resume. That afternoon, everyone left early except John and me. I came upstairs from the photocopier, thinking about the pile of applications I wanted to review before I went home. I was in no rush to leave, eager to avoid Ben as much as possible until we went our separate ways. John stood in the doorway to my office, blocking the entrance.

'Why were you in James's office for so long this morning?' he said, smiling.

'I can't tell you yet.'

'Tell me or I won't let you pass.'

'I can't, James wants to tell everyone at the same time tomorrow.'

'So what? You know I won't tell.'

I shook my head. 'Come on, move. I have stuff I need to do.'

'Tell you what, you can either tell me or kiss me and I'll let you pass.'

After two years of similar games and resistance, I'm not sure who was more surprised when I jumped up to the top step and held his face in my hands, slowly pulling it down to mine for a long kiss.

For the first time since we met, John no longer looked so damn sure of himself, surprise and delight written across his face. Across both our faces.

'Now move,' I said and shoved past him, grinning.

I didn't know if anything would ever come of our friendship, but it didn't matter. The kiss, the promotion, the warm tingly feeling on my lips that lasted for days, it all cemented in my mind that there was no turning back with Ben. My heart felt young and free, and I knew that *this* was what being twenty-two years old was supposed to feel like.

———

In the first few weeks that I acted as Executive Officer, I gave a month's notice on our place at Maroubra. I had just found an amazing loft apartment across the park from Grandpa at Redfern and I was convinced that if I could ever get hold of the agent to see it, it would be my new single girl's pad. As I hung up the receiver again with no luck, John appeared at my office door and took a seat across from me without being invited. 'Make yourself at home.' I smiled, ready for our usual banter.

'I'm leaving,' he said, his face serious.

'What do you mean you're leaving? For the day?' He didn't look exactly like himself, I supposed, he looked upset. 'Are you sick?'

'No. I'm not sick, I'm resigning.'

'You can't resign when I'm acting as the EO!'

'I knew you would say that! But I am. I'm moving to Perth, I just can't work here anymore.'

'Perth? Why Perth? And why can't you work here anymore?'

'Perth, because me and a mate are going across to try and find some work. And why? You know why I can't work here anymore. I've told you a hundred times before I can't come to work and be this close to you every day and not actually be with you.'

'I know you've said that, but I never thought you would actually leave!'

'For two years I've been chasing you. For two years there has been something between us and you keep standing in the way of it. I *know* you feel the same way about me.'

'I know! But everything with me is so complicated, I've only just ended things with Ben, I haven't even moved out yet. You're my best friend . . . I don't want you to leave!' I felt miserable at the thought of not seeing his face every day.

'You're my best friend too,' he said, 'but it's not enough. I can't see you day in, day out anymore because it's too much, too painful.'

'I don't want you to go!'

'I know you don't, but I have to. For me. We're still going to talk all the time, we'll still be best mates, we just won't work together.'

'Yeah, *and* you'll be on the other side of the country.'

'You could always come and visit me.'

I moved around the desk and took the typed resignation from his hand, pulling him up to hug me. I wanted to cry, but instead I shut my eyes tight against his chest and said, 'I'm going to miss you so much.'

———

'Come away with me for one night, my friend has a caravan up near Avoca Beach, so let's go on the last day of work. It can be our last beach trip before I leave.'

On the final day of work for the year we locked up the office together. Next year when I opened the office, John would be gone. We got in the car and headed north, and the further we drove the less anything outside the two of us existed.

That night I slept entangled in John's arms and dreamless. When we woke, John smiled at me and said what I had been thinking most of the night: 'Seriously, Ren what took you so frickin' long?'

———

In the lead-up to John flying out, we were inseparable. I had worried so much about ruining the friendship, about there being no spark if we ever did cross the line and sleep with each other, but like most things I have worried about in life, it was wasted energy. The transition was seamless. The humour, easiness and fun of our friendship moved with us from the bed to the shower and back to the bed again. I never thought I would ever *want* someone to touch me again after Jay; I had thought that sex would always just be a duty that I would have to perform to make things right in a relationship, but in the days before John left I experienced what all-consuming desire was like. We would leave the house only to have to go back home again. Never more than an arm's distance apart, we listened to Jeff Buckley's 'Last Goodbye' on repeat and kissed each other passionately to avoid talking about what would happen when there were four thousand kilometres between us instead of just twelve narrow terrace stairs.

The night before John was to leave, we waved goodbye to all of his friends in the driveway of his parents' house, both of us tipsy and flushed from a fun afternoon of drinks and shenanigans in the backyard. When his friends had gone we walked the streets, talking. What had the last few weeks meant?

'People do the long-distance thing all the time, you know,' John said as we started around the block again.

'I know, but you need to go and do your thing without feeling anchored to me and I need to get my shit together. I'm moving tomorrow. '

'You're talking like nothing is going to happen with us.'

'You're moving to Perth tomorrow.'

'Not forever.'

'No, but let's just see how things go.'

'That's what we've been doing for two years!'

'You might find the love of your life in Perth.'

'You're ridiculous,' he said to me.

'There are lots of things you still don't know about me, things that might change your mind about how you feel about me –'

'Try me.'

We sat down on some stranger's front fence and John squeezed my hand tightly as I let all of my secrets spill from my tongue as freely as the tears flowing from my eyes: a six-year-old me finding out about my dad; my father's unforgivable crimes; Canberra; nightmares of Jay; the pregnancy; Ben. My whole life summarised in minutes.

'These are the things you should know about me before you decide if you really want to be with me. I'm really not that normal –'

'What even is normal? Nothing you've said makes me feel differently about you. Maybe it just makes me understand you a little better, why you're a bit crazy sometimes and why it's been so hard for you to leave Ben. I still want to be with you.'

'Don't say that now. It's a lot to take in. I think you should wait until you're settled in Perth and have some headspace – four thousand kilometres should do it, huh? See how you feel when you're in Perth, when I'm not sitting right in front of you.'

The next morning we kissed each other as if we would never see each other again, because neither of us was really sure if we would.

That afternoon I closed the door for the final time at our Maroubra house. Ben and I stood in the driveway saying our goodbyes.

'I never thought we would actually break up,' he said.

I looked at his unshaven face. 'Really? We've both known for weeks this goodbye was coming. Neither of us has been happy for a long time.'

'Yeah, maybe, I don't know, I guess I always thought we'd just end up getting married and having kids.'

'For a long time I thought that too, Ben.'

'You know I almost asked you to marry me once. Remember when I took you skydiving for your birthday? You caused that fight on the way, so I didn't ask you, but I was going to propose to you when we jumped out of the plane.'

I don't know what he wanted me to feel as he was telling me that – regret, remorse, a desire to stay? But as I remembered wandering alongside the freeway feeling so defeated, I wondered how we could have each been feeling so differently that day? Me full of self-loathing, caged in a relationship I didn't know how to escape, and him on the verge of proposing a lifelong union.

Standing in the drive, I was relieved that he had never asked, that I'd never had to say yes or no, because I really don't know if I ever could have said no to him. More than anything, I felt so overwhelmingly grateful that I was about to walk away from it all.

'I've got to go,' I said. 'Grandpa is waiting at my new place to help me unpack.'

He leaned forward to hug me. 'I'll call you,' he said and I nodded.

'We'll still be friends,' he said as I let go of him and walked away.

# 34

'You said to call once I was in Perth, once I'd had time to think.' His voice sounded secretive, quiet. 'Well, I don't know if I'm supposed to be using my phone yet because the plane's still taxiing to the gate, but anyway, I'm technically in Perth and I don't want to just see how things go, I want to be with you, properly. I want to give this long-distance thing a shot.'

I smiled as I remembered John's words, my own plane now on the same tarmac, waiting for the doors to open. It had been six weeks since he'd left and he had no idea I was coming. Six weeks since we decided it was silly to pretend that, after all these years, we didn't owe it to ourselves to give this whole love thing a proper go. But now that I was here I wondered if it would be the same. I should have told him I was coming, we should have planned it together. Coming like this left me vulnerable, laid all my feelings bare. What if he saw me and changed his mind? What if we saw each other and it was really nothing more than friendship?

As I followed the other passengers though the airport towards the luggage carousels, I wondered if Daniel, John's cherished, no-bullshit friend and my accomplice, would have managed to convince him to come to the airport. I'd been working hard to win Daniel over as being worthy enough for his best friend and I wondered what sort of lie he would've had to conjure up to get John to come.

I stood tall on the giant descending escalators, searching the crowd below, my heart pounding in anticipation. Would he be here or wouldn't he?

And then I saw him, strolling up to Daniel without a care in the world. He had a freshly purchased Slurpee in his hand and was wearing his favourite 'One Love' T-shirt. His tanned, unshaven face broke into a casual smile as he reached Daniel and then he laughed, probably at his own joke. He was completely unaware I was watching him. My best friend. How could I not love him? Lifting his head, his eyes met mine and the airport chaos fell away. His beautiful face broke into a wide smile as he started to bound towards the escalator.

In each other's arms again, tears in our eyes. 'Look at you being all romantic and surprising me,' he said. 'You must really love me to come all this way.'

'I must,' I said and then, quieter, 'I do,' I said into his shoulder.

'I can't believe you're actually here,' he said and then just like in the movies he picked me up and swung me around as he shouted to the airport, 'I love this girl!'

While my cheeks burned and I laughed and cried and begged him to put me down because this was all very embarrassing, I realised I was happy. Such a small, simple word that had been eluding me for so long. What an idiot I was to question whether I should have come.

Over the next ten days we planned our lives. We spent hours playing all our old games, mapping out exactly where we could probably afford to buy a pub so that we never had to come back to Australia, challenging each other as to who would eat and drink the most pasta and wine when we finally made our way to Italy, and arguing vehemently over which way around the world was the best way to go – finish or start in India? The only difference was that this time it didn't have to be a game, there was literally nothing standing in our way to make it all come true – except living thousands of kilometres apart, that is. We decided to give ourselves six months: John would make a go of it in Perth; I would keep clocking up my experience running ESRHA. And in six months we'd work out what to do next. In the meantime we set up our rendezvous schedule: Bali, Perth, Sydney, every six weeks. And we'd write to each other. A love letter each way for every day we weren't together.

When the final boarding call was made for my flight back to Sydney we faced each other for the goodbyes. Again. We'd get good at them if all our plans eventuated, but for the moment it was still too new, too raw, too hard. My eyes filled with tears and I tried to stop them spilling over by channelling my mother and looking up to the ceiling, trying desperately to stop my face from crumpling. We kissed each other goodbye and as I turned to board, John stopped me and held my shoulder.

'Remember when we first started working together and I told you that one day you'd end up marrying me?'

I smiled. Our old jokes. Our standard go-to when things were too hard. This I could do.

'Let's not get ahead of ourselves.' I winked.

'Why do you keep pretending that you weren't wrong all those years ago? Just admit it, please, before you get on the plane, just say, "John was right and I was wrong."'

Our eyes locked, sparkling, laughing, until I had to look away, redirecting my smile to my shoes because, in spite of myself, I knew that there was a pretty good chance he might just be right.

'I'll see you in Bali,' I said instead.

'It's only six weeks —'

'I love you,' I said, meeting his eyes.

'I love you, too.'

And as the plane sped down the tarmac I tried to distract myself by counting out exactly how many hours there were in six weeks.

# 35

'Seven,' she said, holding up one splayed hand and two fingers. 'That's how many times the average woman leaves a violent relationship before she leaves for good.'

'Really? That seems a lot! Leaving once took me long enough.' I sat back in the chair and immediately started thinking about all the places Ben and I had lived together. I counted once in my head and then twice more on my fingers, to be sure. Seven places. Seven places in four and a half years. But it was not the same. I didn't leave seven times; I just started over seven times. Letting it all sink in, I decided that what I did was worse because seven times I just drew a line in the sand without ever seriously staging an ending.

'Oh God,' I said, 'I'm a statistic.'

Sitting in the big wingback chair in Robyn's inner-city counselling suite, I felt even more ridiculous because now I wasn't even unique in my failures. And stupid, because I felt my reasons for staying were nowhere near as credible as the other women who made up those statistics – they probably had children to consider, no financial means to support themselves, maybe no career to hide behind. Of course it took *them* seven times to leave, but what excuse did I have? Why had it taken me so long?

I tried to work it out with Robyn.

'Maybe I wouldn't have allowed the violence to escalate the way it did if I had dealt with the rape better. I probably would have left after Thailand, or maybe even before.'

'Why do you say you didn't deal with the rape well?'

'Because it was my fault it happened . . . Because I still can't forget about it. I still have those dreams now and it's been years. It's my brain punishing me!'

'Why do you think it was your fault?'

'Because I would have sold my soul to pay for my law degree, and if I hadn't been so desperate to have a dazzling career, I never would have crossed paths with Jay, never would have even been in that room, in that place to be raped.'

'What happened with Jay was not your fault. You were an eighteen-year-old girl, alone in a new city, in a very vulnerable situation, with absolutely no support. The sooner you realise this, the sooner we can move on to trying to resolve the dreams –'

'But it was my fault!' I felt compelled to convince Robyn, hot tears stung my eyes as I conjured an image of my eighteen-year-old self, so cocky and sure that everything would all just work out. 'If I hadn't been so preoccupied with trying to prove how smart I was, with trying to show everyone that I could have this amazing life just to spite them, then perhaps I would never have been so desperate to be a lawyer! Maybe I could have just been happy being a teacher and living on the Northern Beaches forever!'

'And maybe you wouldn't have been! You will never know! I think your drive to succeed has been your salvation; you could have chosen to be anyone, but you chose to try to break the cycle. Try to think about it from another perspective. Imagine you hadn't been coached to keep everything about yourself a secret from the age of six; perhaps you wouldn't have felt so insecure about who you are, maybe you wouldn't have felt so desperate to overachieve as a means of absolution for who your parents are. Maybe you would have reported the rape, or you might have confided in someone about the violence. I know you think the buck starts and stops with you, but you are only twenty-two, you can't take responsibility for everything.'

We were a few months into the counselling relationship, a relationship that would never have happened if I hadn't just been permanently promoted to Executive Officer at work. Because my predecessor had eventually left due to stress, a board requirement of me stepping into the role permanently was that I saw a counsellor once a fortnight during the time that I took the organisation through a major period of change and growth. I guessed it was to make sure I didn't leave in the same burnt-out fashion.

I saw Robyn for almost a year and for the first time in my life I began to talk about things in a way that I never imagined talking to anyone. I began to feel things that I had never really allowed myself to feel, about my dad, my family, my tendency towards self-destruction when I felt trapped. I talked about Canberra, the rape, and my fears of being forever ruined, but particularly I found myself talking about my relationship with Ben. Memories of the violence, the forced sex, the years of emotional manipulation, truly filled me with shame. It made my skin crawl to think about how crippled I'd been, and now that I'd finally left I found it incredibly hard to forgive myself for how long I'd stayed. I hated how much power I'd allowed Ben to wield over me, how much his words, his presence still permeated my days. I had thought being removed from the physical abuse and from Ben would mean I could put the experience behind me, the way I had become so accustomed to doing. But it wasn't like that. The violence had eaten away at my heart and mind, shaken my faith in thinking it was okay to live my life hiding all my imperfections and emotions behind a smile, because with Ben that hadn't served me very well, in fact it had only fed the destruction.

It became apparent that the only way to 'fix' it was to stop trying to pretend that nothing had ever happened in my life and try to accept it all, try to truly make peace with all that I am. I had to find a way to reconcile Renee and Ruby and stop pretending that if I simply pasted a smile on my face then everything would be all right. Somehow I had to unlearn a whole lifetime of behaviours and be honest with myself and others about all the ugly, painful things that I so badly wanted to forget, so that I could become one completely whole person for the first time in my adult life. Sure, a mosaic of a person, but whole all the same. It was at this time I realised the task ahead of me and I accepted that even after walking away from Ben, it was all still so very far from over.

Slowly, in my sessions with Robyn, we began to explore my feelings and my life. And I began to realise just how abnormal my normal had *always* been. It might sound strange, but sometimes when it's your life you really just don't notice.

# 36

## Rishikesh, June 2007

Just as the rain begins to fall in fat, furious drops against the tiled balcony floor where I sit writing, the call to evening prayer sounds out across the Ganges. Splotches hit the shoulders of my green Indian tunic and I see my fresh blue-inked thoughts smudge across the page. I snap my journal shut, but instead of moving out of the rain I shut my eyes and tilt my head back, letting the cool drops hit my face. I poke my tongue out and catch them, like I used to do when I was a child. The air smells of monsoon and I know that there are just mere moments until the gentle wind caressing my skin will start to howl in a glorious symphony with the light and sound in the sky.

Over the last three months I have become accustomed to the orchestra of monsoon, because it has chased us all over the continent. South, west, east, and now all the way to here in the north, in the foothills of the Himalayas.

I would loathe to be as clichéd as to say that I have 'found' myself in India, because if anything I have always known exactly who I am and in my desperate attempts to hide all my secrets, I vehemently tried to lose myself behind the well-constructed mask of Ruby. But here in India, just a few weeks away from turning twenty-five, I have finally made peace with just being me. I have realised that Ruby and Renee have always been the same person, neither of us perfect, but together perfectly flawed. And perhaps that's even better than perfect, because it's human.

'Babe, why are you sitting in the rain with your tongue out?'

I open my eyes, smiling at how ridiculous I must look as I turn to face John. He is standing against the doorframe in his oversized 'poo catcher' hippy pants that I bought him in Goa, purchased partly so he could attempt to blend in with the crowd, but mostly for my own daily amusement.

'Never mind the explanation. Put your tongue in and let's go!'

'Go where? The storm's about to start!'

'I know, that's the point, remember? The prayer is on and everyone else will be rushing to get out of the rain, so it's perfect timing. Stand up! Let's go!'

The first bolt of lightning electrifies the heaving sky and then a crash of thunder follows so close to us that it makes me jump.

'Okay,' I say, a little reluctant to be struck by lightning but unable to say no to a life experience because I have promised myself I will live every moment of this life with no regrets. 'Let's go.'

We race out of our room as the power to the village goes out, but the darkness is no big deal to us – the power always fails here. Continuing up the already muddy dirt path, we trip all the way to Lakshman Jhula, the iron suspension bridge that hangs twenty metres above the Ganges and allows the two sides of the gorge to meet. The bridge is the pulse of Rishikesh. Day and night the bridge is like a mosh pit, bursting at the seams with disfigured beggars, peddlers, milky-skinned bodies with their oversized backpacks and of course the devoutly faithful, but right now it is empty. Except for John and me.

The rain is teeming down so forcefully it is impossible to open my eyes for any longer than a few seconds at a time without having to swipe the water away. My Indian dress, designed to protect my modesty from prying eyes, is now anything but modest, clinging to my chest, my hips and my thighs like a second skin.

I can't see John's face in the blackness, but I can feel him next to me. The sky cracks open, illuminating his face, his smile. His hand reaches for mine. The bridge is swinging wildly in the wind, and we cling to each other, exhilarated by the moment, the storm, the intimacy of being alone on Lakshman Jhula. We are but two tiny specks, swinging beneath this spectacular show of life. No one in the world knows where we are or what we are doing, no one else will ever see what we are seeing right now. It's just us.

There is nowhere for us to be, we have no more than a bag of belongings between us; no ticket home. And it is in this moment, despite having already been married for three months, that I now accept my heart is safe. This man, this love, this life we are building together; I am loved and I am free. No more secrets, no more hiding behind Ruby. There is just me and John swinging in the storm.

# Epilogue

In the years since John and I married, I've gained some much needed perspective on what happened in the early years of my life. To me, everything still feels like it was normal. But I now accept that it wasn't. I know that most children aren't told lies by the adults in their life, and that if they are told lies they aren't so fundamental in shaping that life.

At times it has been hard for me to accept that everything I thought about my early life was built on lies. But I also know that I am only who I am today because of everything that has happened in my past. If my life had started differently, I would not have been so determined to change it. If I hadn't faced so many challenges in life, maybe I wouldn't appreciate the true beauty of what I have now.

At times it can be hard for any of us to look in the mirror. I know because for so long I didn't like what I saw, because that person – that Renee – had been tossed around on the waves created by the thoughts and actions of those around me. For years I struggled so hard to be in control of my life, and for so many years other people fought hard to take that control away from me.

Now, when I look in the mirror, I see the person I have become. I see a woman who has created her life the way she wants it. I have a career I am passionate about. I have a husband I adore. And I have three cherished sons whose lives started and continue in honesty and love. If I had to go through everything I went through in order to achieve this, it's been worth it. Painful, often overwhelmingly so, but worth it.

Now my life is lived on my terms. I'm in charge. No more lies – only freedom.

# Acknowledgements

First and foremost, thank you to Hachette Australia and the exceptional team who worked so hard to make this book a reality. Specifically to Sophie Mayfield, Nathan Grice, Alex Craig, Kylie Mason, Christa Moffitt and Laura Boon, your hard work and expertise in your respective areas has been both essential and greatly appreciated. To Sophie Hamley, if I could have dreamed up the perfect publisher to work with me on my book it would have been you. Your continual hard work, incomparable expertise and absolute faith in my story from the mentorship phase to the final version has been a constant source of confidence and comfort. I will be forever grateful.

To the Faber Academy, Patti Miller and the Life Stories team, I am truly indebted for all that you shared and taught me in the initial days of my writing. To the Northern Territory Writers Centre, thank you for the gateway to publishing my book and for all that you offer to Northern Territory writers.

To my writing gang, thank you for your unwavering support and enthusiasm for my writing journey from our very first Faber encounters. Special thanks and gratitude to Tanya, Kahla, Jill, Dianne, Olga, Nat and Tina for the countless hours of reading, edits and advice long before the single chapters of my life formed this book.

To my stepdad Peter, I am so grateful for your support of my writing and for the relationship we have built. Thank you to my sister Analiese for believing my story should be out there from the very beginning; and to the baby of the family, Ashleigh, for always being a constant source of inspiration, humour and love. I am so proud of you both.

Thank you to Julie, for both the practical and emotional support in writing this book and for loving me like your third child. There isn't a daughter-in-law alive luckier than me. And to my sister-in-law, Sally Kate, your advice, support and love is essential, and valued – always.

To my tight circle, had I known I would thank you in a book one day I would have insisted upon a classier group name, but alas, hindsight . . . thank you to the Tbags and Habots for being my secret keepers, supporters and cherished friends. Especially thanks to my first 'proper' readers and best friends, Michelle and Kellie, for being my unshakeable pillars of support, honesty and love. It would be impossible to do life without you two.

Thank you to Shelly, for being there back in the dark days and staying for the sunny ones.

To my late grandparents, every day I feel fortunate that you both made me your entire world, especially you, Michael Kevin Neville; you were always my 'normal' and are still my inspiration for kindness and loyalty.

To my mum. Even when the skies are grey, the sun still shines just as brightly. Sometimes hidden, always constant. Just like love. I love you and I hope you read this one day.

To my precious boys, Harry, Finn and Jack. From the first moment I held each of you in my arms, you have given my life a meaning and purpose that is more fulfilling and beautiful than anything I could ever have imagined. Thank you for filling my days with joyful chaos and my heart with a love like no other. There is simply no greater privilege in life than being your mother.

And finally to my husband, John. Thank you for being exactly who you are. Thank you for always believing in me, always loving me and always rolling your eyes and getting on board with my next 'big thing'. I am quite certain the world would stop spinning without you.

KE 6/17

**hachette**
AUSTRALIA

If you would like to find out more about Hachette Australia,
our authors, upcoming events and new releases you can visit
our website, Facebook or follow us on Twitter:

hachette.com.au
facebook.com/HachetteAustralia
twitter.com/HachetteAus